Post-Marxism Versus Cultural Studies

Titles in the *Taking on the Political* series include:

Post-Marxism Versus Cultural Studies

Theory, Politics and Intervention

Paul Bowman

Edinburgh University Press

© Paul Bowman, 2007

Edinburgh University Press Ltd
22 George Square, Edinburgh

Typeset in 11 on 13 Sabon by
Iolaire Typesetting, and
printed and bound in Great Britain by
Biddles Ltd, King's Lynn, Norfolk

A CIP record for this book is
available from the British Library

ISBN 978 0 7486 1762 3 (hardback)

The right of Paul Bowman to be
identified as author of this work
has been asserted in accordance with
the Copyright, Designs and Patents Act 1988.

Contents

Acknowledgements

For permission to incorporate works I have previously published elsewhere, my thanks go to the following: the editor and Edinburgh University Press for permission to reproduce elements of a chapter originally entitled 'Ernesto Laclau, Chantal Mouffe, and Post-Marxism', first published in *The Edinburgh Encyclopaedia of Modern Theory and Criticism*, edited by Julian Wolfreys (2002); the editors of *Culture Machine* for permission to use elements of the article 'The Task of the Transgressor', first published in *Culture Machine* (issue 6, 2004: http://culturemachine.tees.ac.uk); and Taylor & Francis/Routledge (http://www.tandf.co.uk) for permission to reproduce elements of three articles: 'Promiscuous Fidelity to Revolution: Or, Revaluing 'Revolutionary' Left Intellectualism', first published in *Contemporary Politics: New Agendas and Global Debates* (Vol. 9, No. 1, March 2003); 'Proper Impropriety: The proper-ties of cultural studies', first published in *parallax* (Vol. 7, No. 2, April–June 2001); and 'Between Responsibility and Irresponsibility: Cultural Studies and the Price of Fish', first published in *Strategies: Journal of Theory, Culture and Politics* (Vol. 14, No. 2, November 2001).

For numerous forms of assistance and support, I also owe thanks to Barbara Engh, as well as to Mark Devenney, Thomas Docherty, Jeremy Gilbert, Gary Hall, Kurt Hirtler, Ernesto Laclau, Martin McQuillan, John Mowitt, Griselda Pollock, Adrian Rifkin, Richard Stamp, Marcel Swiboda, Joanna Zylinska, and my long-suffering editors Benjamin Arditi and Jeremy Valentine. Jeremy Valentine in particular commented extensively and invaluably on each of the several versions of this work.

Even though he would have been extremely unlikely to have read even this far into this book, my dad, George Bowman (1937–2003), always cared, supported, approved, and accordingly, helped. Finally, I owe many thanks to my family, the Bowmans and the Hamiltons, and, overall, to Alice.

Preface

In an essay on 'university responsibility', Jacques Derrida said, 'I do not know if there exists today a pure concept of *a* university responsibility, [and] I do not know if an ethico-political code bequeathed by one or more traditions is viable for such a definition. But', he continues, 'today the minimal and in any case the most interesting, most novel and strongest responsibility, for someone attached to a research or teaching institution' is to make 'as clear and thematic as possible' the 'political implication' of the key and complex insight that all interpretation, 'the interpretation of a theorem, poem, philosopheme or theologeme is only produced by simultaneously proposing an institutional model, either by consolidating an existing one that enables the interpretation, or by constituting a new model to accord with it' (Derrida 1992: 21, 22). This is the same as saying that *all* interpretation – of anything – requires that the interpreter 'assume one or another institutional form'. 'This', Derrida adds, 'is the law of the text in general'. The book you are reading is concerned with this 'law of the text'. Derrida continues: Interpreters are not 'subjected passively' to the dictates of an institutional form, however; and all interpreters' 'own performance will in turn construct one or several models of community'. But nor is interpretation 'free': reading, or interpretation, cannot be extricated from the complex snares of the institutional practices and protocols of the contexts within which it occurs. Nor is reading or interpretation 'natural', or necessarily 'true'. Rather, it is always in some sense institutionally located and (over)-determined. Indeed, Derrida goes further: institutions themselves are not simply free or unrelated, but they too are complexly ensnared, imbricated or reticulated within, and articulated to yet other institutions. There is a fundamental complexity and textile-like interimplication between institutions, the acts within and of them, and other contexts, sites and scenes. Derrida puts it provocatively: 'When, for example, I read some sentence from a given text or in a seminar . . . I do not fulfil a prior contract, I can also write, and prepare for signature, a new contract with an institution, between an institution and the dominant forces in society' (21–2). It is the 'political implication' of this complex textuality that Derrida demands should be made 'as clear and thematic as possible', in terms of 'the most classical of norms':

> By the clearest possible thematization I mean the following: that with students and the research community, in every operation we pursue together (a reading, an interpretation, the construction of a theoretical model, a rhetoric of an argumentation, the treatment of historical material, and even of mathematical formalization), we argue or acknowledge that an institutional concept is at play, a type of contract signed, an image of the ideal seminar constructed, a *socius* implied, repeated or displaced, invented, transformed, menaced or destroyed. An institution – this is not merely a few walls or some outer structures surrounding, protecting, guaranteeing or restricting the freedom of our work; it is also and already the structure of our interpretation. (Derrida 1992: 22–3)

Derrida views this as a primary concern of deconstruction. In this sense, deconstruction is far from simply 'theoretical'. Rather, as Derrida continues to argue, if 'it lays claim to any consequence, what is hastily called deconstruction *as such* is never a technical set of discursive procedures, still less a new hermeneutic method operating on archives or utterances in the shelter of a given and stable institution; it is also, and at the least, the taking of a position, in work itself, toward the politico-institutional structures that constitute and regulate our practice, our competences, and our performances' (23). Moreover:

> Precisely because deconstruction has never been concerned with the contents alone of meaning, it must not be separable from this politico-institutional problematic, and has to require a new questioning about responsibility, an inquiry that should no longer necessarily rely on codes inherited from politics or ethics. Which is why, though too political in the eyes of some, deconstruction can seem demobilizing in the eyes of those who recognize the political only with the help of prewar road signs. Deconstruction is limited neither to a methodological reform that would reassure the given organization, nor, inversely, to a parade of irresponsible or irresponsibilizing destruction, whose surest effect would be to leave everything as it is, consolidating the most immobile forces of the university. (23)

With this argument in mind, this present work engages with 'deconstructive' post-Marxist scholarship and 'deconstructive' cultural studies. What demands this engagement derives directly from Derrida's argument about university responsibility, in that it alerts us to the *political* implication of university academic and intellectual work. Indeed, as will be shown in Chapter 1, cultural studies is to be regarded as being precisely the same sort of ethically and politically motivated institutional practice as Derridean 'deconstruction', in this regard. Neither ought simply to be formal and procedural, but rather both seek to intervene into their immediate and extended institutional socio-political contexts, in the hope of making a difference 'that counts', in Stuart Hall's (1992) words.

Given Stuart Hall's rightly influential status in cultural studies, Chapter 1 clarifies Hall's important and influential conception of cultural studies' *raison d'être* and *modus operandi*. It clarifies that the foundations of his views relate fundamentally both to deconstruction and, crucially, to the deconstructive post-Marxist political theory of Laclau and Mouffe (1985), *etc.* This 'post-Marxist' theory is a perspective which views history, culture, society and politics as being irreducibly 'discursive'. It was from the outset and continues to be characterised by taking a view of culture, society, subjectivity and even all intellectual and political categories that is enabled and informed by an irreducibly deconstructive optic: central to it are notions of the contingency, bias and politicality of construction, the 'impossibility' or 'constitutive incompletion' of identities, and so on. As Chapter 1 also clarifies, Laclau and Mouffe's (1985) theory that culture and politics are contingent and hegemonic has become strongly influential within cultural studies. The influence of Laclau and Mouffe's theory on cultural studies in itself has often been overlooked. But, rather than merely seeking to point up this relation, this work seeks to show that it is in this profound 'influence' itself that a first problem resides. This relates to the Derridean deconstructive complication or complexification of the idea of the political that we began with. As has just been seen, Derrida extends the consideration and conception of the political in such a way as to make it inextricable from the institutional and ultimately even the textual. In light of this contribution, the 'problem' of post-Marxism and cultural studies that this work engages relates to the question of academico-political responsibilities. What are the responsibilities of post-Marxism and cultural studies? To what are they to be responsible? What is it to be responsible and to intervene responsibly, significantly, effectively, anyway? Into what, and how? These are important questions, and as this work argues, they ought in fact to be regarded as a cortical problematic of cultural studies and post-Marxism. However, although it is 'theoretical', this problematic is not 'merely academic'. Rather, the conflict that arises between post-Marxism and cultural studies in light of the question of 'university responsibility' is ultimately a matter of political consequentiality. It is about what happens.

However, for many the more basic question is *why* they should be related together anyway; *why* post-Marxism and cultural studies should be articulated in terms of a Derridean emphasis on and problematisation of 'university responsibility' (of all things!). In this work I argue that relating these putatively discrete approaches is eminently justified and actually even called for, because both post-Marxism and cultural studies in a strong sense came into existence in response to a certain deconstructive 'crisis' in (and about) politics and knowledge. As will be argued, both post-Marxist theory and cultural studies as institutions initially and constitutively orientated themselves as interventional efforts, as wanting to challenge, dislodge, or at least develop, existing and often broadly Marxist models of political causality, of intervention, and of what determines the character of conjunctures, identities and objects. Both cultural studies and post-Marxism, that is, sought to establish precisely what effective and responsible, intellectually justifiable and rigorous ethico-political in-tervention could be. In other words, both sought to intervene. In this sense, both are of course obviously 'theoretical', yet guided by the aim of establishing ethico-politically responsible and effective 'practical' intervention. In both cases (to the extent that they are separable), this required and has resulted in an important and often refined rethinking of politics, theory, and institution. But this still needs to be taken further, both theoretically and practically. Ultimately, I argue, both rely heavily on the theoretical (broadly deconstructive) concept of '*articulation*', especially as it has been theorised by Laclau and Mouffe (1985), as well as on the general sense that '*hegemony*' – again, especially as theorised by Laclau and Mouffe – names and describes the logic of political and cultural articulation, and accordingly the movements and processes according to which meanings, values, relations, identities, orientations and institutions, are established. These insights offer the ingredients for a revivified theory and strategy of responsible intervention.

Now, it should be clear that something very like this notion of hegemonic articulation is strongly at work in Derrida's understanding of the relations and effects within which academic work finds and constitutes itself. So, this movement of rethinking that can be seen in the impetus to and of deconstruction, cultural studies, and post-Marxism can also be said to oblige the rethinking of the nature of intellectual institutional practice itself. Derrida is most clear on this point. In light of this, I argue that post-Marxism in particular – as well as many tendencies within and styles of cultural studies – have yet to fully acknowledge the importance of, let alone actually to undertake and act upon, such a rethinking and reorientation. Nevertheless, both post-Marxism and cultural studies encounter and, in their best moments, try to negotiate the problems introduced by an acknowledgement of the uncertainty or undecidability of 'university responsibility'. That is to say, the undecidability of responsibility that Derridean deconstruction identifies suggests the *failure* of any straightforward causal notion of politics and (accordingly) of intervention. The logic of political causality and therefore the answer to the question of how to intervene 'successfully' must be engaged. This book argues that cultural studies and post-Marxism are constitutively orientated by the aim of intervention when what intervention should and could be is undecidable. Its aim is to clarify the extent to which both remain unclear about precisely how to intervene: this central 'concept', or impulse, remains under-theorised. *Post-Marxism Versus Cultural Studies* seeks to help reactivate the theory and orientation of intervention.

However, and in a sense that Derrida's argument helps to draw out, there are many aspects of an uneasy and problematic conflictual relationship between post-Marxism and cultural studies. The nature of this conflict is established in Chapter 1, after some key dimensions of the historical, ethico-political, and conceptual imbrication of cultural studies and post-Marxism are laid out. First, the historical and conceptual coincidence of post-Marxism and cultural studies is considered, and the post-Marxist paradigm of 'discourse analysis', as elaborated by Laclau and Mouffe (1985), is explained. The importance of this paradigm for politicised cultural analyses of all kinds, and indeed for all efforts to understand the political, is emphasised as being extremely important and productive for cultural and political studies. Next, the specificity of the problematic of cultural studies is mapped out and engaged. From this position, it becomes possible to begin to clarify the character and stakes of the conflict between post-Marxism and cultural studies. What must be emphasised, though, is that this conflict is neither *merely* academic, nor *merely* theoretical, nor is its significance limited to this 'case study'. It is rather, I argue, crucial to an understanding of the matter of political intervention itself, as intervention is a fundamental raison d'être of cultural studies and post-Marxism. It is the most important thing to be theorized.

Chapter 2 deepens the consideration of the conflict, by examining the differends between the post-Marxist notion of 'discourse' and the deconstructive notion of 'text' in relation to problems of knowing (and) the political. It explores the problems of establishing what is political, what the political is, and the political dimensions of all *establishment* (with 'establishment' read as both noun and verb). Organised by an analysis of Stuart Hall's exemplary politically-inflected concerns with post-Marxism's 'textualism' and its theory of 'discourse', this chapter is supplemented by John Mowitt's important re-theorisation of the importance of what he calls the 'textual paradigm' (1992). This paradigm is deemed by Mowitt to be of immense ethico-political consequence when it comes to the question of 'university responsibility', and specifically the responsibility of post-Marxism and cultural studies. Crucial here is Mowitt's notion of the 'disciplinary object', or the productions (or, indeed, *inventions*) of disciplinary knowledge that are effective institutionally and that are circulated or disseminated discursively. This approach, I argue, offers a uniquely important way to make sense of the political dimensions and ramifications of academia within hegemony, as well as providing a key way to read the post-Marxist theory of hegemonic politics, as it were, 'against itself' and towards a more generative politicised paradigm. Informed by both the post-Marxist theory of hegemony and the concept of the disciplinary object, the chapter considers the hegemonic, institutional, academic and ethico-political position of cultural studies and other such subjects constituted through reference to 'interdisciplinarity'. Derrida (2002) suggested that cultural studies and interdisciplinarity may quite often be 'confused' and 'good-for-everything' concepts. Nevertheless, the chapter argues, Derrida's own readings, in *Dissemination* (1981) and elsewhere, provide a clear way to make sense of the institutional, structural, discursive, and political 'plight' – and importance – of a subject like cultural studies. With the matter of hegemonic and institutional location firmly foregrounded, the chapter goes on to interrogate some key (problematic) conceptualisations of intervention and politics, with a view to reconceptualising and reorienting notions of what academico-political intervention might possibly be. These relate to a 'microscopic', 'micropolitical' *antidisciplinary strategy* of *interdisciplinary intervention*, derived directly from deconstruction (Derrida: 1996; Mowitt: 1992).

Chapter 3 follows on from this by examining some key ways that post-Marxist and related intellectual work (such as that of Judith Butler and Richard Rorty) conceives of itself *as* intervention. This is a different issue to that of how post-Marxism theorises intervention as such. Indeed, theorising intervention in general is something that it can all too easily do, by invoking 'articulation', for instance (as in: 'intervention is successful motivated articulation'). Rather, this chapter pursues the matter of how institutional intellectual work construes *itself* whenever it seeks to *be* or affect an intervention (How and with what is it actually 'articulated'?). The chapter explores this by considering some exemplary encounters at the borders of post-Marxism that take us to the heart of the problem. These encounters and accounts, I argue, reveal the form, orientation, hopes, and often less than explicitly declared or avowed metaphysical rationales, fantasies and presuppositions of much theory about political practice. The chapter explores the way theory and practice are thought (or left unthought), examining the way that certain of Laclau's key engagements with other approaches have been orientated, organised and executed. So, although it explicitly only looks at encounters at the borders between post-Marxism and other paradigms, the chapter is actually an engagement with works to be taken as representative of a wide spectrum of conceptualisations of intervention, conceptualisations that can be discerned widely throughout cultural and political studies. The chapter examines Laclau's engagements with Richard Rorty's unapologetic anti-theoretical pragmatism, Žižek's equally unapologetic 'high theory', and Butler's attempt to negotiate between such positions, and it is supplemented by Derrida's comments on the encounter between Laclau and Rorty (1996). The chapter thereby seeks to delineate and engage with the limits, problems and possibilities of such paradigms, and with the ethico-political implications of such styles of thinking and orientation. The contention is that the limits, problems and possibilities seen here are exemplary illustrations of the paradigms of a great deal of works of both 'anti-' and 'high' theory circulating in cultural studies, political studies (post-Marxism included), and academia generally.

But where does such a project take us, or leave us? The concluding chapter, Chapter 4, reiterates what is at stake in the 'versus' of *Post-Marxism Versus Cultural Studies*, by clarifying that the question of the 'paradigm' or of the theoretical orientation is something that is far from being of merely theoretical or 'merely academic' consequence. It argues that post-Marxist political theory in particular must now attend to the challenge and criticisms laid down by deconstruction and cultural studies if it is not, paradoxically, to disengage from the possibility of intervening politically in anything like the way that was its own initial *raison d'être*. In light of this consideration of post-Marxism and cultural studies as interventional efforts, Chapter 4 takes issue with the agenda proposed by the most recent work of Laclau, as well as with the arguably rudderless drift of cultural studies away from engaging with political responsibility, and proposes a rearticulation with the shared and constitutive problematic of both and a reorientation *vis-à-vis* the demands of any project of responsible intervention. Responsible intervention today requires an explicit problematisation of disciplinarity as 'enclaving', and an interdisciplinary strategy that is antidisciplinary. (This paradox is engaged in Chapter 4.)

If this work primarily identifies and explores an 'academic' conflict between post-Marxism and cultural studies, it seeks to show that this conflict is not merely academic, in the pejorative sense; nor merely inconsequentially abstract, theoretical or intellectual; but rather that it is a conflict that has more than one political implication (Derrida 1992: 21–2). In order to argue this, it is first necessary to establish more fully what post-Marxism and cultural studies are, what the nature of their relationship is and what their wider importance or significance may be. So, the first chapter will delineate the key features of the post-Marxist political theory of discourse and hegemonic politics, and indicate the ways that this approach to understanding culture and politics is an invaluable resource not only for cultural studies, but also for many other academic and political projects more broadly.

Focusing first on the influential post-Marxist work of Ernesto Laclau and Chantal Mouffe, especially their groundbreaking co-authored work, *Hegemony and Socialist Strategy: Towards a Radical Democratic Politics* (1985), the chapter stresses the importance not only of Marxism but also deconstruction for this post-Marxist theory. This is because post-Marxism proceeds from a deconstruction of Marxism, a deconstruction aimed at reconstructing and revitalising Marxism so as to re-affirm Marxism newly construed, and to revivify it as a relevant and active force within today's 'postmodern' or indeed 'deconstructive' world. Post-Marxism, then, is shown to be a deconstructed and deconstructive version of Marxism, a political theory whose validity is held to be more clear, demonstrable and appropriate within the context of the contemporary world. As Nicholas Royle argues, 'deconstruction' is a term that should not be limited to

describing the work of a few academics, but should rather be understood as a term that actually indicates 'what is happening today in
what is called society, politics, diplomacy, economics, historical
reality, and so on' (Royle 2000: 11). Indeed, Royle's point here
can perhaps most readily be understood in terms of post-Marxist
deconstruction: for, the reason why the world is construed as one of
'discourses' in post-Marxism is because, within this theoretical paradigm, 'history and society are an *infinite text*' (Laclau 1980: 87) – a
perspective clearly related to Derrida's important argument that '*there
is nothing outside of the text*' (Derrida 1974: 158). For reasons that
will return regularly throughout this work, deconstruction is cortical
to post-Marxism's understanding of the political. It is also cortical to
cultural studies' understanding of culture. However, it is in their
differing relations to or appropriations of deconstruction that the
nature and stakes of their conflict congregate.

As will become clear, though, deconstruction is always a double-
edged sword; never simply a 'medicine' but also a poison; never simply
a 'solution' but also the deepening and radical development of any
problem. Thus, even though post-Marxism as a project is enabled by a
simultaneously controversial and productive deconstruction of Marxist categories, values, assumptions and rationalities, this does not
mean that post-Marxism itself cannot be deconstructed and be shown
to be limited, partisan, incomplete, 'constitutively impossible', and
indeed perhaps even what Derrida (1995) would have called 'violent'.
So, after spelling out the immense importance and value of post-
Marxist theory, this work undertakes a deconstruction and critique of
post-Marxism. This process also takes up Derrida's injunction always
to invert and displace a problematic (1977; 1982), not simply for
reasons of intellectual or academic rigour, or as an upshot of any
reading's thoroughness or fidelity, but as a way of identifying ethical
and political stakes and consequences. Accordingly, one thing that is
inverted and displaced in this process is the commonly held assumption that post-Marxism 'teaches' and cultural studies 'does'; or, that is,
that the political theory expounded by post-Marxism is merely a 'tool'
to be 'applied' by cultural studies (see also Hall 1996d: 149). In other
words, the argument is that whilst it is true in one sense that post-
Marxism is indeed primarily a political *theory*, and that cultural
studies does in a similar sense aspire to be a politically significant
intellectual *practice* (Hall 1992; 1996), this schema in which the one is
theory while the other is practice is a perspective that is actually facile,
partial, limited, limiting, and arguably even debilitating for cultural

studies, and indeed, even for political or politicised practice of all orders. It is vital to think about theory and practice, to think about what (we think) theory is and does, and what (we think) practice is and does. For there is no escape from 'theory', and it is of course a kind of practice in its own right, one which moreover orientates any practice. But this work does not merely intend to upturn the commonsense assumption that 'theory informs practice but *proper* practice is more important than theory' into an easy 'theory is a more important practice than other kinds of practice' – as provocative and challenging as this might be. (This is a proposition which will return and be examined in terms of the analyses of Slavoj Žižek's idiosyncratic post-Marxist thinking on politics and political action, and in the examination of Laclau's attempts to articulate his theory *as* practice, in Chapter 3.) Rather, Derrida regularly reiterates the important political stakes and consequences of the displacement of the terms, assumptions and focus of any debate (See Protevi 2001). So here, in deconstructing easy notions of theory 'versus' practice, the aim is not point-scoring, score-settling or one-upmanship for or against cultural studies or post-Marxism, or for or against 'theory' or 'practice'. Rather, the aim is for a revaluation and a reconceptualisation of the ways in which such intellectual work is construed and orientated as politicised practice. This is about responding to the demand of taking on the political. It is an interdisciplinary intervention with antidisciplinary aims.

Being-heard is structurally phenomenal and belongs to an order radically dissimilar to that of the real sound in the world.

Jacques Derrida,
Of Grammatology (1974: 63)

One – Cultural Studies *and* Post-Marxism

On the day of [The Centre for Cultural Studies at Birmingham University's] opening, we received letters from the English department saying that they couldn't really welcome us; they knew we were there, but they hoped we'd keep out of their way while they got on with the work they had to do. We received another, rather sharper letter from the sociologists saying, in effect, '. . . we hope you don't think you're doing sociology, because that's not what you're doing at all'.

(Stuart Hall 1990: 13)

Introduction: Of Deconstruction into Politics

Post-Marxism and cultural studies both explicitly engage with and take on the question of the political, of political engagement, and of ethical, political and university responsibility. Both are interested in intervention. But their relationship is far from simple, and the intellectual and political costs of ignoring its complexity are high. This chapter will explain why. First, let us examine the usual view. In this, the importance of post-Marxist political theory for cultural studies is regularly affirmed (Morley and Chen 1996: 1–2; Hall 1996c: 40; Sparks 1996: 90–5; Daryl Slack 1996: 117–22). Rarely has anything like the reverse been suggested. However, the need for just such a revaluation, or inversion and subsequent displacement of this schema is great. The usual interpretation of the relationship between cultural studies and post-Marxism is regularly conveyed in works of or about cultural studies (it is rarely mentioned or acknowledged within post-Marxist scholarship), and it has several often problematic but nonetheless important dimensions. Jeremy Gilbert clarifies these, by noting firstly that:

During the 1990s a number of essays by key figures speculated as to the desirability of explicitly designating 'post-Marxism' as a theoretical paradigm for 'cultural studies'. It might well be argued that this was always an unnecessary move, that both the *de facto* post-Marxism of Stuart Hall, along with all of those for whom 'cultural studies' only ever came into existence as a critique of Marxist economism, and the (closely-related) official 'post-Marxism' of Ernesto Laclau and Chantal Mouffe had been so thoroughly absorbed by the mainstream of cultural studies that there was little point in bothering to formulate this position in any more explicit or elaborate fashion. (Gilbert 2001: 189)

Gilbert acknowledges the historical, intellectual and political scope of the influence of Marxist theory for ('new') left wing political thinking in general, and cultural studies in particular. The implicit impetus to and logic of the constitution of both cultural studies and post-Marxism in this account is that they both come as a response to perceived problems in Marxist economic reductionism and Althusserian structuralism. According to Jennifer Daryl Slack, both cultural studies and post-Marxism amounted to the 'struggle to substitute the reduction that didn't work' – namely Marxist economic reductionism and structuralist theory's reductionism – 'with . . . something'. The problem with theories saturated in economic or structuralist determinism is that they are fatalistic or even anti-political in that they determine *in advance* that individuals, groups, agents, and indeed culture and politics in their entirety are epiphenomenal and inconsequential. This, says Daryl Slack,

> pointed to the need to retheorize processes of determination. The work of cultural theorists in the 1970s and early 1980s, especially the work of Stuart Hall, opened up that space by drawing attention to what reductionist conceptions rendered inexplicable. It is as though a theoretical lacuna develops, a space struggling to be filled . . . In theorizing this space, a number of Marxist theorists are drawn on: most notably Althusser (who drew on Gramsci and Marx), Gramsci (who drew on Marx) and, of course, Marx. Its principal architects have been Laclau and Hall. (Daryl Slack 1996: 117)

Daryl Slack finds it remarkable that 'in spite of the importance of Laclau's formulations, he has been excluded – as has Mouffe – from most of the popular histories of cultural studies' (Daryl Slack 1996: 120–1). This work will consider more fully this aspect of the peculiar relation of post-Marxism to cultural studies, and Daryl Slack's diagnosis of it, in the following chapter. But what is first to be emphasised here is the importance of the post-Marxist theory of Laclau and Mouffe for cultural studies. Morley and Chen, for instance, begin their 'Introduction' to *Stuart Hall: Critical Dialogues in Cultural Studies* by reminding us that 'back in the mid-1980s, as an alternative to formalist and positivist paradigms in the humanities and social sciences, British cultural studies, and Stuart Hall's work in particular, began to make an impact across national borders, especially in the American academy' (Morley and Chen 1996: 1). Immediately after making this contextualising point, the very first point that they mention – the very first book, the very first problematic, and the very first orientating discussion within cultural studies – is Stuart Hall's discussion of Laclau and Mouffe's 'seminal book, *Hegemony and Socialist Strategy* (a key statement of postmodern political theory)' (1). They conclude: 'When we look at it retrospectively', this engagement 'can be seen as a starting-point' (2), a constitutive cultural studies engagement with the 'postmodern' political theory of post-Marxism. However, and quite problematically, Morley and Chen are prepared to deem this encounter something 'from which cultural studies moved on, through another round of configuration' (2). But Stuart Hall himself is not prepared to do this. For him, the problematic established by this encounter with post-Marxist political theory is *constitutive*, and hence *ineradicable*. Indeed, Morley and Chen also deem Laclau and Mouffe's theory to be '*seminal*', like Stuart Hall. But Hall insists on the need to maintain fidelity and reference to this 'starting-point', arguing:

> one cannot ignore Laclau and Mouffe's seminal work on the constitution of political subjects and their deconstruction of the notion that political subjectivities [were hitherto thought to] flow from the integrated ego, which is also the integrated speaker, the stable subject of enunciation. The discursive metaphor [central to post-Marxist theory] is thus extraordinarily rich and has massive political consequences. For instance, it allows cultural theorists to realize that what we call 'the self' is constituted out of and by difference, and remains contradictory, and that cultural forms are, similarly, in that way, never whole, never fully closed or 'sutured'. (Hall 1996d: 145)

Hall even declares, 'if I had to put my finger on the one thing which constitutes the theoretical revolution of our time, I think that it lies in that metaphor' (145): the metaphor of 'discourse'. This work will keep returning to different dimensions of the possibilities, problems and problematics that 'the discursive metaphor' introduces for cultural and political studies. But at this stage what is important to note is that, for Hall, something that is seminal, generative, or constitutive – a starting-point – is not something from which one can simply move on. For Stuart Hall, then, the question of the political, of intervention and responsibility that comes to light in the cultural studies engagement or encounter with post-Marxism is not something that will – or should be permitted to – simply go away. This is why, after some qualifications and caveats, Hall maintains that he remains 'a post-Marxist and a post-structuralist, because those are the two discourses I feel most constantly engaged with. They are central to my formation and I don't believe in the endless, trendy recycling of one fashionable theorist after another, as if you can wear new theories like T-shirts' (Hall 1996d: 148–9). The problematic of post-Marxism is in fact central to cultural studies.

Before delving deeper into post-Marxism 'proper' or the constitutive encounter of cultural studies with it, though, it might reasonably be asked: never mind *post*-Marxism, what's the problem with *Marxism*? Furthermore: if Marxism is or was such a problem, then why maintain *any* reference to it at all? As has already been seen, one prime problem with Marxism relates to reductionism in its theory of determination. In other words, in Marxism, the determination of more or less everything is related to something 'essential' about classes and the economy, viewed as a closed system (Daly 2002). For both Hall and Laclau, among others, class essentialism and economism are unsatisfactory simplifications that cannot explain everything, and that are, accordingly, suspect. Nevertheless, their quests to re-theorise processes of determination more adequately are therefore marked by and hence retain a constitutive reference to Marxism. According to Hall, it was Laclau's rethinking of Marxism that offered a way out of Marxian dead-ends: 'Laclau', he argued, 'has demonstrated definitively the untenable nature of the proposition that classes, as such, are the subjects of fixed and ascribed class ideologies' (Hall 1996c: 40). Colin Sparks explains that 'Hall's road away from Marx lay through the writing of Laclau . . . Laclau provided a significant weakening of the rigours of the Althusserian version of Marxism "from within"'. The important feature here, according to Sparks, is that 'Laclau was concerned to produce a "non-reductive" theory of ideology and the mechanisms by which it functioned in society' (Sparks 1996: 89). So, by 'adopting the formulations of Laclau', Sparks concludes, 'it became possible' for Stuart Hall and cultural studies 'to give equal weight to each of the members of the "holy trinity" of race, class and gender'

(Sparks 1996: 92). Indeed for Angela McRobbie, the post-Marxist theory of Laclau and Mouffe therefore actually provided 'the theoretical underpinning for what has already happened in cultural studies' (McRobbie 1992: 720). This is an observation that Jeremy Gilbert proposes 'could actually be taken further', to suggest that post-Marxism's theorisation of discourse and 'radical democracy is a theoretical formulation of the already-emergent practice of many diverse new forms of political/social/cultural practice' (Gilbert 2001: 191).

Accordingly, the important status of post-Marxist theory for cultural studies may seem clear. This is what was termed earlier the 'usual interpretation' of the relationship between cultural studies and post-Marxism. Indeed, the validity of this is not something that this work will contest, in this obvious regard; for post-Marxist theory has been and remains indubitably important and enabling for cultural studies. However, the contention of this work is that this 'importance' is not straightforwardly unproblematic, nor is it straightforwardly 'enabling'. This contention itself may hardly appear straightforward. But it can begin to be explained by noting that, as Gilbert observes, despite her *celebration* of Laclauian post-Marxism, nevertheless 'what McRobbie is also looking for in Laclau and Mouffe's post-Marxism is an *absence*, a gap for cultural studies to fill, a work for it to do' (Gilbert 2001: 191). In other words, that is, *if* post-Marxism is everything that cultural studies has deemed it to be – namely, a vital and vitalising paradigm for rethinking the political – then is it actually a 'sublation' of cultural studies? Now, 'sublation' is a Hegelian term, meaning to complete and surpass or supersede (Mowitt 2003: 175–88). So, to sublate something is not simply to affirm it. It is also a double-handed or double-dealing change. For, if cultural studies has been completed *and thereby surpassed* by post-Marxism, then what place is left for cultural studies? Where is there 'a gap for cultural studies to fill, a work for it to do'? If post-Marxism is said to vindicate, justify, and (however retroactively) 'underpin' cultural studies, it also thereby *trumps* cultural studies, and usurps or obviates its role and position. So, one important set of questions is: Is cultural studies ultimately just more or less the same as post-Marxism? Should everyone involved in cultural studies simply 'do' post-Marxism? Is the post-Marxism of Laclau and Mouffe in fact '*better*' cultural studies than cultural studies? Does this post-Marxism provide a *better* way to do cultural studies than any other possible paradigm?

The Stuart Hall kind of answer would be: *both yes and no (but ultimately no)*. Hall's specific problems with and relationship to post-Marxism will be examined in due course. But, it should be affirmed from the outset that what is most important in examining this debate is not simply to arrive at a decision about whether to prefer post-Marxism *or* cultural studies, but rather to explore the question of the political *consequences* of these – and of all – academic intellectual efforts. This refers us back to the importance of the Derridean injunction introduced in the Preface, to attend to the 'political implication' of institutional/intellectual 'paradigms', with which we began (Derrida 1992). In cultural studies, this problematic takes the form of theoretico-practical questions of political intervention: questions about how to intervene, and into what; questions about what political intervention *is*; questions about what and in what way academic work should and could intervene, etc. (Hall 2002). In deconstruction and broadly 'Continental Philosophy'-informed work, these are formulated as questions of 'responsibility'; and for Derrida, as also introduced in the Preface, as questions of 'university responsibility' in particular. However it is formulated, this problematic is crucial for cultural studies, because it is arguably the very question of *how to do cultural studies*, if anything like 'responsible intervention' is indeed an ambition.

This problematic immediately opens onto such questions as those of what cultural studies is meant to be and do, and on what justification – what it is meant to be *for* and how to establish the rectitude, validity and legitimacy of this or that answer. Of course, there is a logical or epistemological problem, an anachronism or tautology discerned, of inevitably relying on opinions already held in order to arrive at desired or expected conclusions – what might be termed '*ex post facto* rationalisation' or retroactively 'positing the presupposition'. Yet it nevertheless seems important to establish what cultural studies is supposed to be doing before it could be possible to determine what kind of paradigm or orientation it should adopt, even though such a verdict will have been arrived at by way of an already adopted paradigm and orientation. This is to acknowledge the disjointedness introduced into rationales by the inevitability of an 'originary' and ongoing bias. The problematic tautology or anachronism at play, Derrida (1977) calls the skewing work of the 'nonconceptual order' upon which concepts and preferences are established. Jeremy Gilbert puts it rather more bluntly: 'everyone has a theory, they just don't always know what it is' (2003: 151). This is the same as saying that the determination of the point and purpose of anything is always-already arrived at under the sway of a particular interpretive paradigm. Paradigms are what guide and perhaps even determine interpretations, values, the formulation of questions and the establishment of answers. Indeed, ultimately the paradigm adopted actually determines *in advance* the answer to the question of *what* 'activity' and 'orientation' are, could and should be. In other words, the problem is that every paradigm, insofar as it offers a different worldview from other paradigms, entails different conceptions of what is analytically relevant, a different model of causality and relation, and a different understanding of the status and effects of particular events, phenomena, institutions and activities (and indeed different understandings of *what* events, phenomena, institutions, and activities *are*). Construed like this, there is clearly nothing outside of the paradigm; and each one – however conscious or unconscious of it one may be – always-already implies its own answers to the question of which activities, projects and orientations are 'proper', 'right' and 'best'.

This problematic will not go away, and will inform Chapters 2 and 3. At this murky, opaque and indecisive moment, with the what, why and how questions of cultural studies clearly foregrounded, a consideration of the post-Marxist paradigm ought to be undertaken, not to sidestep the problematic of the paradigm of cultural studies, but actually to deepen it. For, when it comes to post-Marxist theory, one key question for cultural studies is: If post-Marxism were to be a – or the – paradigm *of* cultural studies, then what orientations, protocols, aims and objects would it oblige cultural studies to adopt? (Mowitt 1992) Post-Marxist political theory is a paradigm of and for analysis, and analysis that extends to embrace the cultural. But is it *the* paradigm of cultural studies? How can and should one adjudicate? This book is preoccupied with these questions, and with their 'political implications'.

The following section clarifies the strong sense in which, and the compelling reasons why, Laclauian post-Marxist discourse analysis can be construed as a vital paradigm of cultural analysis, and why it has rightly been extremely influential within cultural studies. Its 'influence', as has already been indicated, extends from the explicit adoption of post-Marxist language, concepts, categories and frameworks by Stuart Hall from the 1980s onwards, to the contemporary proliferation of works not always but often called cultural studies, works that are increasingly carried out precisely as 'discourse analyses' and which are clearly extremely indebted to post-Marxist discourse theory. Indeed, the influence of post-Marxism as a paradigm of cultural studies (and beyond) is extensive, and growing. And as this work will argue, it will always be extremely valuable for cultural studies. But this influence is not without its limitations, problems, or indeed its political implications.

To return to the Derridean question of the 'political implication', a crucial argument has been offered by John Mowitt (1992). Mowitt proposes that one key problem is that the concept of 'discourse' as used by post-Marxism tends to assume that 'discourse designates how a particular type of phenomena presents *itself* such that it can become the focus of cultural studies' (Mowitt 1992: 16–17). What Mowitt alerts us to here is a problematic that relates to that of 'representation', central both to and beyond cultural studies and post-Marxism, regarding the establishment of knowledge. Mowitt cautions against the making of any assumption that 'phenomena' *ever* as if naturally or neutrally 'present themselves' to the scholarly gaze. Indeed, he argues, things are never so simple. Accordingly, Mowitt's concern is with the orientating role that paradigms play in establishing not only what we *think* we 'know', but also with 'the *way* cultural research is designed, legitimated, and conducted' (16) in light of this. This is a direct political implication of the work of paradigms. The political implications extend deeper and further than this. But for Mowitt, they all hinge on the institutional context of the establishment of knowledge. His worry is that the post-Marxist discourse paradigm actually *occludes* certain crucial dimensions of the problematics and political significance of academic intellectual practices, and their ability to think and to work towards or as 'intervention'. For Mowitt, what is crucial for all politicised intellectual activity is to maintain a vigilant attention to the matter of the role that all institutions, including academic institutional contexts, play within what post-Marxism calls 'discourse' and 'hegemony'. Such an institutional focus, which Mowitt is far from alone in seeing as being central to cultural studies – a focus that needs to be explicitly maintained and developed within cultural studies – is, he argues, distinctly lacking in post-Marxism. In terms of this argument, then, it is post-Marxism that would seem to have a lot to learn from cultural studies.

Now, if both cultural studies and post-Marxism share the 'political' problematic – as it were, sharing 'Gramsci', and sharing the concern for a non-reductive understanding of 'ideology' and a more complex grasp of cultural-political determination – then the relationship between the work of Hall and Laclau constitutes an important index of the relationship between cultural studies and post-Marxism in terms of the question of intellectual orientation and of the political. As has already been indicated, the influence that Laclau's work had on Stuart Hall, and the once central – and still strong – influence of Hall's work on cultural studies, is considerable (Morley and Chen 1996). Thus, considerations of the work of Stuart Hall and Ernesto Laclau and other key figures from cultural studies and post-Marxism will structure this work in terms of the question of responsible academico-political engagement, insofar as they can be taken to represent exemplary positions within and around which many problematics cluster and condense. Yet this work is not primarily 'about' Hall or Laclau, or indeed any named thinker. It is rather about the question of establishing responsible academico-political engagement or intervention, or indeed university responsibility. This is taken to be the key problematic of cultural studies. However, because the post-Marxist paradigm has already been introduced as being at once highly influential and somewhat challenging, both enabling and problematic, both to cultural studies and to the Marxism that was once so central to them both, it should now be established more fully what is meant by 'post-Marxism', what it is and does. The problems to be discerned within the post-Marxist paradigm will serve to enable a fuller consideration and clarification of what is to be understood by 'cultural studies', what it is and does; their relationship, and the importance of the problematic that their differences point to, not merely for them both but for all thinking of the cultural, the political, and the questions of responsibility and political intervention.

It is helpful to remember that, very much like Laclau (1999; 2000), Stuart Hall maintains that he is ' "post-Marxist" only in the sense that I recognize the necessity to move beyond orthodox Marxism, beyond the notion of Marxism guaranteed by the laws of history. But I still operate somewhere within what I understand to be the discursive limits of a Marxist position. And I feel the same way about structuralism' (Hall 1996d: 148). It is helpful to remember this because one crucial relation between cultural studies and post-Marxism can be found in their respective post-Gramscian engagements with questions of politics, hegemony and 'culture', or 'ideology'. What will come to be significant here relates to two key differences in the orientations of cultural studies and post-Marxism in the face of these questions. Where they are most different is, first, on the question of 'culture', which is deconstructed in cultural studies yet barely mentioned in post-Marxism; and second, on the question of 'politics', which is theorised rigorously in post-Marxism and is adopted – with reservations – by cultural studies. As will be explored below, post-Marxism works with a straightforward model of political causality and refers to normal (macro-)political phenomena 'out there'. Cultural studies work often proceeds in this manner, too (something that is problematic in itself); but cultural studies moves away from reductive Marxism by way of a detour through questions of culture. What is significant about this 'detour', though, is that however much it could be said to have been enabled or theoretically justified by Laclauian theory, it can also have the effect of problematising to the extent of weakening and jeopardising the normal post-Marxist notion of politics. Now, as will become important, this is most palpable and comes most to the fore in the different deployments of 'deconstruction' in cultural studies and post-Marxism, as well as the way that deconstruction has been mobilised in John Mowitt's critique of the post-Marxist discourse paradigm to forward a different ('textual') paradigm for cultural studies. Indeed, as will also hopefully become clear, deconstruction is to be viewed as irreducibly cortical to both cultural studies and post-Marxism – and nowhere more importantly than in the thinking of responsibility and intervention. In other words, for post-Marxism and cultural studies, there is no getting away from deconstruction. Bearing this in mind, this work will explore the key features of the post-Marxist discourse paradigm and convey its importance for cultural studies, before introducing the problematics for cultural studies that it poses.

The Discourse of Post-Marxism

As post-Marxism is an explicitly *political* theory, it may come as a surprise to some to learn that the post-Marxist political theory of Laclau and Mouffe is perhaps more indebted to putatively literary theory, Continental philosophy, deconstruction and semiotics than to political theory 'proper'. But it was actually by applying deconstructive, literary theoretical, psychoanalytic and semiotic concepts and techniques to the analysis of the political that Laclau and Mouffe developed their self-proclaimed 'radical' version of Marxist political theory, which found its first thoroughgoing articulation in *Hegemony and Socialist Strategy* (1985). This work carried out a methodical historical critique and deconstruction of 'classical Marxism' (1985: 3), enabling them to claim to identify why classical Marxist theory could not predict, account for, nor adequately explain the behaviour of political struggles and socio-political or economic classes. This failure, becoming increasingly apparent throughout the twentieth century, represented a severe challenge to both the (rhetorico-) political force and the intellectual validity and viability of Marxism; challenging its credibility as a political position and as an academically plausible paradigm. Even though many, including Robert J. C. Young, have rejected the need to call such Marxist theory post-Marxism, by arguing that 'after all, capitalism transforms itself often enough without becoming "post-capitalism" (and, it might be added, enough capitalist states have collapsed without it being subsequently assumed that this signals the end of capitalism)' (Young 2001: 7), nevertheless the apparent inaccuracies of Marxian predictions about the world have initiated something of a 'crisis' *within* Marxism itself. Its predictive and even descriptive failures ran entirely contrary to the claims that Marxism could be the objective science of history (2).

So Laclau and Mouffe orientated their analysis by identifying a discrepancy between Marxism's claims about the socio-political world, on the one hand, and the 'reality' or observable development of actual societies, on the other (122). For, as 'objective science', Marxism aimed to predict the course history must necessarily take, culminating in the revolution of a universal class. In the face of the failure of this prediction, Marxism could most readily survive by recourse to a rearticulation of the emphasis of its claims; by moving away from claiming to be the declarations of an objective science (of the order: 'This *will* happen'), and changing to those of injunctions made in the name of an ethical programme (of the order: 'This *should* (be made to) happen') (Laclau 1996a: 66; Devenney 2004: 125). However, for Laclau and Mouffe (1985), any move which entails abandoning the idea of Marxism's apodicticity (absolute indisputability), and sees Marxism as *merely* ethical, was simply unsatisfactory – intellectually and politically (Laclau 1996a: 66–7).

Although they would not disagree that Marxism entails an ethical dimension, especially regarding the primary question of justice (or any claim regarding justice), which they argue is always in some measure at the heart of democratic struggles (1985: 174), and ultimately all politics (Laclau 2005), their analysis does not remove itself from the matter of the mechanisms *governing* social and political 'reality'. However, where classical Marxism concerned itself with 'objective reality', Laclau and Mouffe see objectivity itself as only one part of reality. So, as objectivity is only one part of a social totality, it is not coterminous or coextensive with 'reality' as such, and any analysis of the *totality* should not therefore concern itself with only that one part

(1985: 111). Accordingly, their emphasis moves from the objectivity of that which exists, 'is', or has being or presence (Spivak 1974: xiv), and focuses instead upon the 'logic' of the socio-political. They do not ignore 'the objective' and 'objectivity', but focus more upon the ways that 'objective reality' actually gains that status of being – or what they term 'the *conditions of possibility* of any objectivity' (Laclau 1989: xiii). But this logic is neither commonsensical nor metaphysical; not, that is, organised by notions of simple 'identity', 'presence' and the law of non-contradiction (Laclau and Mouffe 1985: 124). It is rather a deconstructive logic, intelligible most readily in terms of the Saussurean semiotic notion in which the identity of any sign (or, in Laclau and Mouffe, any entity at all) is constituted on the basis of defining and asserting itself in terms of that which it is not – that is, on the basis of difference. (In fact, it is rather to be understood in terms of the *failure* or limits of this model of structure, in the move taken by Derrida from thinking structures of *difference* to thinking in terms of the ultimate impossibility of 'pure presence', and hence the failure of any structure, or *'différance'*.)

Their overhaul of Marxist theory constitutes an attempt to 'save' the project of Marxism – or its object, socialism – from obsolescence, whilst not abandoning its telos, the hope of egalitarian radical democratic emancipation for all from exploitation and subjection, whether that attendant to capitalist production or otherwise. Hence the term 'post-Marxism': the reference to the telos of Marxism remains in place, as a guiding idea, but the 'post-' signifies after, more than, other than Marxism (Laclau 1993: 329). They abandon the idea of some inevitable process of the unfolding of historical 'necessity', in favour of stressing the contingency of social-political organisation, and the belief in the need to struggle, politically, for emancipation. The 'post-' signifies the abandonment of axioms that they call essentialist (1985: 47).

Their deconstruction of these has caused much controversy among other Marxist theoreticians (Geras 1985; Forgacs 1985; Sim 1998), and in a sense this controversy exists actually because their analysis of the social, political, ideological and economic takes the form of a deconstruction. For, deconstruction itself remains controversial. Often, it is not deemed 'political' at all, or of any 'use' to political analysis – especially not before Laclau and Mouffe's intervention (Bennington 1994: 6). As a tool for literary analysis, and occasionally for drawing out philosophical themes within texts, deconstruction is often construed as being worthwhile only insofar as it constitutes a radical form of *reading* (Weber 1987). But Laclau and Mouffe use deconstruction to read the texts of classical Marxism and the political world, and to reassess everything according to what is suggested by using this particular reading practice. So, already, post-Marxism is far from being *proper* Marxism: the way that it apparently denies some of the central tenets or mantras of Marxism and applies a form of analysis often deemed anarchic and even irrational to political texts, has led post-Marxism to be received as a transgression of Marxism, or even as not Marxist at all. But, their critical analysis of Marxist categories and their subsequent construction of a post-Marxist paradigm (Mowitt 1992: 17) constitutes for them a reinvigoration and radicalisation of the tradition, which they deem to be the only way to keep open the possibility of the socialist objectives of the Marxist project, as a valid and viable political force.

Let us briefly retrace the outline of their argument, as presented in *Hegemony*, indicate some of its key subsequent development, and the ways it has contributed to contemporary conceptualisations of the nature of the political (Beardsworth 1996: xi), before opening the question of its limitations. In the opening movement of *Hegemony*, Laclau and Mouffe focus on the social conditions characterising 'revolutionary situations'. Reading Rosa Luxemburg's analysis of these situations, they argue that:

> in a revolutionary situation, it is impossible *to fix the literal sense* of each isolated struggle, because each struggle overflows its own literality and comes to represent, in the consciousness of the masses, a simple moment of a more global struggle against the system. And so it is that while in a period of stability the class consciousness of the worker . . . is 'latent' and 'theoretical', in a revolutionary situation the *meaning* of every mobilisation appears, so to speak, as split: aside from its specific literal demands, each mobilization represents the revolutionary process as a whole; and these totalizing effects are visible in the overdetermination of some struggles by others. This is, however, nothing other than the defining characteristic of the symbol: the overflowing of the signifier by the signified. *The unity of the class is therefore a symbolic unity*. (10–11)

Here, the 'literal meaning' of an event is shown to depend on the context in which it occurs, or in which it is interpreted and given meaning. The literal meaning of anything cannot be divorced from its 'connotation' (Hall 1980: 133), and both the connotation and denotation of a signifier (or, more precisely, of its 'articulation') will always be established within the confines of a certain context: the same signifier will connote and denote very different things in different contexts, depending on the context in which it occurs, as well as the infinite range of possible contexts in which it could thereafter be reinterpreted (Derrida 1977: 1–25; Laclau 2005: 25). In the case of a revolutionary political situation, they argue, any particular event in that struggle will ideally attain a meaning in which it is equivalent to all other events in that struggle, no matter how different it might *literally* be. The meaning of any event will arise as a result of the 'overdetermination' of the context in which it occurs, and/or the context in which it is interpreted.[1]

In the revolutionary situation, the event and its interpretation take place in the same context – that of the revolutionary situation itself. But the meaning of an event is open to the possibility/inevitability of being re-narrated in different contexts, so that it will *mean* – indeed, '*be*' – something entirely different, elsewhere. In this example, though, they are concerned with the meaning of an event *within* the interpretive context of a revolutionary situation, and not with its meaning outside or after that situation. Later on, they consider the importance of the reiteration of an event's meaning into different discursive contexts, as a key moment of articulating a certain desired meaning to any event, so that its meaning becomes relatively fixed within the socio-political imaginary, thus enabling it to (tend to) work for the purposes of a certain political project. So, in a non-revolutionary situation, were a group of workers to strike for better pay or better working conditions, then that strike would not necessarily symbolize any general cause or struggle. In a revolutionary situation, in which an entire society has become polarised into two opposing camps (say, 'the people' versus the aristocracy or '*ancien régime*', as of the French Revolution), then when a particular group strikes, it will symbolize the entire struggle, the entire plight of the people. In Laclau and Mouffe's terms, in such a situation or context, whatever the people do – however *different* each act is – it will be *equivalent* in status and meaning when considered in terms of the general struggle: it will be a symbol of and for it. For as long as the struggle persists, it will be immensely important to each side of the struggle to reiterate a certain meaning for these events, in order that, over time, and through the 'regularity in dispersion' of these reiterations, the meaning which best serves the cause will become consolidated and sedimented as 'true' in the mindset, or imaginary, of as many people as possible. The meanings which tend to become dominant in the social-political imaginary, and which work to strengthen a particular cause, political position, or power structure, will, in their terms, have become hegemonic, working to constitute, represent, and perpetuate the dominant hegemony or dominant hegemonic political position.

It is important to note that processes of the overdetermination of meaning take place in all contexts. In fact, the tendency to establish (to 'articulate') certain meanings in certain ways can be viewed as one of the ways of defining or delimiting the notion of 'context' itself. For post-Marxism, then, 'objectivity' or 'truth' themselves are – and are permeated with – 'floating signifiers' (Laclau and Mouffe 1985: 171; Laclau 1996: 36–46, 2005). They are not necessarily attached to any particular final or transcendental signified, or necessary referent. It all depends, for Laclau and Mouffe, on 'precise discursive conditions of emergence'. In the discourse of what Laclau and Mouffe call orthodox or classical Marxism (as found in the likes of Plekhanov and Kautsky), the 'truth' of society lies with the economic base of any given society, where the putative *real, fundamental, structural* situation of human societies is that there are, first and foremost, material economic factors, determining everything important about that society. So, the location of a source of raw materials, along with the viability, presence, or possible presence, of the other factors of production (land, labour, capital, legislation, confidence, etc.), will govern the decision about whether to locate, say, a factory thereabouts, and hence constitute the conditions of possibility for a certain kind of society's development there also. As such, it is by way of the dictates of the economic base that the presence and form of any social activity is determined. For such Marxism, then, it is true to say that the economy is determinant in the first and last instance of social relations, felt nowhere more profoundly than in a society operating under a capitalist economy, where population is displaced and located according to the dictates of profitability, and where the fate of nations is determined according to decisions made by capitalists.

In terms of this 'truth', then, some classical Marxism sees a distinction between the constitutive factor of the 'economic base', and the subordinate element of the 'ideological superstructure', or the lived relations and fantasy life of a society; its beliefs, practices, and relationships – the family structure, the educational apparatus, religious institutions, media, the whole infrastructure, and its attendant systems of values, truths, or ideology. But, immediately, post-Marxism points out, it is really quite impossible to maintain the distinction between base and superstructure, as they are symbiotic, overlapping, and non-separable, which is why they offer the term 'discourse', to indicate the entire open-ended structure, rather than maintain otherwise impossibly essentialist distinctions (Laclau and Mouffe 1985: 174) and/or any belief in the simple fixed identity of notions like 'individual', 'class', and 'society'. For, instead of preserving the kind of thinking which takes an 'individual' to be a member of a 'class', a class which is itself a coherent part of a coherent 'society', Laclau and Mouffe focus on these terms themselves. What is an 'individual'? What is a 'class'? And what is 'society'? They expose such notions as essentialist by inquiring into the relationship between the concept (for example, the concept of 'working class') and the referent thought to be signified by that term (in this example, the concept or signifier of 'working class subject' would be tied necessarily to some specific living person, exemplifying and representing *the* 'working class'). The first essentialism is this kind of referential thinking: namely, *that* someone who occupies at certain times what is thought to amount to a (or *the*) 'working class subject position' *is therefore* 'a member of the working class', purely, simply, and entirely. They argue that whilst it is true that at certain times in certain people's lives, they may quite literally occupy what are deemed to be working class subject positions, it is equally likely that such a person will at other times occupy incommensurable subject positions, not consistent with being a 'working class subject'. They argue that this is a theoretical 'confusion' of Marxist theory (119), which has led either to the 'logically illegitimate conclusion . . . that the other positions occupied by these agents are also "working-class positions"' or, alternatively, that these contradictions in the variety and inconsistency of subject positions occupied by 'working class' subjects are the result of some separating power of capitalism, working in the superstructure. That is to say, Laclau and Mouffe argue that it is never simply the case that there is an essential or substantial unity to the working class, a unity extending to all the possible subject positions occupied by all the 'individuals' who make up the class. Whereas earlier Marxist theory would consider ideological contradictions to be the result of the divisive power of capitalism, used in order to perpetuate the mystification and delusion of subjects who would otherwise be able to see the truth of their situation as the exploited, Laclau and Mouffe disagree. They argue that many of the problems of theoretical Marxism have been brought on by Marxism's own manner of theorising: Marxism, they argue, theorises the 'individual' as a referent, 'individuals' as being the 'origin and basis of social relations' (115), and 'society' itself as actually *being a 'thing'*, a referent.

However, as the passage quoted above reveals, Laclau and Mouffe contend that any class unity that might occur – a unity in which individuals see themselves as part of a class, and act as a class, in unity – will only be a symbolic identification, related to signification and not to some presumed innate properties of referents. Indeed, the so-called inherent properties of any referent are, in Laclau and Mouffe's terms, produced in and through signifying practices – practices which are inherently contingent and therefore immanently political. Indeed, Laclau (2005) argues that the true or most salient 'referents' of political ontology and political force are political *demands* rather than 'people' or 'groups', because it is through the work of the shared political *demand* that identities are constituted (Laclau 2005: 224). This means, in this case, that it is the work of symbolic signification that has the power to make or break the notion of 'class' as a valid political force. What this also means is that, in stark distinction to traditional Marxist theories of political action and transformation, it is quite possible that members of many different socio-economic classes can identify with the symbol of a political struggle, and become identifiable as a consciously unified group, struggling for a particular political transformation. 'Valid' political groups need not essentially consist of members of the same class. Nor are political groups total, complete, or 'natural': they are not 'naturally arising' (or ontological referents); rather they are produced within discourse and signification: the 'referent' is *produced* – meaning that political identities and groups are partial and provisional identifications with a cause. Unity will not be complete, total, or permanent. As soon as the cause (the political antagonism) is lost, won, or dissipates, the group will effectively cease to exist, as the identity of the group has no essence outside of the antagonism, around, against, and in terms of which it constructed itself. Thus, they argue, one should not identify political agency with named referents. A political identity will be formed in relation to a political issue (an antagonism); that identity is not the whole or entire identity of the person or persons who hold it, even though some political antagonisms persist to such an extent that the identities of certain people and groups will be dominated and overdetermined to a massive extent by these political antagonisms.

Thus, a theory of the political should not theorise in terms of 'individuals'. For the 'identity' of an individual depends on the discursive/contextual factors of its emergence. But this insight into the constitution of subjectivity does not constitute the totality of post-Marxism's contribution to political theory. For it also explores the

roles played by the imaginary, fantasy, institutionalisation, legislations, and so on, within the political domain (Žižek: 1989), and
thereby expands the conceptualisation of 'the political' itself, as well
as transforming the nature of any consideration of the socio-political,
away from simply thinking about 'individuals' in 'society'. For, just as
looking at individuals misses relevant discursive or structural elements
(because the notion of the individual implicitly takes the identity of
that individual to be set and already established, while Laclau and
Mouffe argue that any individual identity will be constituted by
factors such as the very fact of their involvement in a struggle or
context), the post-Marxists also point out that the object of political
analysis termed society, the social or the socius, is not only *not* pre-
given, already-existing, established, unified and objectively real, but
that, actually, *society does not exist* (Žižek 1990: 249). For 'society' or
'the social' is not a *thing* (or *referent*). It is a construct, or a 'figure',
without a final signified. You cannot put your finger on any object and
declare that *it is society*. There is no object which objectively *is* society.
'Society' functions as a signifier, but it has no final signified. Everyone
'knows what it means', although this meaning will differ in its
representation, from context to context, but no one could put their
finger on some *thing* that 'is' the essence or substance of the social.
There are *figures* of and for the social/society (metonyms, metaphors,
symbols, allusions, etc.), but 'society' is itself already a figuration or a
construct for something that is constitutively absent (Laclau and
Mouffe 1985: 125).

But, of course, 'society' or 'the social' *does exist*. (At least, as far as
we're concerned!) It is just that political thinking of what it means to
say that something exists has to be reassessed (Derrida 1974; Spivak
1974: xiv). 'Society' does not exist as an essence residing somewhere,
fully present and intelligible in any way. It is rather, according to the
post-Marxists, an ideological fantasy. So, whenever a signifier of
society or the social is presented as being *the* signifier of society –
examples might include the figure of the monarch or a rebel, the
results of a census or a table of statistics about a society, etc. – it is
immediately obvious that this representation is not that society *itself*,
that it in no way captures the 'essence' of the society, that there would
seem to be so much more to it than that. This is because, as Laclau and
Mouffe point out, 'the totality is not a datum but a construction'
(1985: 144; Laclau 2005: 224), and always both less and more than
any given signifier of it. They refer to this effect as that of the 'surplus
of meaning', an effect resulting from the fact that because 'identities

are purely relational . . . there is no identity which can be fully constituted' (1985: 111). The production of any identity is contingent, partial, antagonised (to the extent that something 'blocks' it), and political.

This formulation applies not only to the identity of individuals, but also to that of institutions, and even of historical events. None of these identities are fixed, but rather are the effect or result of their relationships with other identities, and the relationships between identities (it being the *relationship* in which an identity is placed or articulated that determines the meaning and being of that identity) are established in what Laclau and Mouffe term 'discourse'. To stay with the concept of the social or society, it can be said that, because it is intelligible, or because everyone 'knows' what it is, even though 'it' is a construct with no ultimate referent, this intelligibility has been constructed by discourse: discourses of value, which assert what society *is like* or *should be like*, using the term rhetorically (through analogy), and empirical discourses, using statistical constructs which take parts as indicators of the whole (metonymically). The features of rhetorical or value-based discourses and those of empirical discourses mark key coordinates of all discourses of the social. Historical, literary, anthropological, governmental and bureaucratic discourses, and so on, all incorporate the evaluatory and the ostensibly referential in order to suture the meaning of 'society'.

The suturing of 'society', so that it means something whole, complete, knowable, etc., implies the 'regularity in dispersion' of certain articulations, their reiteration in many and varied discursive contexts (1985: 142); the signification of 'society' (or any term) becomes *partially* fixed only on the basis of its regular deployment in familiar ways, in everyday discourses (educational, governmental, familial, media, etc.), throughout time and space. Laclau and Mouffe invoke the Lacanian concept of the *point de capiton*, or 'quilting point', to explain the way that meaning becomes relatively fixed within different discursive contexts. These quilting points are overdetermined by their status within discourses (examples might include the idea of 'Man', the 'Individual', or 'God'), and they prevent the slippages of meaning that would occur in interpretation were there no relatively stable terms to refer to in communicative or interpretive predication. Their stability is a result of the work of their regularity in dispersion throughout dominant discourses. But a deconstruction of the situations in which they are used to structure meaning reveals that, despite their putatively obvious intelligibility, or their putative transparency of meaning, it remains impossible to identify a concrete signified or referent for them other than through connotation, metaphor, metonymy, symbol, and other literary or poetic devices. This leads to the peculiarity in which even the ostensible literality of speaking about 'the individual' reveals itself to be figurative. Thus, even the objectivity of objective language is itself a construction relying on rhetorical, textual, poetic, and otherwise literary techniques; or, as Laclau and Mouffe say, 'all discourse of fixation becomes metaphorical: literality is, in actual fact, the first of all metaphors' (111).

In a sense, all of this now runs contrary to discourses that claim to be objective (Devenney (2004) even claims this to be the key achievement of Laclau's political theory: that ultimately it demonstrates the impossibility of positivism in the field of cultural and political study). It goes against such discourses, and rejects all claims made in the name of neutral or natural objectivity. Objectivity, for the post-Marxism of Laclau and Mouffe, is never neutral, but is rather contingent, contestable and political; and this subverts the notion of objectivity *and* challenges the authority of discourses claiming to be objective. Indeed, one of the key interests of post-Marxist theory is in exploring the conditions of possibility for objectivity: for post-Marxism, like a lot of so-called postmodernist thought, objectivity is not naturally occurring, but is rather something that is *forcefully established*; something that is, as such, contingent and variable.

This may sound – and indeed it is – controversial, especially when as a proposition it is brought into contact with that putative pinnacle of objective knowledge, *scientific* objectivity and truth. For 'science' is often taken as a signifier of our ability to *know* the truth. However, many scholars since Thomas Kuhn (1962) have argued that in any effort to produce truth, science constitutively requires the production of systems. This inevitably involves exclusions, reductions, the imposition of conventions and limits, and ultimately therefore the production of knowledge that, given its conventional, contingent, and limited requirements, has a peculiar status – the status of a kind of fiction. For, in a strong sense, even scientific systems too are irreducibly theoretical, speculative constructions, relying on paradigms, and hence subject to the kind of legitimation problematics discussed above. Lynette Hunter, for instance, argues that scientific 'models' (paradigms) – scientific discourse's 'tautological worlds' – acquired the status of 'neutral fact' only 'in the late 18th to 19th century' when science started to become increasingly hived off into discrete disciplines. Hunter's argument is that although it may well be that science has always desired to achieve the status of 'neutral fact', it is actually the demands of 'technological application with its particular requirements for commercial exploitation that pushes the wider scientific discourses into claims of neutrality' (Hunter 1999: 33). This is of course a litotes restatement of the condition or 'crisis' described most famously by Lyotard in *The Postmodern Condition: A Report on Knowledge* (1984). Apropos science and its relation to economics, technology and capital – or, in other words, on the subject of the conditions of possibility for objectivity, and relating the partiality and constructed character of objectivity to techno-capitalism – Lyotard offers this concise formula: 'No money, no proof – and that means no verification of statements and no truth. The games of scientific language become the games of the rich, in which whoever is wealthiest has the best chance of being right. An equation between wealth, efficiency, and truth is thus established' (Lyotard 1984: 45).

Lyotard's rightly famous work elaborates at once the tautologies, circularities and aporias of legitimation, value and truth, as well as their reciprocal interimplication and socio-institutional imbrication or sedimentation – their reticulation or articulation with each other – within, throughout, and as, the entire hegemonic field of discursivity, or, that is, the entire social and cultural terrain. Objectivity is 'produced' by interested parties. Lyotard argues this in order to characterise what has now become generally known, following his own work's title, as 'the postmodern condition'; and he presents this condition as being one of a crisis beginning in the question of how to legitimate knowledge, and reciprocally therefore becoming a problem of how to establish *any* truth, including *the truth of reality itself*. The crisis consists of how to establish the reality of what appears to be reality and the truth of what claims to be truth, and its effects radiate and permeate the social in myriad ways. Lyotard infamously paints a picture wherein science, reliant on technology, is immediately beholden to the powers of capitalism. Thus, capitalism becomes for Lyotard something of an all-pervasive power, immediately ensnaring not just the means of establishing objective knowledge, but also the means and mechanisms of making 'good' judgements, 'sound' legal and moral pronouncements, and other prescriptives. He argues that:

> since 'reality' is what provides the evidence used as proof in scientific argumentation, and also provides prescriptions and promises of a juridical, ethical, and political nature with results, one can master all of these games by mastering 'reality'. That is precisely what technology can do. By

reinforcing technology, one 'reinforces' reality, and one's chances of being just and right increase accordingly. Reciprocally, technology is reinforced all the more effectively if one has access to scientific knowledge and decision-making authority.

This is how legitimation by power also takes shape. Power is not only good performativity, but also effective verification and good verdicts. It legitimates science and the law on the basis of their efficiency, and legitimates this efficiency on the basis of science and law. It is self-legitimating. (1984: 47)

Accordingly, for any discourses claiming to be objective, this anatomy of the inescapably biased 'conditions of possibility' for objectivity – an objectivity that henceforth becomes construed as constitutively contingent, even in its scientific variants – will be inadmissible. For, were it accepted, then it would enable the contestation of the authority of objective discourses and therefore also of sedimented structures of power and knowledge. This is precisely what Lyotard calls the 'postmodern condition', or 'postmodern legitimation crisis'. In Laclau and Mouffe's terms, this is now the terrain of *antagonism* (1985: 122).

'Antagonism' in Laclau and Mouffe is the limit of objectivity. In a paradoxical sense, in fact, it is for them the *only* objectivity, even though antagonism, in their thinking, *cannot* 'be objective'. Rather, antagonisms arise in the face of putatively objective relations that are experienced as being contingent, *unjust* or *wrong* (1985: 125; Laclau 2005). Now, in discussing 'antagonism', Laclau and Mouffe explore the example of the development of feminism (1985: 154), in which the claims for the equal rights of women were articulated with reference to the *ethos* and *telos* of equality and democracy. But, they point out, 'in order to be mobilized in this way, the democratic principle of liberty and equality had first to impose itself as the new matrix of the social imaginary; or, in our terminology, to constitute a fundamental nodal point in the construction of the political' (154–5). Thus, it was the institution of 'democracy' as a *point de capiton* which paved the way for the possibility of the birth of feminism. In their terms, it was the democratic revolution which constituted the conditions of possibility for the emergence of many antagonisms *as* antagonisms and for the construction of, in this example, a democratic feminist struggle. In fact, Laclau and Mouffe locate, in the democratic revolution, and indeed in the concept of democracy itself, a profound transformation of the range of possibilities for politics, a radical extension of the entire political terrain, which moves the political into every relation and institution which has a place (or does not yet have a place) in every aspect of every sense that can be signified by the notion of 'society'. As they argue:

> the 'democratic revolution', as a new terrain which supposes a profound mutation at the symbolic level, implies a new form of institution of the social. In earlier societies, organized in accordance with a theological-political logic, power was incorporated in the person of the prince . . . the radical difference which democratic society introduces is that the site of power becomes an empty space . . . The possibility is thus opened up of an unending process of questioning . . . (1985: 186)

The ramifications of this argument are significant. However, in discussing them, it is important to note that despite Laclau and Mouffe's preferred choice of example (feminism, democracy), there is no *necessary* relation between antagonism and the experience of injustice in Laclau and Mouffe's thought. Injustice might be an example of where antagonism happens, and Laclau and Mouffe do wish to tie their political colours to the mast of 'justice'. But, even though 'relations' are not objective, it does not follow that they are 'unjust' or 'antagonistic'. Non-objectivity is indeed the condition of antagonism for Laclau and Mouffe, but antagonism doesn't *necessarily* follow from it. What is crucial for politics is that any actually existing relation or state of affairs has to be *represented as* 'unjust' or 'wrong' (Laclau 2005). In this sense, hegemony is the act of representation of non-objectivity in a particular way, and it may or may not succeed. So, just because discourses are not objective, just because their referents are constructed, it does not follow that they will actually be contested. In fact, in the vast majority of cases they are accepted (See also Rancière 1999). As will be seen in the ensuing discussions in the following chapters, this is one of the key reasons why Richard Rorty (1996) rejects deconstructive post-Marxist theory, and indeed rejects all 'high' philosophical political theory. As will be clarified, Rorty's 'pragmatist' argument is that there are enough pressing problems to deal with without getting involved in incessantly debating the fundamentals of ontology, or indeed their mirror opposite, the *lack* of ontological fundamentals. For Rorty, pragmatism is superior to all 'deconstructionism' and 'high theory' precisely *because* it is unconcerned with theoretical matters; Rorty's reply to Laclauian theory is, basically, *so what* if there is no ground under our feet; let's just get over it and get on with things! In general, cultural studies, like Slavoj Žižek, has always been very suspicious of this sort of argument, and has taken it as evidence of the existence of 'ideology' – in which positions like those of Rorty, insofar as they appear content with the status quo, are deemed to be ideological. The Žižekian Marxist response to positions such as Rorty's is to denounce them as ideological and as trying to cover over the 'radical antagonisms' of capitalism. Similarly, thinkers like Judith Butler mistrust any denials – such as may perhaps be discerned in Rorty's position – of the political significance of cultural *difference*. The arguments, and the status and significance of the arguments, of these thinkers will be discussed more fully in the following chapters, especially Chapter 3.)

What Laclau and Mouffe take to be vital here is that when society is no longer considered to be organised according to some theological or 'natural' hierarchy based on divine right or nature, then the members of that society must bear the responsibility for its (*their own*) organisation. If society's hierarchies and institutions are deemed to be unjust, then democratic principles enable the contestation of that situation on the basis of appeals to justice and equality. In post-Marxism, then, democracy is deemed to be the best means of assuring that any injustice, exploitation, and oppression can be countered, and that *all* power be accountable, precisely because democratic principles contain within themselves the basis of their own critique and interminable contestation. Of course, the non-objectivity of society – its 'always-constructed' character – does not necessarily lead to the inevitable institution of democracy as a mode of organisation. Thus, it is clear that post-Marxism does have an ethical stake in radical democracy, because arguably bearing responsibility for the non-objectivity of society does not necessarily mean being democratic: it can just as easily mean blaming 'the other' (for example, 'the Jews' (See Žižek 1989)) for all of society's problems. Indeed, the championing of democracy in this sense does assume that all subjects *know* that non-objectivity is the case. However, non-objectivity is the condition of what Laclau and Mouffe call hegemony and hegemonic politics, and this form is given a historical purchase with reference to modern democracy. The advent of this kind of politics, Laclau and Mouffe argue, enabled the proliferation of the political logic that they term 'hegemonic'.

Their theory of hegemony and hegemonic politics clearly and avowedly takes its inspiration from the work of Antonio Gramsci (1971: 181–2), but the key difference between Gramsci's model and that of Laclau and Mouffe lies in the latter's emphasis on the discursive construction of every political identity, in that identities do not exist *before* their construction around antagonisms. This is the reason why the post-Marxists talk of subject positions or identification or interpellation as opposed to subjects, because they construe political identities and meanings to be partial, provisional, and constantly (potentially) in a state of flux. Accordingly, their emphasis is on the prime importance of the *tendency*: the tendency to represent certain issues or figures in a certain way, the tendencies by which certain issues are articulated as equivalent or different, related or separate, and so on. For it is the regularity in dispersion of manners of representation, modes of articulation, and conventions of interpretation, that govern the character of a political hegemony, and so any changes at the point of representation or articulation can effect changes throughout an entire hegemonic structure – a structure that encompasses all areas of the social, political and institutional make up of a society.

The Text of Cultural Studies

Strong criticisms of post-Marxism have come from within Marxist political theory itself, and these have been widely detailed (see, for instance, the summaries given by Lechte (1994: 191) and Sim (1998)). But one of the most challenging, yet widely unacknowledged critiques of post-Marxism actually comes from within the very field of literary, textual and cultural studies that post-Marxism mined heavily in its formation and development. As you will recall, post-Marxist political theory developed by way of recourse to literary theoretical and deconstructive techniques of textual analysis. Yet, in reading Laclau and Mouffe, the debt (Derrida 1994) that they owe to the theory of the text, as developed by Barthes, Derrida, Kristeva, Sollers, and so on, is given little attention. John Mowitt argues that this inattention, coupled with post-Marxism's championing of the notion of 'discourse' instead of 'text' (even though post-Marxism actually used the notion of 'text' to define what it means by 'discourse' (Mowitt 1992: 15)), constitutes a limitation of the radical political implications of the theory of the text, or of deconstruction – an innovation that was already, from the outset, profoundly political and subversive. It is therefore important to specify the core significance of the theory of the text, and why Mowitt insists that it has such a crucial status within cultural studies, and poses such a challenge to post-Marxism.

On Mowitt's account, the importance of textuality or textualism on cultural analyses of all orders cannot perhaps be overstated. The construal of objects of study as being textual – as being constructions whose identities, features, properties and characteristics are established through inter-*textual* reference of similarity and dissimilarity and through reciprocal relations with other objects, and whose meaning and status is at least influenced by con-*text* (the objects' contexts and the observers' contexts) – is a (broadly semiological) commonplace – in cultural studies, at least. However, the textual approach to cultural studies, argues Mowitt, should not stop at textualising the external object or field. Rather, what Mowitt sees as key here relates to the implications that the textual insight has for the understanding of the ways that *disciplines themselves construct or establish their own objects of study*. Crucial in the view that disciplinary fields are textual, 'textile', 'woven' (1992: 98), complexly inter-imbricated, is the point that therefore the 'closure of [any] text can only be understood as a mutable effect of a social configuration that embraces language and its various actualizations, and not as an ontologically grounded formal property. In short, the closure of the text is coordinated with the socially constructed perception of its limits' (1992: 7–8). In other words, the textual approach must insist upon the contingency of constructions not only externally ('out there'), but also – and significantly – 'internally' ('in here'). It is because of this that Mowitt argues that 'the text thus appears as irreducibly entangled in disciplinary politics and not merely as the articulation of an effort to reorganize disciplinary boundaries . . . but as a critical practice seeking to problematize the cultural work effected by the disciplines' (14). Derrida calls this 'the law of the text in general': all interpretation 'is only produced by simultaneously proposing an institutional model, either by consolidating an existing one that enables the interpretation, or by constituting a new model to accord with it'. Therefore, in this view, all interpretation constitutes something of 'a new contract with an institution, between an institution and the dominant forces in society'. Interpretation is institutional: both institutionally constituted and operative within an institutional and ultimately political context (Derrida 1992a: 21–3). So, Mowitt's (Derridean, deconstructive) argument is that, in more than one register, 'textualism' is something that can seriously problematise post-Marxist 'discourse'.

Indeed, Mowitt contends that 'the text emerges to name the alterity that simultaneously constitutes and subverts the context of disciplinary reason' (Mowitt 1992: 25). It only does this, however, to the extent that it is deployed to 'pose questions that bear on the institutional maintenance of the hermeneutical field as such – questions which quickly center upon the political problems of how institutions are constituted, reproduced, and transformed' (215; See also Weber 1987). If it is *not* deployed to pose questions about the establishment of the institutional maintenance of the hermeneutical field, however, then 'we gain access only to the comparatively homogeneous tissue of intertextual references that constitutes the hermeneutical field of a particular textual example':

> These are not concerns which come *after* the particular text in question or which are properly 'extrinsic' to it – they are concerns which address the very definition of the textual artefact as an artefact. Insofar as the artefact is meaningful to a particular social group, it is because its members continue to support the disciplinary structures (many of which are not 'merely' academic) which read the artefact on their terms. (Mowitt 1992: 214–15).

Mowitt's contention, in this regard, is that post-Marxist discourse does not – at least, hasn't yet, and perhaps cannot – do this as thoroughly or adequately as what he calls the 'textual paradigm'. (This is otherwise known as deconstruction. Mowitt prefers to keep explicit reference to textuality because of the foregrounding effect this has on the work of the *institutional* construction of what he calls 'disciplinary objects'. This is discussed more fully in Chapter 2). The argument here is once again that disciplinary paradigms play a primary role in constituting precisely what disciplines think they know, what they think that they *can* know, and orientate what they think they can or should do and the way they think they ought to do it. For Mowitt, the emergence of the concepts of the text and textuality through the work of intellectuals associated with the *Tel Quel* journal, particularly Derrida, Kristeva, Barthes, and Sollers, represent a vital ethico-political advance, in that 'the text gives academic intellectuals on the Left a way to conceptualize the link between the struggle to make sense of a particular artefact, and the struggle to transform the general conditions under which that construction takes on its cultural value' (220). In this, a thoroughgoing textual approach to knowledge establishment or production would be one *obliged* to 'confront the problem of disciplinary power as such' (219–20).

What should be emphasised here is the sense in which Mowitt's argument explicitly asserts 'education's role in the formation of cultural hegemony'. Indeed, one of his clearest calls is for academics to endeavour 'to make education into an openly insurgent practice and break the hold that the vocational or professionally oriented disciplines have had on the commerce between the university and society' (218). So, Mowitt should in fact be read as endorsing a model of politics as institutional, disciplinary, and hegemonic, in a sense consistent with yet not limited to post-Marxist (particularly post-Gramscian) theory. This apparent proximity to post-Marxism, though, is not simple contiguity; but is rather a site of disagreement and conflict. Mowitt construes it as a conflict that plays itself out in the tension between 'textual' versus 'discourse' approaches to intellectual work. Attendant to his argument is the observation 'that the historical institutionalization of textuality conditioned the emergence of discourse' (15): that the development of the concept of 'discourse' *relied on* the 'prior institutionalization of textuality' (16). Mowitt draws attention to the fact that, in a relatively early essay called 'Populist Rupture and Discourse' (1980), Laclau specifies how the term 'discursive' is to be understood. He does so by characterising it entirely in terms of 'textuality'. Laclau writes, 'By "discursive" I do not mean that which refers to "text" narrowly defined, but to the ensemble of the phenomena in and through which the social production of meaning takes place, an ensemble which constitutes society as such . . . History and society are an *infinite text*' (Laclau 1980: 87; quoted in Mowitt 1992: 15). Two things in Laclau's orientation strike Mowitt as pertinent. The first is that the characterisation of discourse *as* text demonstrates the prior institutionalisation of textuality ('why would one invoke a concept that was even more obscure than the one s/he is attempting to clarify?' (16), he asks). The second is that talk of discourses 'obscures an important tension between the discursive and the textual' (16):

> To specify what is at stake in this tension, it helps to begin by underscoring the fact that discourse is typically used, as is the case with Laclau, to characterize both the medium and the nature of sociality. Insofar as society is interpretable, it presents itself as an ensemble of discourses. In addition, all that is analytically relevant about society is that which can be interpreted. From this perspective discourse serves as a general name for the class of practices (what, in an older vocabulary, might have been called behaviours and institutions) that define the perceptible surface of society. Cultural analyses conducted from this angle tend to locate particular embodiments of discourse, that is, discourses whose properties and functions are then detailed. For example, all the various 'moves' defining a particular style of dress characteristic of a youth subculture might be read as an expression of resistance to the sartorial norms of the dominant class. However, what is clearly not emphasized here is the status of discourse as a

disciplinary object, a paradigm that organizes the *way* cultural research is designed, legitimated, and conducted. Instead, discourse designates how a particular type of phenomena presents *itself* such that it can become the focus of cultural studies. What remains obscured in the concept of discourse is its relation to an enabling paradigm – a paradigm which, I would argue, derives from the institutionalization of textuality as an interdisciplinary object. Laclau acknowledges this, but shifts the accent in his discussion onto the sociohistorical dimension which, implicitly rests underdeveloped within the concept of the text . . . This is a maneuver that harbors a problem . . . (Mowitt 1992: 16–17)

The problem with this manoeuvre is that, unlike encountering 'discourses' ('out there'), wherever any discipline encounters *textuality*, this encounter is at once productive and yet threatening, disruptive, and (disciplinarily-speaking) dangerous. For, to construe any object as textual immanently draws the contingency of the constitution and limits of that object into sharp relief and, potentially, crisis. It is to transform and to risk 'impossibilising' the object, or at least the stable knowledge of it. The textuality of any object reciprocally thereby risks drawing the limits (and, hence, the very 'heart') of the discipline into question and, again, potential crisis, because the text constantly begs the question, the interrogation, of the determination of any object and any limit (Mowitt 1992: 5–6). The emergence of 'text', then, immanently confronts *every* discipline with the task of rethinking itself, rethinking its own protocols and limits (and reciprocally, once again, its very 'heart'). To view everything as textual demands an account of that discipline's determination of its own protocols and limits. On the other hand, Mowitt contends, something different takes place with the institutionalisation of 'discourse', or with the manoeuvre from a textual (anti-)paradigm to a discursive (disciplinary or disciplining) paradigm. For, quite the opposite of *problematising* limits, discourse preserves the integrity of the disciplinary subject-object divide, and as such 'confirms' the discipline in its security or legitimacy as being a subject that knows this or that field or object 'out there'. For Mowitt, then, the political significance and resources of the text derive from what he calls its potential deployment as an 'antidisciplinary object', which may precipitate productive and ethico-politically consequential crises within and across disciplines and their institutions. The 'discourse paradigm' of post-Marxism, on the other hand, is 'disciplinary', and works to maintain established disciplinary organisations and relations. Textualism for Mowitt is therefore of prime value for what might be called the micro-political perspective that is absent from post-Marxist work. However, not everyone within cultural studies views textuality as simply promissory or politically enabling, beneficial, or advantageous.

The Problem with the Text

Stuart Hall, for instance, does concur that 'culture will always work through its textualities'; but asserts 'at the same time that textuality is never enough' (1992: 284). So it is important to establish what it is about textuality that Hall sees as never enough, and what it is that textuality is never enough for. Simply put, for Hall, the problem with the text relates to politics. In the most direct sense, the problem he discerns is that 'if we are concerned to maintain a politics it cannot be defined exclusively in terms of an infinite sliding of the signifier' (Hall 1996b: 258). In other words, Hall considers the text to constitute a – if not *the* (at least 'theoretical') – problem for cultural studies; a problem that devolves on the troublingly 'infinite' slipperiness introduced by the text. Of course, it is only if 'history and society are an *infinite text*' (Laclau 1980: 87), or in other words, if one already concedes that '*there is nothing outside of the text*' (Derrida 1974: 158), that the problem arises of 'an infinite sliding of the signifier'. In other words, Stuart Hall simultaneously acknowledges the veracity of deconstruction, but also nevertheless *resists* it, viewing textuality ambivalently, as a curiously necessary but unstraightforward enabling and frustrating *problem* for cultural studies (or, indeed, in Derrida's sense, a 'dangerous supplement').

As will be seen in Chapter 2, Hall's peculiar simultaneous subscription to and resistance of deconstruction and textuality is not evidence of any confusion. It is rather that Hall wants the text to remain a *problem* rather than develop into a *problematic*, because, for Hall, the important problematic for cultural studies to engage with is first and foremost always to work out how to intervene consequentially into mobile *political* problems ('out there'). In other words, Hall sees it as important that cultural studies does not get too fixated on and involved with the theoretical question of the 'infinite sliding of the signifier' at the expense of involvement with real political problems. (In this regard, Hall has a strong pragmatic impulse, which relates him, at least 'sentimentally', to another of Laclau's erstwhile interlocutors, Richard Rorty. Indeed, because of post-Marxism's engagement with 'pragmatism', Rorty's position will soon be taken as an exemplary rendition of the impulse towards establishing a 'university responsibility' which does not digress into 'over-philosophication' and excessive theory, in Chapter 3.) As soon becomes apparent, Hall's chief criticism of Laclau relates precisely to the perception of a subordination in Laclau of a proper concern with political issues and an excessive/digressive elevation of theoretical discussion about abstract political logics. Given Hall's ambivalence about textuality (and, by extension, about deconstruction), and given post-Marxism's use of deconstruction as its enabling gesture, as well as Laclau's definitional recourse to infinite textuality as a synonym of the form, character and logic of 'history and society' or 'culture', coupled with Mowitt's arguments about the text as offering an intellectual-political tool that not only challenges the post-Marxist paradigm but that might also be deployed politically, the text deserves further attention. It is worth remaining with Stuart Hall's indication of both the necessity of the textual and the problems for cultural studies that he sees lurking within textuality. He argues that:

> the refiguring of theory, made as a result of having to think questions of culture through the metaphors of language and textuality, represents a point beyond which cultural studies must now always necessarily locate itself. The metaphor of the discursive, of textuality, instantiates a necessary delay, a displacement, which I think is always implied in the concept of culture. If you work on culture, or if you've tried to work on some other really important things and you find yourself driven back to culture, if culture happens to be what seizes hold of your soul, you have to recognize that you will always be working in an area of displacement. There's always something decentred about the medium of culture, about language, textuality, and signification, which always escapes and evades the attempt to link it, directly and immediately, with other structures. And yet, at the same time, the shadow, the imprint, the trace, of those other formations, of the intertextuality of texts in their institutional positions, of texts as sources of power, of textuality as a site of representation and resistance, all of those questions can never be erased from cultural studies. (Hall 1992: 283–4)

As with so much of his work, Hall's argument here is clearly saturated in deconstruction, representing cultural studies' understanding of 'culture' in language that is clearly indebted to Derridean deconstruction, and arguably to a Laclauian understanding of discourse. (However, unlike Mowitt, and in a way that actually supports Mowitt's argument, Hall somewhat conflates and collapses the textual and the discursive: for Hall, the 'metaphor of the discursive' is the same as that 'of textuality'.) In other words, as deconstructive as Hall's depiction of the textuality and/or discursive character of culture is, there nevertheless remains a hesitation, an invocation of a sense in which cultural studies is not simply deconstruction and should, or must, be more and other than deconstruction. But the claim that cultural studies must locate itself and operate somehow 'beyond' or 'after deconstruction' seems deeply problematic, especially when one understands culture the way Hall represents it here: namely, as something pointedly textual and *in différance* (deferral, difference, delay, displacement). Given that Hall's understanding of deconstruction (not to mention 'culture') is evidently far from naïve, we should enquire as to where or what this 'beyond deconstruction', or 'beyond the textual' *is* that cultural studies should be. We should also work out how to make sense of Hall's simultaneous acknowledgement of cultural studies' deep and profound indebtedness to deconstruction, of its *having* to think questions of culture deconstructively, of textuality *'always'* being 'implied in the concept of culture', with this assertion of the need for cultural studies *necessarily* to be 'beyond' deconstruction and textualism. As noted above, Hall's concern relates to politics; that 'if we are concerned to maintain a politics it cannot be defined exclusively in terms of an infinite sliding of the signifier' (Hall 1996b: 258). For him, cultural studies is concerned with – indeed, is even a form of – politics: *cultural politics*, that is; not politics 'proper'; not necessarily parliamentary or state politics. Rather, it is intimately interested in the fundamental *contingency* of culture, its *changeability*, its *imposed-ness*, and the alterability which attests to what is often termed culture's constitutively political character (Arditi and Valentine 1999). Laclau and Mouffe, who strongly influenced Stuart Hall – at least in terms of providing a comprehensive, fluid and fluent-making post-Marxist paradigm and vocabulary of discourse analysis – regularly use such formulations. Jeremy Valentine explains why cultural studies tends to subscribe to such a perspective:

> Because cultural studies maintains that action is meaningful, and is thus not simply behaviour, and that power is structured, and is thus not simply random, political action necessarily entails a cultural dimension. By the same token, because the referent of culture is by its nature limitless, the relation between culture and politics extends beyond the restricted domain of politics understood as the mechanics of a formal system so that culture entails a political dimension. One might say that cultural studies reaches the areas of politics that Political Science does not, and succeeds in this ambition to the extent to which a relation between meaning and power can be shown. I think that Stuart Hall and those influenced by his work have

incontrovertibly established the necessity of this perspective . . . (Valentine 2003: 191)

This sense of 'cultural politics' – that is to say, the understanding that institutions, beliefs, practices, and arguably even our very sub-jectivities and identities are contingent and alterable, the insistence on the political character and consequences of cultural formations, and the understanding that, as Hall puts it, 'culture will always work through its textualities' (1996b: 271) – clarifies why connections are claimed between the political (in this extended 'discursive' sense) and culture, and why representatives of cultural studies and deconstruc-tion often feel themselves to be *doing* something political. This may strike many as either delusional (as in 'but it's merely academic!') or controversial (as in 'academia *should not* be politically motivated or tendentious!'). But it is based on an understanding of cultural, political, and social reality as discursive and hegemonic, meaning that even the 'merely academic' is an active part of the circuits, networks, relays and forces of culture (perhaps particularly in 'making meaning'), and is therefore always already politically consequential. This is the cultural studies (and) post-Marxist answer to Marxian reductionism and determinism, of course. It also means that every-thing, including academia, is to be construed as inescapably politically motivated and tendentious (however 'unconscious' this may be). In this view, reality is at once material and textual, as Hall intimates, or as Laclau and Mouffe express it, discursive: constituted in both material and textual ways.

However, without denying materiality, the textual supplement to reality and to any understanding of it, arguably engenders something of a doubly deconstructive situation. For, even though 'reality' is also material, it is nevertheless discursive and therefore always either imminently or actually *in deconstruction* (Royle 2000: 11). In this sense, one will never be able understand, grasp, express or articulate 'reality' adequately *without* deconstruction. But, Mowitt explains, one problem here, as has been noted at least since Jameson in 1975 (Jameson 1988) is this:

On [Jameson's] account, textuality is nothing but an intellectual expres-sion of what [he] later calls 'the cultural logic' of the latest phase of capitalism . . . The point is not that textuality is simply ideological (Jameson accepts Marx's and Engels' discussion of ideology as the struggle for hegemony in the realm of ideas), but that in its putative bracketing of history (*the* referent), textuality cannot help but affirm those social changes which condition its emergence. The model of the text is therefore problematic because it is incapable of either generating or sustaining a *critical* ideology. Here we have the deepest aspect of Jameson's concerns about modernism and, for that matter, postmodernism. Obviously, insofar as textuality can be affiliated with modernism in this way, then it too can be reduced to sheer, that is capitalist, ideology. (Mowitt 1992: 12–13)

Jameson's problems with textuality therefore also relate to politics, connecting with Hall's problems with deconstruction and textual understandings, as apparently being unable to maintain a politics, or as being 'incapable of either generating or sustaining a *critical* ideology'. So the question is what it is that seems to make deconstruction both so appropriate and so inappropriate, both necessary and insufficient, for cultural studies and for post-Marxism, intellectually and politically speaking. This question is particularly important if cultural studies is indeed construed as 'a practice which aims to make a difference in the world' (Hall 1992: 278). In this respect, then, the archive of explicitly deconstructive thought, deriving from the *Tel Quel* group (Derrida, Barthes, Kristeva, Sollers) who rigorously theorised and provided the now familiar, ubiquitous, and arguably indispensable concepts of text, textuality, intertextuality, and so on, seems to offer something singularly appropriate to Hall's and cultural studies' very conceptualisation of culture and the political. He insists that 'culture will always work through its textualities – and at the same time that textuality is never enough' (1992: 284). The answers to the immediately arising questions of 'never enough of what' and 'never enough for what' refer, as mentioned above, to *politics*, and specifically to the matter of establishing and maintaining a politics, to trying to make a difference that counts. For this, Hall argues, is the particular and acute obligation, orientation and defining aspiration of cultural studies:

That is to say, unless and until one respects the necessary displacement of culture, and yet is always irritated by its failure to reconcile itself with other questions that matter, with other questions that cannot and can never be fully covered by critical textuality in its elaborations, cultural studies as a project, an intervention, remains incomplete. If you lose hold of the tension, you can do extremely fine intellectual work, but you will have lost intellectual practice as a politics. I offer this to you, not because that's what cultural studies ought to be, or because that's what the [Birmingham] Centre managed to do well, but simply because I think that, overall, is what defines cultural studies as a project. Both in the

British and the American context, cultural studies has drawn the attention itself, not just because of its sometimes dazzling internal theoretical development, but because it holds theoretical and political questions in an ever irresolvable but permanent tension. It constantly allows the one to irritate, bother, and disturb the other, without insisting on some final theoretical closure. (1992: 284)

To argue that textuality is never enough is far from a straightforward call to 'return to reality' or to return to 'real political practice', as if there were a clear-cut choice between theory and practice, or a clear division between academic work and political work. Indeed, to conceive of culture and politics as complex discursive formations implies rejecting such distinctions as facile simplifications. (However, the theory/practice schema is not an easy metaphysical binary to step out of, as will be argued in Chapter 3.) Instead, what is at stake here might be clarified by making a distinction, between 'politics' and 'the political' (Beardsworth 1996). In terms of this distinction, one could say that everything is contingent and alterable (the political), and that cultural studies desires to alter it, to intervene (politics). Thus, anything new or different, anything which might alter a state of affairs, might itself be or become 'political'.[2] But, invoking the *possibility* of politicality is not good enough when one's concerns and aspirations are interventional, specific, pressingly present and real (*whatever* they may be). Maintenance of this 'metaphysical' desire could represent one difference between deconstruction and cultural studies, if cultural studies is something that understands culture and politics deconstructively but nevertheless desires the very thing that it understands to be 'constitutively impossible'. That is to say, for Hall, what is definitional of cultural studies 'as a project' is the aim of definite, precise, certain, fully present and knowable, unmediated interventional power and agency in the present of the institutional terrain of culture and society. This desire is 'impossible' and 'metaphysical' because the institutional terrain of culture and society is never fully present, constitutively mediated, in deferral, relay, and referral (*différance*), prone to the 'slippage of signification' (Laclau and Mouffe 1985) and dissemination (Derrida 1981). It should be noted, though, that in maintaining this frustrated tension *as* a tension, Hall thereby actually (paradoxically) remains impeccably deconstructive, insisting as he does upon the 'double bind' of this situation. This explains his assertions that cultural studies must operate on 'two fronts at one and the same time' (1992: 282), maintaining a deconstructive understanding of the political that problematises all metaphysical notions of politics, hand in hand with metaphysical political desires and orientations that that very deconstructive understanding would seem 'logically' or 'necessarily' to forbid.

For Hall, a deconstructive understanding of culture (Laclau and Mouffe's 'discursive terrain') is the condition of possibility for establishing 'the way things are'. As introduced earlier, establishing the way things are is in a sense 'necessary' before one can possibly *know* how to confront, engage with or intervene in reality properly (politics: intervention). But a textual understanding actually makes the aim of a (knowledge of) decisive intervention impossible. Moreover, as Hall points out, in cultural studies this double bind runs deeper or more palpably because, he claims, 'it has always been impossible in the theoretical field of cultural studies – whether it is conceived of in terms of texts and contexts, of intertextuality, or of the historical formations in which cultural practices are lodged – to get anything like an adequate theoretical account of culture's relations and its effects' (1992: 286). Textual understandings (if this is not ultimately an oxymoron) are not amenable to grand system-building unlike, say, dialectical or positivist understandings: the only universally true picture or system that deconstruction might claim to be able to draw would be the picture or system that clarified how and why universally real and true pictures and systems are impossible. As Derrida once put it, deconstruction is not formalisable, but for reasons that can be formalised (1981: 52); or, as Slavoj Žižek less hospitably argues:

> the ultimate lesson of deconstruction seems to be that one cannot postpone the *ontological* question *ad infinitum*, and what is deeply symptomatic in Derrida is his oscillation between, on the one hand, the hyper-self-reflective approach which denounces the question of 'how things really are' in advance, and limits itself to third-level deconstructive comments on the inconsistencies of philosopher B's reading of philosopher A; and, on the other, a direct 'ontological' assertion about how différance and archi-trace determine the structure of all living things, and are, as such, already operative in animal nature. One should not miss the paradoxical inter-connection of these two levels here: the very feature which forever prevents us from grasping our intended object directly (the fact that our grasping is always refracted, 'mediated', by a decentred otherness) is the feature which connects us with the basic proto-ontological structure of the universe. (Žižek 2001: 204)

Žižek's arguments and position will be considered more fully in the following chapters. Here what is salient is that Žižek's claim is that deconstruction (and 'deconstructionist cultural studies') can be construed as entailing 'prohibitions' against enquiring into the truth and reality of things (2001: 204–5), because such enquiry would be 'metaphysical', and because deconstruction and deconstructionist cultural studies claim not to trade in undeconstructed metaphysics. However, even if Žižek's characterisation is appropriate or fair, which is doubtful, the problem is that Žižek never really pursues the question of *why* deconstructively orientated work might insist upon such 'prohibitions'. To clarify what is at issue here, it could be noted that Žižek's own (postmodern) bricolage of Lacanian psychoanalysis, Hegelianism, and Marxism, amalgamated into a new paradigm, illustrates the universal problem of all paradigms: they offer a particular perspective/construction that masquerades as *the* way to see 'how things actually are'. Accordingly, all different paradigms provide different versions of what proper intervention and political agency are: change the ingredients, and the answers change too. (This is the 'decentred otherness' that Žižek prefers to evoke as if some kind of irreducibly mysterious enigma). As Derrida apostrophised: 'whence the abyss – that's the whole problem'! (1998: 9–10) That is to say, because all paradigms offer different answers, therefore *certainty* is the very thing that becomes dubious. This is what both Hallian cultural studies and Derridean deconstruction wrestle with. In this sense, Žižekian certainty is the antithesis of a deconstructive (or) cultural studies relation to questions of knowledge, orientation and agency. However, as a certain deconstructive understanding of the 'undecidability' of knowledge and effect (regarding political causality) might seem to apply equally to *any* articulation, to *any* statement, or to *any* act, then the question returns as to *why* cultural studies *should* exist in and as the kind of frustration that Hall seems to insist upon. If *anything* might be consequential, then mightn't anything be an intervention? Why not be content to produce 'extremely fine intellectual work'? What's the difference, the specificity, the challenge, the task, for cultural studies?

Gary Hall argues that, 'by definition, cultural studies is . . . a politically committed questioning of culture/power relations which at the same time theoretically interrogates its own relation to politics and to power' (Hall 2002: 10). The reasons for the definitional status of this apperception relate to cultural studies' construal of modern cultures and societies as being constituted in, on and as contingent institutional bases and relations, which means that they are fundamentally political. As John Protevi reads this, through a deconstructive optic therefore *everything*, even 'writing', or any other act of 'inscribing a mark to render it iterable, is a performative signifying and a meaningful performance – we could call it *making sense*. Making sense is the construction of a hegemonic formation of forces in which meaning or iterability is produced from the clash of force vectors' (Protevi 2001: 63). This specifies further the deconstructive radicalisation of the politicality of the cultural: 'the reading of marks is institutionally enforced. Reading strategies outside the institutionally enforced reading code make no sense, as anyone who reads the bewildered responses to deconstructive readings can tell you' (Protevi 2001: 64). The impossibility of ever occupying a position or perspective *outside* of the contingent cultural-political terrain is precisely why cultural studies views itself as Gary Hall says it does, and as Stuart Hall implies it must. The justification for explicitly adhering to the double bind that Stuart Hall identifies relates to remaining frustrated with what seems to be merely 'theoretical' or entirely 'academic' work, but never deluding oneself that theory could somehow be *dispensed with*. To reiterate Jeremy Gilbert's observation: 'everyone has a theory, they just don't always know what it is' (2003: 151); or as Godzich renders this: 'knowing is essentially theoretical' (1987: 163). Accordingly, academic institutions and their productions do not amount to nothing. One is always in the 'game of hegemony' (Hall 1992: 281). And according to the implications of the deconstructive understandings of Stuart Hall and Gary Hall, cultural studies must never simply occupy either end of the binary that constitutes the parameters of, for example, Žižekian thought, which oscillates between two equally unsatisfactory positions: either an *academia-is-everything* position or an *academia-is-nothing* position. Žižek will be explored further in the following chapters, but Mowitt points out one relevant problem about such a reductive schema as Žižek's. He argues:

> Once we acknowledge that what enables a reading to 'make sense' reaches well into the institutional field of the social, then it becomes possible to extend the range of what a reading ought to concern itself with . . . [As such, we should not believe] that 'mere readings' must give way to action when 'real' social issues are at stake. This perspective has already produced enough intellectual paralysis within the academic Left, and it is no more worthy of perpetuation than is the self-indulgent complacency that leads academic intellectuals to think that simply writing a textual analysis of a Hitchcock film is tantamount to the articulation of an oppositional politics. (Mowitt 1992: 217)

Indeed, Žižek often actually holds quite traditional understandings of the political, of agency and of intervention, when compared to deconstructive cultural studies or other post-Marxism: sometimes he advocates a 'to the barricades!' notion of political action, whilst at other times he seems to believe that revolutionaries 'out there' require academics 'in here' to be their teachers or consultants, providing academic texts as revolutionary pamphlets; or even at other times viewing academic work itself to be somehow revolutionary political action, *in and of itself*. (Because such assumptions and positions about the relationship of academic practice to the political are so widespread and entrenched, they shall be returned to and explored more fully, via readings of Žižek, Rorty, Butler and Laclau, in Chapter 3.) In this regard, Mowitt offers a much more 'transgressive' understanding of the political force and propensities of academic intellectual work, hinging on what he calls a politics of 'antidisciplinarity':

> What antidisciplinarity . . . depends upon is a notion of reading that understands how its specificity as a practice derives from the institutional field which surrounds it. Since this means that all readings have institutional implications, isn't it time that we began reading it so as to undermine the institutions of disciplinary power at the very points where they have typically reproduced themselves with the greatest efficiency? (Mowitt 1992: 218)

Mowitt's injunction here amounts to a strategy of pressuring borders, boundaries, demarcations, conventions, limits, and established facts, values and proprieties, of all orders; a pedagogical-political strategy of transgressing norms – not simply for the ('tactical') sake of it, but rather, as John Protevi explains in his account of why anyone might ever feel the need to 'deconstruct' (Protevi's account arguably characterises an impetus that is discernable equally in Derrida, Hall, Mowitt, Laclau and Mouffe, and others):

> *why* deconstruct . . .? In the name of what does deconstruction release its forces of rupture? Derrida answers: in the name of justice. Derrida's political physics looks like a 'might makes right' position. And in one sense indeed it is, in the sense that might makes *droit*, that is, the fact that positive law can be analysed in terms of social power. Derrida reminds us, however, that might does not make justice. Instead, 'Force of law' tell[s] us that 'deconstruction is justice'. Institutions, or sets of positive laws [*droits*], are deconstructible because they are not justice. Deconstruction is justice, that is, 'deconstruction is already engaged by this infinite demand of justice'. Deconstruction also finds its 'force, its movement or its

motivation' in the 'always unsatisfied appeal' to justice . . . We might want to say here that *democracy* is the future, the 'to come' of this transformation, intensifying itself to the point where instituted bodies that muffle or distort the calls of others are overflowed and reinscribed in other contexts. Deconstruction is democratic justice, responding to the calls from all others. (Protevi 2001: 69–70)

In this regard, deconstruction, as (*strategic*) infinite demand for justice, is another name for the radical democratic element of the project of post-Marxism, as well as arguably being very closely related to cultural studies' much-invoked openness to alterity. (It is for this reason that Joanna Zylinska, for instance, argues that 'a sense of duty and responsibility has always constituted an inherent part of the cultural studies project' (Zylinska 2001: 177).) But such justifications notwithstanding, the Jamesonian objection keeps returning, which runs as follows: because capitalism itself might be construed as a radical form of 'deconstruction', therefore deconstruction might be a symptom of capitalism. In this spirit, Hardt and Negri famously argue that the dominant form of power today is *itself* deconstructive and anti-essentialist. Power 'itself', they say, chants along with anti-essentialists and post-modernists, 'Long live difference! Down with essentialist binaries!' (2000: 139) 'Power', they contend, 'has evacuated the bastion [that anti-essentialist intellectuals] are attacking and has circled round to their rear to join them in the assault in the name of difference' (2000: 138. See also Bewes 2001: 92). So, the problem remains the one that Mowitt says many have discerned in textuality (when textuality is taken as being exemplary of all that is problematic in 'postmodernism' or 'deconstructionism'): that it appears to be 'incapable of either generating or sustaining a *critical* ideology' (1992: 12–13). In the face of this problem, the 'solution' that Mowitt proposes devolves on 'what may strike some as the unlikely matter of disciplinarity' (13): by 'securing theoretically the text's link to disciplinarity and . . . drawing the practical consequences of this linkage as they manifest themselves within the institutional domain of disciplinary power' (14). Indeed, Derrida too connects deconstructive, 'textual' practice to the practical consequences of institutional and therefore wider discourse; for example when he contends:

If it were only a question of 'my' work, of the particular or isolated research of one individual, this [scandalised denunciation of deconstruction] wouldn't happen. Indeed, the violence of these denunciations derives from the fact that the work accused is part of a whole ongoing process.

What is unfolding here, like the resistance it necessarily arouses, can't be limited to a personal 'oeuvre', nor to a discipline, nor even to the academic institution . . . If this work seems so threatening to them, this is because it isn't eccentric or strange, incomprehensible or exotic (which would allow them to dispose of it easily), but as I myself hope, and as they believe more than they admit, competent, rigorously argued, and carrying conviction in its re-examination of the fundamental norms and premises of a number of dominant discourses, the principles underlying many of their evaluations, the structures of academic institutions, and the research that goes on within them. What this kind of questioning does is to modify the rules of the dominant discourse, it tries to politicize and democratize the university scene . . . (Derrida 1995: 409–10)

The Institutional Articulation and Dissemination of Texts and Discourses

It is important to emphasise the often tacit but nevertheless significantly and clearly shared agreement among the post-Marxists Laclau and Mouffe, and Hall, Mowitt, Derrida, and beyond, about the interlinked *institutional* character of culture, society and politics and the conviction that institutions such as the university have a position and doubtless a role, or multiple roles, within hegemony and hegemonic politics (Readings 1996; Peters 2001). The shared conviction is of the ethico-political importance and consequentiality of university practices of the production of knowledge; that knowledge may affect institutional and ultimately ethico-political cultural practice more widely (Mowitt 1992: 27). Thus, the stakes devolve on what academic disciplines and practices do, how they do it, and how this relates, links, connects, or is articulated with other scenes.

Thus a key concern should be that of establishing what disciplinary activity is to be, what it is articulated with, how and in what ways. For, what is an academic discipline or academic subject anyway? What is its hegemonic 'position', and what are its 'structural' limits, or what is the logic of its constitution within the university institution, itself within hegemony? This, the final section of this chapter, will explore these questions, but will do so – crucially, yet perhaps surprisingly – not primarily through reference to empirical examples (for which, see instead Readings 1996; Kilroy et al. 2004; Rutherford 2005); but rather by examining the deconstructive logic of *dissemination*, as proposed by Derrida in the book (or 'text') of that name (Derrida 1981), and as discussed by other deconstructive thinkers. The reason for taking this perhaps peculiar detour through an apparently 'quasi-transcendental' moment in Derridean deconstruction is double: it is at once to reemphasise, performatively, the institutional articulation of text and discourse within hegemony, and to propose, again performatively, one way in which Derrida's supposedly 'philosophical' readings of even the texts of ancient philosophy reveal and cast new light on political-institutional questions. Derrida himself always asserted 'the necessity of posing transcendental questions in order not to be held within the fragility of an incompetent empiricist discourse' (1996: 81); and, as Protevi makes clear:

> That the basic problem of deconstruction, even in Derrida's technically detailed readings of phenomenology, is thus basically political is clear: the names of philosophers as signatories are indices of texts which are indices of real history. The role of presence in the West is the target; philosophy texts are only paths to this target. The long-debated relation of philosophy and politics, the difference between the history of the West and the history of metaphysics, is thought by Derrida under the rubric of 'force'. (Protevi 2001: 20)

To begin a deconstructive reading of cultural studies in terms of *dissemination*, it can first be noted that it is clearly like other proper academic subjects at least in that it putatively 'takes' external objects as its focus of study. It speaks *of* and *for* them (in what might be construed as something of an unethical opening of the ethical (Derrida 1995a: 67)). Arguably, it must *always* study 'other things', things 'out there' – even if the theory of the text immediately problematises and complexifies this – because to be an academic subject proper could be said to require as much. Textuality notwithstanding – or indeed, even as a consequence of the adherence to textuality as that which 'emerges to name the alterity that simultaneously constitutes and subverts the context of disciplinary reason' (Mowitt 1992: 25) – the specificity of cultural studies is said (by cultural studies, at least) to devolve on an openness to other topics. In one familiar respect, cultural studies is said to study objects hitherto excluded or not accorded any worth *as* objects of attention within the academy (popular culture, subcultural practices, marginalised and excluded identities, 'trivia', etc.). In another, related, respect, it is said to at least seek to revalue and to reappraise the knowledge that circulates *as* knowledge within other already institutionally legitimated subjects, disciplines and public discourses (Young 1999: 3–16; During 1993; Storey 1994; 1996). Both of these procedures might, of course, count as valid and important interventions; because, on the one hand, studying the different is to bring into visibility things that had hitherto lacked representation, and, on the other hand, critiquing extant knowledge can again bring into visibility excluded differends, and thereby in turn come to influence or modify the production of knowledge about these things – knowledge that, as deconstruction, cultural studies, and post-Marxism all agree, must in some sense affect institutional and political cultural practices (Mowitt 1992: 27).

However, any such effort or orientation could be construed as making a difference, as 'counting', *only if* it, as it were, *made any difference*: *only if* it came to be counted – or could be *made* to count. Arditi and Valentine's (1999) concept of 'polemicization' is important here; for it proposes a logic whereby *relevance* is established only through a rhetorico-political struggle. In other words, to evoke one of Spivak's important questions, the vital question here is *who will listen* (Spivak 1993: 194)? What consequences will that listening have? As cultural studies predominantly takes place within or around the university context of the interdisciplinary arts and humanities, one should not ignore this scene, this location, and should evaluate its status as a political locus or site of potential antagonism. For the scene in which any interventions of cultural studies are to be staged, regardless of what anyone thinks they should be, is irreducibly related to the university, before and after any other form of publicity, publication or mediation.[3] This is because it is the university, primarily, that confers any authority or legitimacy onto the identity and voice of cultural studies that it may have (although the subject itself will always make appeal to some little other object which also called it into being, as if in response to the question 'how can you/we, the university, have excluded *this*?'). Its speech is directed *to* the university, all other intentions notwithstanding. It comes from and goes to the university, *first*.[4] (Derrida 1992; Godzich 1986; 1987) Its discourse is structured like that of the Greek *theoria* as described by Godzich (1986: xiv–v; see also Chapter 2), although it is not simply a discourse *of* a *theoria*, but rather a discourse that first and foremost appeals for recognition and legitimation as itself being of the same standing as the *theoria* that it implicitly addresses. According to Godzich, the archetypal 'theoria' was a hegemonic social institution within ancient Greek society, whose function was one of regulation, stabilisation, verification and legitimation. Godzich explains:

[T]he act of looking at, of surveying, designated by *theorein* does not designate a private act carried out by a cogitating philosopher but a very public one with important social consequences. The Greeks designated certain individuals, chosen on the basis of their general probity and their general standing in the polity, to act as legates on certain formal occasions in other city states or in matters of considerable political importance. These individuals bore the title of *theoros*, and collectively constituted a *theoria* . . . They were summoned on special occasions to attest to the occurrence of some event, to witness its happenstance, and then to verbally certify its having taken place. (We may recall here the role of witnesses to the execution of death sentences in the American judicial system.) In other words, their function was one of see-and-tell. To be sure, other individuals in the city could see and tell, but their telling was no more than a *claim* that they had seen something, and it needed some authority to adjudicate the validity of such a claim. The city needed a more official and ascertainable form of knowledge if it was not to lose itself in endless claims and counterclaims. The *theoria* provided such a bedrock of certainty: what it certified as having seen could become the object of public discourse. The individual citizen, indeed even women, slaves, and children, were capable of *aesthesis*, that is perception, but these perceptions had no social standing. They were not sanctioned and thus could not form the basis of deliberation, judgement, and action in the polity. Only the theoretically attested event could be treated as a fact. The institutional nature of this certification ought not to escape us, as well as its social inscription. Indeed, it may be of more than theoretical interest, in our current sense of the term, to wonder how this social dimension of the certification of events, of the granting of something the discursive standing of 'real', came to be occulted . . . (Godzich 1986: xiv)

Theoria, then, denotes a collectivity or institution functioning as a 'mediating instance invested with undeniable authority by the polity' (xv). The point of evoking the Greek theoria here is neither allegorical nor analogical, but is rather to emphasise the fact that for cultural studies, like any other practice which seeks to be deemed to be speaking truth or reason, responsibility is double, divided, both in respect to the object and also to the institution. For, such an interlocutor must appeal for legitimating recognition that *it itself* is of the requisite probity (xiv) *in order to be* responsible to the other – a responsible witness *of* the other. Thus, its obligations are divided. And this is constitutively divisive. For, the very fact that cultural studies is an *academic* subject obliges or imposes some 'distance' from any other identity. In speaking of any object or topic it must not *simply* 'be' that other thing. It must first and foremost be academic discourse, operating according to precise protocols. This leads to the possibility that, were one to have become involved in cultural studies in order to do justice to, say, ethnic or women's or queer or whatever other concerns, one would also already have in a certain sense 'transgressed' them, or 'hegemonised' them, by subordinating them to other concerns (Derrida 1995a: 68; 1981: 137): academic protocols and demands such as particular versions of 'rigour', 'logic', 'coherence' and 'rationality', etc., which construct any efforts according to criteria alien and quite possibly illegible to the object 'itself'. (In another respect, of course, the academic who valorises 'working class' themes cannot fail to remove themselves from the working class, if only by virtue of occupation and language.) It is first and foremost *study* (or, perhaps, invention, projection or fetishization); *always possibly not* connected to any other ('real') practice at all, and, if connected, the nature of the relation is far from determined in advance. (Marion Hobson (1998) takes this proviso of the 'always possibly not' to be a key moment of any deconstruction.)

In effect, disciplinary activity *performatively* mimes itself into existence and identity according to an interpretation not only of what it should *do*, but also an interpretation of what it should be *like* (Derrida 1981: 75; 1997: 7). For any subject must establish its identity through the double strategy of a polemical distancing or differencing and affirmative affiliation ('I am like this and not like that') which betrays, again, that disciplinary knowledge itself and paradigm formation is double and 'out of joint' (Derrida 1981: 15, 19; Mowitt 1992: 40–1), relying on an inauguration which has nothing to do with 'it itself', but which presupposes and conditionally imposes what it will, should, or must be (like), and will, should, or must know (like). Echoing Derrida, this is the same as to say that the inauguration of cultural studies is not a cultural studies event (Derrida 1992: 29–30). As Mieke Bal proposes, it is all too easy for 'new' disciplines to unwittingly smuggle and to fail to interrogate or critically revise extant 'traditional' values and protocols into their own constitution (Bal 2003). In Derrida's (1981 and 1992) sense, cultural studies is a university modification, albeit also constituted and compromised by that something other, that figuration of something 'outside' the university: its objects of study. It must 'respect' them both. Its loyalties are divided, constitutively compromised, by a *polemos* with and an *eros* for the university and its knowledge (for, otherwise, why insist on being insinuated therein?), and an *eros* or cathexis with something other, that it must distance itself from in order to do justice to, and also therefore to transgress, by moving 'away' from that thing, not being with it 'properly', of it or as it. But this *poleros* (as Derrida (1998a) has termed it) is dissymmetrical: preference always goes to the institution (Derrida 1997: 7, 17, 19–20).

It is important to reiterate that preference always (also) goes to the institution. But it is equally important to hasten to add that this is nothing to lament, for it actually enables a reconceptualisation of the character of academic, intellectual, political practice. Namely, that a primary object of cultural studies must always also be the supposedly secondary matter of the university institution. Now, increasingly, thinkers within cultural studies are explicitly coming to construe cultural studies as a – if not the – place to *think* the university, to make sense of the university and its relationship to culture, politics and society, locally and globally (Hall 2002; Wortham 1999). Rather than simply repeating such undeniably important arguments here, it seems necessary to address the issue not only of how cultural studies 'knows itself' (in both senses: i.e., the way it perceives objects and the way it thinks of itself), but also the issue of how cultural studies is itself known.

In this regard, cultural studies is perhaps most often referred to as 'interdisciplinary'.[5] Indeed, in the essay 'Cultural studies and its theoretical legacies' (1992) that has also informed this chapter, Stuart Hall clearly insists on the need for cultural studies to be excessive, in the sense of not retreating from any limits, borders or boundaries. Now, a deconstructive comprehension of multiplicity and excess – even and especially an excess of *propriety* such as this one advocated by Hall – is one that construes it as inevitably introducing *alterity* (Godzich 1987: 157). Derrida argues that ultimately 'a monster of fidelity [becomes] the most perverse infidel' (1987: 24); that *too much* fidelity becomes a form of infidelity or transgression. (The impossibility of unequivocal self-identity is perhaps among the key insights of deconstruction.) Indeed, if this is true for 'excessive' attention to any one thing, then it must clearly become even more palpable in the case of interdisciplinary activity. This is to say, in the eyes of supposedly 'single' disciplines, interdisciplines will appear to be *less and other* than 'proper' disciplines. For 'proper' mastery or 'proper comprehension' cannot and must not 'comprehend' too many things, or fold too many things together, too much (Derrida 1981: 159). What 'too many' and 'too much' are deemed to be will always, of course, be contingent, conventional norms; generally tacit and unarticulated, and more to do with what Mowitt calls a vague 'feeling of appropriateness deriving from the matrix that bonds the disciples who see themselves as committed to the [intellectual] project that depends on their cooperation' (Mowitt 1992: 26–7), rather than something based purely in 'reason', 'rationality' or 'logic'.

Accordingly, the excessive interdiscipline's attempts to attain too much mastery will make it tend to appear (when viewed from the position of the established 'proper') as what Girard (1977) would term a 'monstrous double' of 'proper' academic practice. As such, it is always possible that the interdiscipline may become a viable scapegoat, or, as Lola Young says of the way cultural studies is often viewed, a 'hate object' (Young 1999: 3). Of course, any conflicts between the sedimented, established or traditional disciplines and the new (such as cultural studies and other such 'new' interdisciplines) could be construed in many ways: Perhaps conflicts between the faculties amount to skirmishes in a more general conflict between an older and a newer 'cultural logic'. In such a view, cultural studies may be construed as representing the capitalist postmodern logic of 'performativity', in which cultural studies' success has arisen because, as Bill Readings (1996) contends, in a (university) world governed by the profit motive, it doesn't matter what is done, taught or researched, as long as it is done 'excellently', that is profitably and auditably. Alternatively, or in addition, hostility to cultural studies may simply reflect straightforward resentment of its success, or be an inevitable expression of the problem of disciplinary knowledge saturation, wherein there is no object 'out there' that could not be said to be colonised, claimed, or even constituted by and as an object of a particular disciplinary gaze. The limitless academic panoptical injunction for disciplines to 'know more', to 'find out more' – indeed, to find out everything – could be said to have met its limit or saturation point when looking 'outside' immediately amounts to looking at the claimed 'intellectual property' of another discipline.

All of this in a sense reaffirms the Lyotardian problem of legitimation in polyvocal postmodernity: the problem of authority and authorisation. Without the validation of some form of recognised authority – as it were, of some kind of 'father' – then *any* entity, *any* identity, has a problem. To Derrida (commenting on Plato's discussion of any new or unusual 'supplement' or 'parasite'):

Not to know where one comes from or where one is going, for a discourse with no guarantor, is not to know how to speak at all, to be in a state of infancy. Uprooted, anonymous, unattached to any house or country, [such an] almost insignificant signifier is at everyone's disposal, can be picked up by both the competent and the incompetent, by those who understand and know what to do with it, and by those who are completely unconcerned with it, and who, knowing nothing about it, can inflict all manner of impertinence upon it. (Derrida 1981: 144)

Derrida is of course 'literally' only discussing the Platonic/Socratic specification of the problem with 'writing' here. But, as Derrida argues in *Dissemination* and elsewhere, and as seen from Protevi's account of the politics of deconstruction, what can be understood by 'writing' should be massively extended, to include everything from marks on a page to speech, memory, and any form of 'inscription', up to and including institutions, their agencies, and therefore, of course, the institutions of disciplines and interdisciplines like cultural studies. In this sense, it is important to regard Derrida's readings even of the texts of ancient philosophy as studies that uncover primarily political force and consequence (Protevi 2001). In Derrida's deconstruction of pho-nocentrism throughout *Dissemination* (1981), that is, connections are established between a thing's difference from or unintelligibility with-in a given hegemonic order, and the inevitability of disdainful judge-ments of it, as well as the tendency to classify the unintelligible/ different as 'unproductive' (1981: 134). In this regard, Derrida's deconstructions of phonocentrism, 'phallogocentricity', and the values of presence and proper productivity, are also political and politicising delineations of the figure and form of contemporary institutional political polemics, disagreements and antagonisms.

Of course, in *Dissemination*, Derrida reads Plato's philosophy and his metaphysical mysticism, including discourses about gods discuss-ing new technological inventions (such as 'writing'). But there are 'gods' in the machine of the university; what Derrida calls 'classical protocols'. These he regards both as potential sources of resistance to change (as in, 'That's not how it's done!') and as radical democra-tising's best chance. As seen earlier, Derrida often optimistically appeals to the 'classical protocols' of intellectual rigour, competence, close and sensitive reading, openness to new thought, and so on, with a view to the institutional transformation of the extant status quo (1992; 1992a). Derrida's optimism rests on a conviction that uni-versity protocols might always have a stake in or appeal to something 'classical', and that this might always possibly be (what he (1997) calls 'teleiopoetically') 'polemicized' so as to deploy the rigorous decon-structive questioning towards the democratising transformation of institutions within hegemony. Such a stake in the radical potential of 'classical protocols' is construed by Derrida as a force of leverage in the face of other, less than ideal forces, such as the corporate or capitalist-performative protocols that the likes of Lyotard (1984) and Readings (1996) have famously directed our attention to.

However, in any eventuality, and whatever the form and values of the 'gods' of the university at any given time, the Derridean argument is that any *hegemon* (leader, guide, prince (Vitanza 1997)) always demands a productivity that it can comprehend and make use of (Young 1992). In this sense, in what might be called the dominant hegemonic context of the contemporary university, it can be seen that if an interdiscipline lies across science, technology, business, or (supplementing Derrida) any permutation of managerio-info-tele-techno-scientific disciplines, then it might always *prove* its worth in terms of intelligibly worthwhile productivity (Lyotard 1984). As such, any scientific, productive, vocational, economically pragmatic or profit-making interdisciplinary development will tend to appear more 'acceptable'. But if the interdiscipline is what is called a 'discursive discipline', producing nothing more tangible than its own discourse, then it will already be immanently contemptible in the eyes of the 'properly' productive disciplines (Young 1992). Furthermore, it should be noted that any 'unproductive' interdiscipline will almost automatically risk 'disdaining' those closest to itself, especially 'in times of crisis'. This is because the arts and humanities that inter-disciplines like cultural studies constitutively 'poach' from can themselves be construed as constituting a threat to the established lines of demarcation and organisation. So, the 'structural' position of any new (inter)discipline amounts to the almost automatic, inevitable, pre-programmed running of a gauntlet. 'In times of crisis', as far as the (properly productive) sciences are concerned, the excessive (and un-productive) interdiscipline can easily come to be taken to be exemplary or representative of everything bad about the arts and humanities (a 'Mickey Mouse subject'); evidence of a transgression of their limited remit, of the exceeding of limitations, of posturing or 'imposturing'[6] – a dangerous or contemptible supplement, happily dispensed with. For the already-established traditional 'discursive disciplines', it will already amount to an agitator, or even an impostor, whose irritations could well be done without (insofar as they jeopardise stability). The immanent scapegoat-status of the un- or improperly-productive inter-discipline might be said to be overdetermined here. As Derrida's reading in *Dissemination* characterises the plight of such an entity:

That representative represents the otherness of the evil that comes to affect or infect the inside by unpredictably breaking into it. Yet the representative of the outside is nevertheless *constituted*, regularly granted its place by the community, chosen, kept, fed, etc., in the very heart of the inside. These parasites were as a matter of course domesticated by the living organism that housed them at its expense. 'The Athenians regularly maintained a number of degraded and useless beings at the public expense; and when any calamity, such as plague, drought, or famine, befell the city, they sacrificed two of these outcasts as scapegoats'. (Derrida 1981: 133)

In the face of the question of what ancient Athenian rituals have to do with cultural studies, it should be reiterated that Derrida is not *merely* discussing Athens or ancient rituals and mythology about 'writing', but is rather also delineating what might be called the quasi-transcendental form of the structural 'reflexes' pre-programmed into or overdetermined within an exemplarily metaphysical system, one that, to the extent that any contemporary context is similarly metaphysical, could still be said to be effective and pertinent. Or, in other words, Derrida delineates the rhetorico-political dialogical structure of the established vis-à-vis the new – the contexts of its 'reception'. Accordingly, the minimal coordinates of this metaphysical structurality – coordinates that Derrida discerns again and again throughout his readings of western philosophers (see Protevi 2001) – are encapsulated by Derrida as designed overwhelmingly 'to keep the outside out', as 'this is the inaugural gesture of "logic" itself, of good "sense" insofar as it accords with the self-identity of *that which is*: being is what it is, the outside is outside and the inside [is] inside' (1981: 128). Thus, the unproductive or improperly productive inter-discipline can be blamed or hated for any number of crimes: for apparently being a poisoner, beguiler, defiler, free-loader or parasite; or what Derrida calls, taking up the ambiguous and ambivalent term used (doubly) by Plato, *pharmakos*: an ambiguous or ambivalent necessary evil, a corrupting element that necessarily intrudes into the body proper. 'The character of the *pharmakos* has been compared to a scapegoat', Derrida tells us (130).

Now, such a supplement, such a new discipline or interdisciplinary entity, will only have been admitted into the institution because of what it promises: new knowledge, more knowledge – more of the same, but differently. The problem is that establishing new knowledge also introduces alterity and challenges the instituted norm. As such, the 'challenger' can be deemed sophist, equivocator, and simulator (Derrida 1981: 68), and always dices with expulsion (Derrida 1981: 130). This risk remains real and pressing until such a time as hegemonic transformations might consolidate its intelligibility or validity, or that is, might make it come to be a representative or respecter of 'classical protocols' themselves. As Derrida puts it elsewhere, 'stabilization supposes the passage through an ordeal which takes time' (Derrida 1997: 15): 'It takes time to reach a stability or a certainty which wrenches itself from time. It takes time to do without time' (1997: 17). In other words, it takes time and effort to seem timeless, permanent, natural, proper, and enduring. This is the same as saying that the new might become hegemonic, part of the hegemonic structure, established as a 'proper' part of the establishment. The nature or orientation of this political transformation is undecidable. But it has little to do with 'conscious intention'. It is a politicality effectively in excess of the subject, of intention, and of 'political will', related more to reiteration, to the 'law' of 'repeating without knowing' (1981: 75) virtual, 'citational' relations (1981: 98).

As such, it should be clear that the *de facto* politicality of knowledge production obliges that those subjects focused on matters of the political and of responsibility should proceed with an acute attentiveness to the matter of their own – knowledge's own – constitutively political institution, in a sense just as thoroughly as political and cultural studies seek to attend to urgent acute or chronic political issues 'outside the university', 'in the real world'. The 'inside-outside' relation is considerably more complex and consequential than is often acknowledged. As the ineradicable ground of any academic polemic or antagonism is the premise of the university, 'our' premises, so any account of cultural studies that disavows or forgets its perhaps *hyper*-academic obligations fundamentally misrecognises its institutional situation. That this bind to the academy seems to foreclose the possibility that cultural studies has any properly direct, correct, neutral, or immediate (and ethico-politically innocent or simple) relation to the 'worldly' may seem frustrating. Yet it enables engaged academics seeking the logic or orientation of 'university responsibility' to figure 'the world' as no longer somehow simply 'out there' to be 'naturally' known and 'simply' intervened in. This thereby enables cultural and politically-orientated work to grasp more adequately the location and relation of intellectual work, in a way that need not produce an ultimately disabling, totalising 'theory of everything'. Such grand theories, as Jameson points out, tend to construe any and every 'us' either as being self-determining and heroic or (as is more usual) insignificant and unempowered in the face of the grand scheme of things and the forces operative in the world (Jameson 2002: 567). The post-Marxist theory of hegemony, however, when supplemented further with Mowitt's attention to the logic and role of disciplinarity and of the production of 'disciplinary objects' and with a thorough-going attention to the insights of Derridean deconstruction, rather opens up possibilities for a reorganisation of political and cultural studies' interventional aspirations and orientations.

Acknowledging and attempting to proceed in the light of an awareness of the institutional basis of academia does not constitute an irrelevant digression into unrelated or narcissistic 'theory', but rather represents an important starting point to a much needed reconceptualisation of practice and intervention. The question of the way to conceptualise politics, political practice, political causality and consequentiality, focusing specifically on the question of what the relationship of academic discourse on the political and on intervention *is* to politics animates the following chapters. Chapter 2 develops and explores the theme of the tensions and conflicts between what Mowitt calls the textual paradigm of (deconstructive) cultural analysis and the discourse paradigm of (deconstructive) post-Marxism, expanding on the problems, possibilities, obligations and limitations of both ap-proaches, when the aim is determining and establishing intervention. Clarifying this sets the scene for a discussion in Chapter 3 of the key influential and orientative theoretical paradigms, as exemplified by those of post-Marxism, of what the political relation of theory to practice actually is for post-Marxism and cultural studies. However, the word 'and' in the phrase 'post-Marxism and cultural studies' actually obscures the fact that the nature of their relation is far from simple, settled, or straightforward. What must now be clarified further, in order to interrogate the question of determining and establishing politically consequential intervention, are the ways in which the 'and' of cultural studies and post-Marxism is actually a 'versus'. What relates them and draws them together is the very thing that separates them and draws them into conflict. The key locus of this conflict is deconstruction: post-Marxism and cultural studies are both overwhelmingly deconstructive, but each deconstructs differently, which overdetermines their different relations not only to Marxism and to politics, but also to the question of orientation and to the political implication of university responsibility.

Notes

1. Overdetermination is a term that derives from Freud which was used by Althusser (1970; 1971). Laclau and Mouffe deconstruct

Althusser by pointing out his simultaneous use and (problematic) limitation of 'overdetermination' and its implications for Marxian thinking. The sense in which overdetermination refers to a multiplicity of determining factors frustrates the classical Marxist belief in the singular determination of everything in the last instance by the economy. See also Laplanche and Pontalis (1988: 292) for its psychoanalytic and potentially socio-political pertinence.

2. This suggests, therefore, that potentially *anything at all* might well be or become political, according to one possible interpretation of this insight, wherein because the ultimate significance, consequences, status and effect of *anything* might always possibly turn out to have been 'in the post' (as the Derrida of *The Post Card* (1987) or *Resistances of Psychoanalysis* (1998a) might have put it, in the awkward-sounding future anterior tense: Derrida uses this tense because it cannot be known in advance what anything may in the future turn out to be, or to have been and to have done), therefore anything might at some point in the future come to constitute or to have constituted a political intervention. The reasons why subscription to such an interpretation is unsatisfactory are engaged in the following argument.

3. Derrida (1992) has deconstructed such arguments as this, pointing out that there is no simple 'inside' to the university. He undertakes this in order to destabilize certain basically Kant-derived or Kantian-esque forms of thinking (See Derrida's 1992 reading of Kant 1979). Nevertheless, because Derrida's argument can be appropriated as a *shield*, *shelter* or *alibi* deployable to *avoid* the task of auto-critique by those who accept it (as in: 'we don't need to worry about what we are doing, because Derrida has argued that academic work always already automatically and consequentially reaches beyond the university and out into the real world'), I want to resist accepting this in any straightforward sense. If Derrida unsettled a complacent element in thinking ('this is merely theoretical, academic, and inside the university; other things are practical, real, reaching out, consequential and political'), it is important not to assume that anything and everything said and done in any context, such as the university, is somehow inevitably, equally, and predictably consequential.

4. I use the words 'first' and 'primarily', etc., here and throughout, not in ignorance of the deconstructive logic of the supplement, or the constitutive character of the secondary, but rather in order to pose as primary what is so often deemed secondary.

5. Derrida even once *equated* (or conflated) 'interdisciplinarity' and 'cultural studies', and provocatively deemed them to be 'often' somewhat 'confused' and 'good-for-everything' concepts: 'This deconstructive task of the Humanities to come will not let itself be contained within the traditional limits of the departments that today belong, by their very status, to the Humanities. These Humanities to come will cross disciplinary borders without, all the same, dissolving the specificity of each discipline into what is called, often in a very confused way, interdisciplinarity or into what is lumped with another good-for-everything concept, "cultural studies"' (Derrida 2001: 50)

6. For Sokal and Bricmont (1998), it is evidently 'excess' that they have the most distaste for, and this always – as they themselves keep saying – arises because they can't comprehend it. At every step their argument runs: (a) this representation of 'science' is an abuse, which (b) we don't understand, so (c) the author too does not understand it, therefore (d) it is 'meaningless'. Despite their declarations about unintelligibility and meaninglessness, they nevertheless proceed to draw 'meanings' from this 'meaninglessness'. (See Derrida 1978: 54; See also Lyotard 1988.)

Two – Cultural Studies versus Post-Marxism

> . . . metaphors are serious things. They affect one's practice
> (Stuart Hall 1996: 268)

Two Texts of Cultural Studies

As introduced in the previous chapter, 'textuality' is often regarded ambivalently, as a dubious achievement, one sometimes even pejoratively held to be directly related to sheer ideology (Bewes 2001; Mowitt 1992: 12–13). As was also seen in that chapter, Stuart Hall, too, views textuality extremely ambivalently.[1] However, John Mowitt unambiguously embraces the challenge of this ambivalence, asking, 'Would it not make more sense to acknowledge that the textual model is internally fissured by a conflicted relation to disciplinarity and that the literary appropriation of this model which has indeed taken place in history has obscured, or at least contained, this conflictual relation?' (Mowitt 1992: 14) For Mowitt, the text is 'irreducibly entangled in disciplinary politics and not merely as the articulation of an effort to reorganize disciplinary boundaries . . . but as a critical practice seeking to problematize the cultural work effected by the disciplines . . . Or, put another way, the text must be made to oppose the discipline(s) that made it' (14). In this regard, Stuart Hall's position surely coincides affiliatively with Mowitt's, because for Hall it is inestimably important that cultural studies maintain a 'real critical and deconstructive edge' in its awareness of its institutional context. For Hall, cultural studies must 'remain a critical and deconstructive project [that] is always self-reflexively deconstructing itself' (Hall 1996d: 150). In terms of the importance of a certain (anti)institutionally directed deconstruction, then, Hall and Mowitt are broadly in agreement. Furthermore, in terms of cultural studies' relation to post-Marxism, both Mowitt and Hall agree that there are important intellectual and political reasons for cultural studies to hesitate before entirely going along with the post-Marxist discourse paradigm of Laclau and Mouffe. Cultural studies and post-Marxism have significant disagreements, they contend, and both Hall and Mowitt insist that the nature and the stakes of the disagreements congregate around the matter of politics, intervention, orientation and its consequences. However, Hall and Mowitt's criticisms of post-Marxism differ somewhat, as do their proposed solutions to the problems of post-Marxism. This chapter will therefore engage more fully with these disagreements and the intellectual and ethico-political issues that they open up, beginning first with Hall and then moving into Mowitt's readings.

Stuart Hall's Closure versus Post-Marxist Discourse

Stuart Hall largely subscribes to the post-Marxist deconstruction of Marxism's class essentialism, economic reductionism and determinism; attesting that 'I think, for example, it's possible to get a long way by talking about what is sometimes called the "economic" as operating discursively' (Hall 1996d: 145). His key problem with Laclauian post-Marxism, though, is this:

> The question is, can one, does one, follow that argument to the point that there is nothing to practice but its discursive aspect? I think that's what [Laclau and Mouffe's *Hegemony and Socialist Strategy* (1985)] does. It is a sustained philosophical effort, really, to conceptualize *all* practices as nothing but discourses, and all historical agents as discursively constituted subjectivities, to talk about positionalities but never positions, and only to look at the way concrete individuals can be interpellated in different subject positions. The book is thus a bold attempt to discover what a politics of such a theory might be. All of that I think is important . . . I like Laclau when he's struggling to find a way out of reductionism and beginning to reconceptualize Marxist categories in the discursive mode . . . But in [*Hegemony*], there is no reason why anything is or isn't potentially articulatable with anything. The critique of reductionism has apparently resulted in the notion of society as a totally open discursive field.
>
> I would put it polemically in the following form: [*Hegemony and Socialist Strategy*] thinks that the world, social practice, is language, whereas I want to say that the social operates *like* a language. (Hall 1996d: 146)

So, although Hall sees the work of Laclau and Mouffe as being 'quite heroic' (148) in *Hegemony and Socialist Strategy*, nevertheless he feels that there are several problems with their approach. All of these problems are said to relate to political consequence, and all relate to Hall's perception of discourse theory's 'textuality', or 'textualism'. The first problem boils down to what Colin Sparks calls Laclau and Mouffe's definitive and 'radical break' from 'any notion of determination' (Sparks 1996: 91) in *Hegemony and Socialist Strategy*. For, Laclau and Mouffe's conclusions about determination are that:

> It is not the case that the field of the economy is a self-regulated space subject to endogenous laws; nor does there exist a constitutive principle for social agents which can be fixed in an ultimate class core; nor are class positions the necessary location of historical interests . . . even for Gramsci, the ultimate core of the hegemonic subject's identity is constituted at a point external to the space it articulates: the logic of hegemony does not unfold all its deconstructive effects on the theoretical terrain of classical Marxism. We have witnessed, however, the fall of this last redoubt of class reductionism, insofar as the very unity and homogeneity of class subjects has split into a set of precariously integrated positions which, once the thesis of the neutral character of the productive forces is abandoned, cannot be referred to any necessary point of future unification. The logic of hegemony, as a logic of articulation and contingency, has come to determine the very identity of hegemonic subjects. (Laclau and Mouffe 1985: 85; also quoted by Sparks 1996: 91)

As Sparks points out, in the face of this, Stuart Hall 'has expressed hesitations about following this logic through to its conclusion' (91). Indeed 'Hall wished to continue to argue for the continuing relevance of the idea of determination' (95). Daryl Slack paraphrases Hall's problem: with the post-Marxist concept of discourse it becomes too 'easy to leave behind any notion that anything exists outside of discourse. Struggle is reduced to struggle in discourse, where "there is no reason why anything is or isn't potentially articulatable with anything" and society becomes "a totally open discursive field"' (Daryl Slack 1996: 120). The issue central to all of this, for Hall, is precisely political:

> the question of political inflection is a very real problem with a lot of people who have taken the full discursive route. But I don't think I would advance that critique against Laclau and Mouffe. [Their work] *does* try to constitute a new politics out of that position. In that sense, it's very responsible and original. It says, let's go through the discursive door but then, we still have to act politically. Their problem isn't politics but history. They have let slip the question of the historical forces which have produced the present, and which continue to function as constraints and determinations on discursive articulation. (Hall 1996d: 147–8)

The problem with Laclau and Mouffe's post-Marxism, then, is that 'they tend to slip from the requirement to recognize the constraints of existing historical formations [because] they don't reintegrate other levels of determination into the analysis' (Hall 1996d: 148):

> You don't see them adding, adding, adding, adding, the different levels of determination; you see them producing the concrete philosophically, and somewhere in there is, I think, the kind of analytic slippage I'm talking about. That's not to say that it's theoretically impossible to develop a more adequate set of political positions within their theoretical framework, but somehow, the route they have taken allows them to avoid the pressure of doing so. The structuring force, the lines of tendency stemming from the implantation of capital, for example, simply disappears. (Hall 1996d: 148)

The problems, however embryonic, that are discernable within Laclau and Mouffe, Hall argues, are actually very serious because their work is and will continue to be influential: ironically, their avowedly *politicised* political theory produces the possibility that future work (by others, at least) may easily cease to be politicised, in various ways, but particularly in losing an awareness and attention to the effects of the economy (however 'discursively' construed). Hall's concern is that 'discourse analysis' might all too easily become totally disarticulated either from any sense of economico-political determination (however complexly reconceived) or from a post-*Marxist* or leftist political position. His concern is that post-Marxist discourse analysis lets us 'off the hook' vis-à-vis political responsibility. Such a disarticulation of discourse analysis from attending to 'historical forces' risks becoming what Hall calls 'a reductionism upward, rather than a reductionism downward, as economism was' (Hall 1996d: 146). Indeed, according to Daryl Slack, Hall views Laclau's insistently theoretical and philosophical tendency to engage in 'producing the concrete philosophically' rather than through historical analysis to be a tendency that in foregrounding *theory* actually has a reciprocal and negative 'backgrounding effect on the very politics that played such a crucial role in Laclau's work to begin with' (Daryl Slack 1996: 120). Indeed, such a divergence of orientation and interest can arguably be clearly discerned when Laclau argues for instance that once we are aware of the discursive constitution of identities and agencies we therefore *should* 'move from purely sociologistic and descriptive account[s] of the *concrete* agents involved in hegemonic operations to a *formal* analysis of the logics involved' (Laclau 2000: 53). This is quite a different kind of work to Hall's advocated 'adding, adding,

adding, adding, the different levels of determination'. On the contrary, Laclau contends that

> We gain very little, once identities are conceived as complexly articulated collective wills, by referring to them through simple designations such as classes, ethnic groups and so on, which are at best names for transient points of stabilization. The really important task is to understand the logics of their constitution and dissolution, as well as the formal determinations of the spaces in which they interrelate. (Laclau 2000: 53)

For Hall, this is precisely *not* the 'really important task'. For him, what is *important* is the 'conjunctural analysis' of the moment. As Sparks reminds us, 'the analysis of the historical moment is the subject of Hall's only major work published during the 1980s', and although 'the theoretical point of reference which Hall used to argue for this position [on Thatcherism] is explicitly drawn from Laclau' (Sparks 1996: 95), the interest lies in understanding the conjunctural moment and working out how to intervene, rather than merely seeking out some perhaps universal logic of conjunctural formation. Thus, for Daryl Slack, 'Hall's model of strategic intervention is not then limited to a kind of theoretically-driven Derridean deconstruction of difference and the construction of discursive possibility, but a theoretically-informed practice of rearticulating relations among the social forces that constitute articulated structures in specific historical conjunctures' (Daryl Slack 1996: 122). The problem with the post-Marxist discursive approach, then, is not only that, according to Hall, it sees 'nothing to practice but its discursive aspect' (Hall 1996d: 146), but also that it sees the 'really important task' of politicised intellectuals to be purely logical, formalising, and analytical. The problem or challenge, then, is to determine the status of *this* orientation, an orientation that claims that the need 'to understand the logics' is *the* task of the politicised intellectual. Perhaps there are good reasons and justifications for arguing that a proper or more rigorously thoroughgoing, exhaustive and complete cultural studies project should – 'logically' – constitute itself as distinctly different in orientation from the discourse analysis approach of Laclau and Mouffe.

In a similar respect, Gayatri Spivak discusses what she calls the 'canny comment' of Hindess and Hirst: that in theoretical and other such intellectual work there is always a risk that 'concepts are deployed in ordered successions to produce [the] effects [of analysis and solutions, but that] this order is the order created *by the practice of theoretical work itself*: it is guaranteed by no necessary "logic" or "dialectic" nor by any necessary mechanism of correspondence with the real itself' (Hindess and Hirst quoted in Spivak 1999: 316). In other words, the problem with the purely logical approach is that it risks introducing the tendency – a tendency that Hall identifies in Laclau and Mouffe – 'to slip from the requirement to recognize the constraints of existing historical formations' (Hall 1996d: 148). Of course, Laclau has and would always dispute this criticism (Laclau 2005), especially given his argument that although he considers culture and society to be a 'hegemonic battlefield between a plurality of possible decisions', this 'does not mean that any time everything that is logically possible becomes, automatically, an actual political possibility. There are inchoated possibilities which are going to be blocked, not because of any logical restriction, but as a result of the historical contexts in which the representative institutions operate' (Laclau 1996: 50; see also Chapter 3). Accordingly, Laclau can dismiss this criticism, and claim that the discursive approach implies attention to variable historical forces of determination. However, the Hallian rejoinder would remain that such a nod in the direction of 'historical contexts' is a far cry from actually engaging in their analysis. In a sort of ironic reversal, one might say that whilst in the past Hall appropriated the Laclauian insight that cultural and political analyses should no longer be structured 'around entities – class, class struggle, capitalism – which are largely fetishes dispossessed of any precise meaning' (Laclau 2000: 201), now it has come to be the case that *Laclau's own logic* could be said to have come to produce theoretical discourses that are perhaps 'largely fetishes dispossessed of any precise meaning' – endlessly talking about 'positionalities but never positions' (Hall 1996d: 146).

The issue here remains that of the question of the orientation (or paradigm) of analysis, what it can do, what the paradigm allows or obliges one to see, value, engage with; or where it 'takes' one's work. For Hall, Laclauian post-Marxism takes work *away* from intervention and into what (in the next chapter) Richard Rorty will call 'over-philosophication'. To reiterate Hall, this is 'not to say that it's theoretically impossible to develop a more adequate set of political positions within their theoretical framework, but somehow, the route [Laclau and Mouffe] have taken allows them to avoid the pressure of doing so' (Hall 1996d: 148). Of course, Hall perhaps ought to concede that, as Daryl Slack argues, 'when Laclau is read without losing grip on the ensemble of forces, by attributing to them something more like equal weight, without privileging the discursive, the [notion] of [discursive] articulation has greater possibilities' (Daryl Slack 1996: 121; see also Laclau 2005). What is distinctive about Hall, Daryl Slack adds, is that 'by insisting on the specificity of practices in different kinds of relations to discourse, Hall contests the move that Laclau and other post-Althusserians have taken' (122). In short, Hall questions the post-Marxist paradigm's assertion that 'there is nothing to practice but its discursive aspect' (Hall 1996d: 146). The issue of 'the discursive', then, clearly constitutes a point of ambivalence for Hallian cultural studies. Hall wants to resist the potentially infinite slippage that the concept introduces, because of the debilitating effects he contends that this has on one's political interventional abilities: recall his claim that 'if we are concerned to maintain a politics, it cannot be defined exclusively in terms of an infinite sliding of the signifier' (Hall 1996b: 258).

Hall's solution to discursive drift of all kinds is strategically to stake an 'arbitrary closure' (1996: 264), to try 'to return the project of cultural studies from the clean air of meaning and textuality and theory to the something nasty down below' (264). Rather than the theoretical fluency of post-Marxism, Hall wants cultural studies to strive to 'connect'. He contends that:

> The aim of a theoretically-informed political practice must surely be to bring about or construct the articulation between social or economic forces and those forms of politics and ideology which might lead them in practice to intervene in history in a progressive way – an articulation which has to be *constructed* through practice precisely because it is not guaranteed by how those forces are constituted in the first place. (Hall, quoted in Daryl Slack 1996: 122–3)

The question is, though, *what is it* to 'construct the articulation'? What is it for 'academic practice' to 'connect', 'interrupt' or 'intervene'? What is the logic, or what are the determinant conjunctural forces, governing the nature of the effects of cultural studies or post-Marxism, as political practice? In order to develop an answer, the next section will reintroduce and discuss John Mowitt's concept of the 'disciplinary object' (first discussed in Chapter 1), in order to further analyse the issue of the political consequentiality of academic activity.

The Political Disciplinary Object

In order to elucidate the notion of the 'disciplinary object', it will be helpful to consider an example given in Glyn Daly's edifying reading of 'Globalisation and the Constitution of Political Economy' (2002). Therein, without ever actually using the term 'disciplinary object' (which is not yet a widely known term and concept), Daly nevertheless shows very powerfully what disciplinary objects are and do. He begins with a consideration of the putatively different perspectives of Marxist and liberal versions of political economy, observing that:

> While the liberal and Marxist versions of political economy construct the 'objectivity' of the economy in characteristic ways, and are totally different in their prescriptions, they, nevertheless, share the same problematic. In both cases, the economy is an a priori unity whose internal logics, or laws, remain constant in every social formation. In other words, the economy exists as a conceptual model that can be specified in advance, an underlying structure of rationality around which a causal topography of the social may be logically constructed. Emancipation and moral progress were rendered dependent on a particular economic model: the free market (for liberalism); the socialisation of the means of production (for Marxism). In this respect, both types of political economy tend to be presented, by their respective advocates, as ultimate rational accomplishments embodying characteristic ends of history. (Daly 2002: 113)

This sharing of the same problematic, the problematic of political economy, amounts to sharing something of the same paradigm, because, as Mowitt explains, 'disciples, that is, the members of a discipline, must have a framework within which even their intellectual differences take on significance, and this is what a paradigm puts in place . . . The point is that even for disagreements at the hermeneutic level to arise there must be an enabling framework that permits the disputing factions to quarrel over the same thing' (Mowitt 1992: 26, 28). What Daly's account of the sharing of the same problematic under the same organising paradigm foregrounds is the way that both Marxism and liberalism construct a notion of the economy as an objective entity, presupposing it, imposing it, constructing it, and imputing or projecting various values onto it. So this is the first sense in which 'the economy' can be said to function as a disciplinary object. Implicitly for Daly here, and explicitly in Mowitt's account, such disciplinary objects are at once not necessarily 'real' but nevertheless they have real 'effects'. As Mowitt explains, 'the object of a discipline is not necessarily real, it is a regulative fiction that nonetheless *really* works to orient research within a particular field – research which may actually lead to interventions in the real that constitute reality as such' (1992: 27). Now, this is not to be read as the claim that nothing is real, or that academic knowledge is fictional, that truth does not exist, or anything of the sort. Rather, this is the invitation to recall that history is littered with countless real paradigms that have purported to study, understand or organise real objects in real ways. So, therefore, disciplinary objects are concepts, entities, identities, fields, and so on, that are not necessarily real, but that are held to be so, and that are as such socially, culturally, politically, commercially, etc., influential. Another way of grasping this is in terms of the Cartesian Ontological Argument, wherein the existence of the concept of something is taken to be proof of the existence of the thing conceptualised – such as, for instance, unicorns, fairies, God (as in Descartes), aliens, human nature, etc., or, as in the case of Glyn Daly's study, the objectivity and logicality of 'the economy'.

Regarding this 'object', and the related notion of the 'economic structure', Daly makes the classic deconstructive move of introducing an element of undecidability. He points out the impossibility of establishing a clear limit, a clear and pure 'inside' to a structure, and a clear and pure 'outside' to it. Thus, Daly reveals an undecid-ability right at the heart of political economy: namely, the forgotten oxymoronic character of the very formulation 'political economy', or rather, the exclusion of *the political* from the putative structure called the economy, in that 'the notion of political economy (in all its variants) has tended to eradicate the dimension of the political': 'Through routine use, the notion of political economy has tended to become sedimented within a tradition in which it has been made synonymous with generalised ideas about objective interests and positivistic truth – thereby concealing the traces of its own philoso-phico-discursive origins' (113). By unearthing this concealed oxy-moronic aspect of the formulation 'political economy', and thereby revealing that an economic 'structure' is rather more the result of a (political) *decision* and is therefore the product of an *imposition*, first conceptual and then of real policy, rather than a neutral reflection of necessary objectivity, Daly is able to argue that the belief in the objectivity of the economy is actually a violent ethico-political im-position. He gives this striking example:

> The liberal idealisation of the free market has been at the root of some of the most authoritarian and inhumane political measures taken against the poor and excluded. One of the most notorious examples is that of the Irish potato 'famine' where, under Whig prime minister, Lord Russell, and in accordance with market orthodoxy, food continued to be exported from

Ireland while a nation starved. While anti-Irish prejudice played a part in this disaster, it was underpinned by an economistic paradigm wherein a laissez-faire strategy was seen as the *only* 'rational' response. The overriding concern was to secure the long-term optimisation of prosperity and employment through a vigorous export-orientated economy. To depart from the 'invisible hand' approach would have been perceived as immoral and irrational. Far from a pathology of racist motivation, the tragedy of the Irish famine was, rather, the result of an economistic conception of the good.

The response of contemporary liberals to such issues as underdevelopment, genocidal conflict and global poverty is that more capitalist modernisation is required. This is indicative of the liberal economistic myth in which the free market is portrayed as a universal panacea and as the very foundation of a holistic and emancipated society – indeed, the foundation for the final society as *the* outcome of history . . . (2002: 116)

As compelling as this account is, however, one must nevertheless still hesitate before accepting this as (if) truth. For even paradigm-knowledge, or 'knowledge of knowledge' (Derrida 1992; 1987: 311), is no less contingent than any other knowledge. So even though any invocation of a paradigm might seem to imply invoking *knowledge fully known* (full 'knowability'), the possibility of complete knowledge is menaced by a constitutive impossibility that is often overlooked, a fundamental contingency that scuppers the possibility that any paradigm simply does the job of 'explaining' anything in either a natural, neutral or a fully adequate sense. In other words, wherever one tries to signify a fully intelligible, fully present and self-present entity or system, this is enabled by something like a second 'structure', one that is never fully knowable. One might call it 'unconscious', 'hegemonic' or the 'nonconceptual order' on which the 'conceptual order' is articulated (Derrida 1977) – the constitutive outside, excess, or incommensurable excluded of 'structure'.

Daly's argument, interpretations, and conclusions are perhaps therefore *necessarily* contestable. Yet it is not the point or the intention to contest them here. For, vis-à-vis the problematic of the textual versus the discursive, or indeed cultural studies versus post-Marxism, John Mowitt insists that 'the crucial point is not to challenge disciplinary readings simply by replacing them'. Rather, 'antidisciplinary research requires that readings reach from within artefacts to the paradigms that govern their interpretation and beyond these paradigms to the structures of disciplinary power that support them' (1992: 216). The first point to note is that paradigms, even those that include an acknowledgement of textuality, or which have acquired the ability to 'view things as texts', nevertheless police their borders, delimit the potential political effects of rounding on their own constitution, and in effect work as an inoculation or vaccination against the radically deconstructive implications that a fuller unleashing or 'application' of a textual paradigm would precipitate (Derrida 1974: 7). Something immanent to the text constitutes the possibility for a politics of antidisciplinarity. It is this that must be scrutinised and worked upon if cultural studies and post-Marxism are to take on the political in a sense arguably more radical than post-Marxism has yet to acknowledge or attempt. Mowitt calls the politically enlivening antidisciplinary force of the textual paradigm 'intratextuality':

> antidisciplinarity [seeks] to oppose disciplinary reason by linking the texture of an artefact to the institutionally mediated social forces that set its limits as a particular embodiment of textuality. The establishment of such a linkage presupposes the ability to gauge how social forces operate in the constitution of borders which, by definition, bring different practices and agendas into relation with one another. In the final analysis this is what is decisive about the notion of intratextuality. Without it we gain access only to the comparatively homogeneous tissue of intertextual references that constitutes the hermeneutical field of a particular textual example. With it one can pose questions that bear on the institutional maintenance of the hermeneutical field as such – questions which quickly center upon the political problems of how institutions are constituted, reproduced, and transformed . . . Insofar as [any] artefact is meaningful to a particular social group, it is because its members continue to support the disciplinary structures (many of which are not 'merely' academic) which read the artefact on their terms.
>   . . . What antidisciplinarity thus depends upon is a notion of reading that understands how its specificity as a practice derives from the institutional field which surrounds it. Since this means that all readings have institutional implications, isn't it time that we began reading it so as to undermine the institutions of disciplinary power at the very points where they have typically reproduced themselves with the greatest efficiency? Those who insist that such an aim is better realized by mobilizing the disenfranchised fail to see that 'we' (Left academics) are to be counted among the disenfranchised – even if, by virtue of our professional status, 'we' stand further away from the centers of misery and suffering. Why not labor to make education into an openly insurgent practice and break the hold that the vocational or professionally oriented disciplines have had on the commerce between the university and society? In this way we 'redeem' (as Benjamin liked to say) the text, and we make its emergence worthwhile. (Mowitt 1992: 214–15, 218)

Now, Daly's discourse analysis is particularly illuminating here, not just because it conveys in a clear sense the real effects of disciplinary objects in wider discourse; but also because it exemplifies the tendency within post-Marxism to engage with blatantly 'serious' *macro*-political phenomena. The question, though, is that of the *work* that such work, with such a focus, might itself do. Both Mowitt and Gary Hall (2002) problematise the necessity and indeed even the validity of cultural studies having to elaborate itself in and as serious and proper political analyses of the political dimensions of cultural discourses. However, there does seem to be a strong compulsion to equate 'discoursing about politics' or 'the political' with *being* political or *being* responsible, or with *actually* intervening or *doing* politics. This is a problematic conflation that, as will be argued in the conclusion, has skewed post-Marxism and cultural studies away from effective intervention.

Textual versus Discourse Analysis

Taking quite a different stance, and as first discussed in the previous chapter, John Mowitt demonstrates that it was textuality that enabled the post-Marxist notion of discourse. He shows, through a genealogy, 'that the historical institutionalization of textuality conditioned the emergence of discourse' (15) – that the development of the concept of 'discourse' relied on the 'prior institutionalization of textuality' (16). To clarify this, Mowitt quotes from 'Populist Rupture and Discourse' (Laclau 1980), in which Laclau specifies how the post-Marxist term 'discursive' is to be properly understood. At this point, the relevant passage deserves to be quoted in full:

> By 'discursive' I do not mean that which refers to 'text' narrowly defined, but to the ensemble of the phenomena in and through which the social production of meaning takes place, an ensemble which constitutes society as such. The discursive is not, therefore, being conceived as a level nor even as a dimension of the social, but rather as being co-extensive with the social as such. This means that the discursive does not constitute a superstructure (since it is the very condition of all social practice) or, more precisely, that all social practice constitutes itself as such insofar as it produces meaning. Because there is nothing specifically social which is constituted outside the discursive, it is clear that the non-discursive is not opposed to the discursive as if it were a matter of two separate levels. History and society are an *infinite text*. (Laclau 1980: 87; quoted in Mowitt 1992: 15)

Mowitt stresses that there is a lot that is of great value here, as there is throughout all of Laclau's work; particularly insofar as Laclau's approach attests to what Mowitt calls the 'triumph of a hermeneutic (as opposed to a positivistic) approach to society'. This is an approach that bears 'testimony to a development within cultural criticism, whose roots are often traced to the work of Michel Foucault, in which discourse is made consubstantial with sociality as such' (16). The important advance over positivism in this position is that, 'from the vantage point of post-Marxism people no longer simply communicate, they arise as "the people" within the practice of communication' (16). This, Mowitt argues, is why Laclau 'moves to dissociate this conception of discourse from the "narrow" sense of the text': 'he is explicitly attempting to evoke this constitutive aspect of the concept [of discourse] since the linguistic text is, after all, [too easily viewed as] something produced by a subject who precedes its production' (16). However, aside from these important advances, Mowitt sees some problems attendant to the move from text to discourse. The most significant is the way that this 'enabling gesture of post-Marxism' at once clearly and constitutively relies upon and yet 'appears nevertheless to subordinate the textual to the discursive' (15). That is to say, in Mowitt's words, Laclau's 'gesture at one level testifies to the prior institutionalization of textuality', but it also 'obscures an important tension between the discursive and the textual' (16). The problem with post-Marxist discourse analysis is that 'cultural analyses conducted from this angle tend to locate particular embodiments of discourse, that is, discourses whose properties and functions are then detailed' as if 'a particular type of phenomena presents *itself* such that it can become the focus of cultural studies' (16–17). This approach is limited and limiting because 'what is clearly not emphasized here is the status of discourse as a disciplinary object, a paradigm that organizes the *way* cultural research is designed, legitimated, and conducted'. The *disciplinary* object of discourse, contends Mowitt, derives from and reduces the interdisciplinarity but ultimately therefore '*antidisciplinary* profile' (14) of textuality.

So, the political dimensions of textuality, 'textual politics', relate to less than consciously explicit matters of institution and institutionalisation. In one regard, then, this means that in reading or interpreting anything (which, because everything becomes textual once one starts to interpret/read it, means any text) (Derrida 1974: 158; 1981: 43, 328), it must be acknowledged that the literality of any 'letter' or any 'message' ever received and taken to be the 'explicit message', is itself an effect produced and imposed by an instituted mode of reading (Derrida: 1987, 81; 1981: 75, 112, 203, 206; Godzich: 1987, 156; Mowitt: 1992, 17–18). Whilst the basic semi-semiotic interpretation of deconstruction, that one 'final' or 'proper' meaning is ultimately impossible (it is deferred, it differs, it keeps slipping, etc.) can be taken as read, it remains the case that final or proper meanings are attempted all the time. The deconstructive lesson that the condition of possibility for something is also, by the same token, the condition of its impossibility, and vice versa, must be remembered. So, the fact that final signifieds, proper meanings, etc., are impossible is what also necessitates and enables their constant attempted production, reproduction and attempted institution or imposition (Derrida 1981: 296). For, contrary to the common sense of the most popular kind of deconstruction – 'deconstructionism' – the impossibility of ever naturally, immediately, spontaneously and universally receiving anything like a stable set of signifieds or proper meanings does *not* mean that these things 'don't exist', but rather that they must therefore be imposed, wherever such closure is deemed necessary (Derrida 1992a: 197–9, 204, 206; 1996: 84). John Protevi has expressed this in these Derridean terms, arguing that 'everything' is (in) a 'general text' of 'force and signification', meaning that 'meaning', sense, *making sense*, entail manipulating forces and exerting pressure and power: sense is *made* (Protevi 2001: 40, 63–5). It doesn't just happen. The explicit message, the literal meaning, etc., is institutionally constructed: convention is constitutive, *institution* conditions interpretation. Without the imposition of some kind of stability (the post-Marxists call this facility the erection of nodal 'points de capiton' enabling predication (Laclau and Mouffe 1985: 112)), no one could ever agree or, indeed, as Mowitt makes clear, dispute. No phenomenon simply 'presents itself', replete with its natural, proper, unequivocal, inevitable interpretation, meaning, or truth. It is determined by what Derrida calls an institution; what Mowitt calls a paradigm.

Indeed, this is one of the key issues on which Laclau, Mowitt, Derrida and others all basically concur. Yet it nevertheless remains the locus or generative matrix of a key disagreement (in Rancière's (1999) sense of using the same terms but meaning different things by them and therefore effectively speaking *past* each other). For, whereas on the one hand, for the post-Marxists, there simply *are* discourses 'out there' which present themselves to be known by us 'in here', for Mowitt on the other hand, the notion of 'discourses out there' is itself a disciplinary construction – and a reductive one at that, insofar as the theory of discourse does not theorise itself as discourse. That is to say, perhaps all within cultural studies, deconstruction and post-Marxism might be able to concur on the contingent institutional-political point, but disagreements and differences arise between them, devolving on the extent to which the ramifications of this perspective are acknowledged and pursued. To reiterate, the point is that whenever anyone says anything explicit about anything – in short, whenever there is some kind of communally intelligible 'explicit message' or 'signified' at all – then this 'message', and at the same time the community which believes it receives it (Derrida 1987: 4, 5, 33, 81; 1998a: 40, 64), are both only possible by virtue of the institutional constructs through which both the message *and* the community reciprocally arise as such. At the every least these are conventions of a presupposed and imposed determination of what clear, proper or valid 'communication' *is*: what genre, mode or manner, protocols of clarity, of allusion, citation, reference, preferred ways of constructing or referring to referents etc., are acceptable, or even legible or intelligible (Mowitt 1992: 16–17; Readings 1996: 181–2). Invoking a related vocabulary, one might say this is what Wittgensteinian language-games also 'do': they produce communities. It is what Judith Butler (1990) or indeed Lyotard (1984) conceive in terms of the generativity or constitutive productivity of 'performativity'. The institution of a community relates to the 'reception' (construction) of a signified. The question, then, is what this adds to the understanding of the orientations, relations and conflicts of post-Marxism and cultural studies.

In one important regard, the concept of the disciplinary object introduces a new dimension to any discussion. For, although as Mowitt observes, the text is an 'appropriate term for what could conceivably have gone by other names' (1992: 5), his concern is that the term 'discourse' as deployed in post-Marxism does not work 'to name the alterity that simultaneously constitutes and subverts the context of disciplinary reason' (25). The text, then, heavily connotes a crisis at the heart of knowledge-establishment, and works to foreground the cultural-political 'work effected by the disciplines' (their place and role in hegemony). On the other hand, the tendency with the term 'discourse' is to suggest that the studier of discourses is somehow exempt from or outside of discourse, or what Laclau will be seen, in the next chapter, to call the 'ideological political field'. Chapter 3 will examine the way that Laclau's categories attempt to preserve the academic discourse analyst from contamination by the 'discursive' (or what he calls the 'ideological-political field'). So this, rather than being an 'academic *discourse* analysis', will be an '*academic discourse analysis*'. Putting it like this will hopefully clarify that the contention here is not to do with the reality or not of discourse as understood by Laclau. The question is not something like: is discourse a property of the world or is it an analytical construct, which may or may not also be a property of the world, and is this analytical construct commensurate with its object, i.e. discourse? Mowitt and Laclau both begin from Derridean deconstruction. Mowitt's critique devolves on the strictures and limitations of the discourse analysis paradigm, and the limiting reorientations that it places on cultural study. Indeed, as the next section will clarify, Mowitt's argument is that the emphatically 'macro-political' tone and orientation fostered by post-Marxist discourse analysis may well be less political, less interventional, less consequential, than the apparently micrological textual analyses of certain kind of cultural studies.

In order to further clarify what is meant by this, one of Stuart Hall's primary criticisms of Laclauian post-Marxism should be returned to, and read in the light of the attention that Mowitt gives to the question of the disciplinary object and the paradigm. To reiterate the Hallian criticism, then: Hall asks whether it is possible to accept the alleged post-Marxist claim that 'there is nothing to practice but its discursive aspect' (Hall 1996d: 146). Daryl Slack argues that, contrary to the post-Marxists, what is distinctive about Hall is that he insists 'on the specificity of practices in different kinds of relations to discourse' (Daryl Slack 1996: 122), and that Laclau remains valuable only if he is read 'without privileging the discursive' (121). Herein consists the disagreement between Hall and Laclau. Again, it is akin to a disagreement in Rancière's (1999) sense: namely, both parties to it are using the same word, and arguing about its status, *but they mean different things by it*. For Laclau, there is nothing outside of the discursive, because this names the logic of all constitution. For Hall, there is *more* to 'practice' than its discursive aspect, because the 'discursive aspect' in itself does not refer to anything specific, and in talking about it one is not talking about anything specific. It seems to refer to everything, but it thereby refers to nothing, and – worse – actually seems to exonerate the cultural analyst from doing any specific analyses of specific 'determinant forces'. Hall's problem, then, lies in the reductivity of the post-Marxist paradigm in which, in Mowitt's words, 'discourse is typically used, as is the case with Laclau, to characterise both the medium and the nature of sociality. Insofar as society is interpretable, it presents itself as an ensemble of discourses.

In addition, all that is analytically relevant about society is that which can be interpreted [and] discourse serves as a general name for the class of practices . . . that define the perceptible surface of society' (Mowitt 1992: 16–17). For Hall, post-Marxism constitutes a reduction, a move from concrete, complex and multilayered analysis of specific things, and a retreat into producing the concrete philosophically, through logic alone. However, it is the dimension added to this debate by Mowitt's attention to the paradigm and the concept of the disciplinary object that is even more vital. For, it becomes clear that whilst what Hall is worried about is the reduction of purview so that the *only* things deemed to be analytically relevant are hidden fundamental logics, what Mowitt contributes is the argument that what needs to be added to any cultural or political analysis is not just more and more 'analytically relevant' factors or a greater enumeration of 'levels of determination', but the question 'what kind of paradigm might support and legitimate the conjunction of these texts?' (1992: 220)

Cultural Studies versus Political Analysis

What is clear in both Mowitt and Hall's critiques of post-Marxism is that they are concerned that the post-Marxist analytical strategy and orientation itself might actually amount to a kind of *avoidance* of the political. So, the contentious issue is that of what is and what should be the orientation and foci (or paradigm) of cultural studies and/or post-Marxism. The (at least erstwhile) post-Marxist cultural analyst Slavoj Žižek weighs in on this debate regularly. According to him, one key and 'well-known thesis' within political theory and cultural studies is that 'the very gesture of drawing a clear line of distinction between the Political and the non-Political, of positing some domains . . . as "apolitical", is a political gesture *par excellence*' (Žižek 2000: 95). He points to one possible conclusion to be drawn from this: that because political power can be shown to be at work even 'at the root of every apparently "non-political" relationship', therefore 'the job of a critical analysis should be to discern the hidden *political* process that sustains all these "non-" or "pre-political" relationships' (Žižek 2000: 234). Certainly, a great deal of cultural, political, and very many other kinds of 'studies' have been orientated by precisely such an aim; and discerning and denouncing hidden or unnoticed power structures, biases, exclusions and the multifarious 'violences' of different cultural institutions, processes and practices has been immensely influential and orientative. So, it seems likely that many working within and around the contemporary interdisciplinary arts and humanities could be able to agree with Žižek's assertion that the 'job', or obligation, and responsibility of such intellectuals is to reveal such hidden power relationships. However, as the critiques of Hall and Mowitt imply, it seems important to pause to consider further whether the task of discerning and revealing the political in the putatively non-political should actually be *the* job of cultural studies *or* post-Marxism.

Now, this should not be construed as a hesitation in the face of the view that cultural studies and post-Marxism should always aspire to be responsible politicised academic practices, but rather as an attempt to interrupt the smooth working of certain types of thinking and intellectual production, based on the proposition that it might be beneficial to interrogate further *what* taking on or engaging responsibly with the political actually means and obliges. For, 'to always aspire to be' should be understood in the wake of Derrida's deconstructions of responsibility as meaning something very different from *assuming that you already are* that which you aspire to (be). The direct question, then, would be: *should* the 'job' of cultural studies or any critical analysis be 'to discern the hidden *political* process that sustains all . . . "non-" or "pre-political" relationships'? In a certain sense, the answer is *yes, of course*; for, the revelation of exploitation, subordination, oppression, injustice, marginalisation, exclusion and 'violences' of all kinds, has been, and remains, an always justifiable political project. But what would be the effect of *generalising* this aim, of placing it as *the* aim of cultural studies? In a first sense, cultural studies would become orientated as a subspecies or strange variant of political studies; and, moreover, one whose tautological start- and end-point would merely be the assertion, as premise and conclusion, 'all of this *is* political (right?)'. Arguably, the positing of such presuppositions is already in play in cultural studies and post-Marxism, especially because, as has often been argued, there are readily discernible tautologies silently circulating within and underpinning perhaps *all* systems, structures and institutions – tautologies of value, point, purpose, legitimacy, legitimation, justification, and so on (Hunter 1999). Such tautologies work as enabling and orientating assumptions, and are often the minimal (concealed) form of justification for an activity: the argument for something's importance, for instance, whilst it may invoke many other things along the way, will always reiterate a (concealed) circularity of justification or of value ('this is important/valuable because this is important/valuable (otherwise I wouldn't be doing it, would I?)'). This can be seen in arguments that attempt to justify a law or a status quo by basically asserting 'the law is justified because it's legal/the law', 'it's legal (i.e., implicitly 'just') because it's the law', or 'things have to be this way because this is the way things are'. (Richard Rorty terms these generally concealed points of argumentative circularity 'final vocabularies', by which he means that they are premises, beliefs, and 'nodal' points, which generally do not rise to the surface and present themselves *as* tautologies, but which constitute fundamental points beyond which those who hold them simply cannot 'go'; points which, if pressured, can precipitate all manner of crisis for the subjects involved.)

So it is possible to see that as well as underpinning systems, structures and institutions, it is always possible that the ultimately tautological dimension of the basis of any institution's justification might return – like the repressed – to haunt, to antagonise, and potentially to *undermine* it, too, wherever the shocking realisation of the circularity of point, purpose, justification or value becomes perceptible. The discernment of a tautological structure to legitimation threatens to precipitate 'crises' such as the revaluation and alteration of an institution, activity, practice or organisation, or the generation of cynicism, nihilism, or outright rejection. Particularly pertinent to note in this regard is that concealed tautological justifications do not only function 'out there', or 'elsewhere': they are discernibly at work underpinning academic and intellectual practices, across the board (See Hunter 1999: 30–57). So this is pertinent, indeed cortical, to questions in and of cultural studies and post-Marxism, and should not simply be a part of their critiques of *other* institutions. Rather, it should be applied as a question *to*, *of* and *in* post-Marxism and cultural studies. For, concealed tautologies, posited presuppositions, *ex post facto* rationalisations or other such circularities can work to reduce knowledge to 'pure recognition', to repetition, or to 'the production again of what we have always known' (Hall 1996: 267–8), related to a desire for 'static self-confirmation' (Mowitt 1992: 27), through the reiteration of one's own rectitude by reducing the new to the known, and otherness to sameness. The possibility that cultural studies and post-Marxism might be involved in such a process is problematic indeed, and should be considered a *fundamental problematic* (in every sense).

Mowitt has even explicitly suggested that certain orientations which directly and explicitly seek to take on the political can themselves work as avoidance, denial, or even foreclosure of that very possibility.

This argument is that in the reduction of the aims and orientations of critical analyses to the mere discernment of political power, then 'in the very worst of cases, this type of analysis sacrifices the texture of any particular production for a preemptory political evaluation of the cultural work performed by the discourse in which the production was realized' (1992: 18). In other words, he suggests, under such a 'political' injunction or orientation, '*Moby Dick* [might be reduced to] little more than the articulation of the contradictions of entrepreneurial adventurism' (18). Once again, he locates the risk in the post-Marxist concept of discourse: 'Again, discourse serves here as the medium of exchange through which specific cultural productions are read as social communications' (18): 'Obviously', he continues, 'I am not opposed to the labor of political evaluation, which strikes me as unavoidable in any case. Rather, I am concerned that [the concept of] discourse often obscures issues that ought to be part of any thorough political evaluation' (18). Mowitt's most serious charge against such an approach arises when he claims, in this regard, that 'implicit here is a certain phobic structure wherein the particular differences that might actually divide and/or galvanize reading constituencies are translated into pretexts for conducting literary interpretation at the level of social analysis alone' (18). The fact that Mowitt singles out the concept of 'discourse' as being something potentially reductive or obfuscatory *for* 'any thorough political evaluation' is perhaps serious enough. For discourse is a notion that has become an absolutely central category both for post-Marxist social and political analysis and for much cultural studies work (McRobbie 1992; Mowitt 1992; Frow 1995; Gilbert 2001; Rojek 2003). Therefore, if discourse, either as a concept within analyses or as a notion that actually orientates analyses, is indeed in any way obfuscatory for 'thorough political evaluation' (that is to say, therefore, if the concept of discourse turns out to be the complete opposite of what it is generally deemed to be), then this is a problem as much for post-Marxist discourse analysis and political studies as it is for any cultural studies – or indeed any other studies – that seek to engage thoroughly with the political. But what should be made of this claim of a 'phobic structure'?

In Derrida's writing, deconstruction and writing are always (among other things) indissociably associated with the 'democratic' (Derrida 1981: 144). This has lead Protevi to conclude that: 'Deconstruction is democratic justice, responding to the calls from all others' (Protevi 2001: 70). On this note, regarding Laclau and Mouffe, it might be said that because of their use of deconstruction and their talk of 'radical democratic politics', then it certainly seems unjust to suggest that their work may in any sense seek to avoid 'responding to the calls from all others'. However, Mowitt is keen to remind us that there's more to radicalising democracy than meets the ear and trips off the lips. What is vital, he argues, is 'inscribing within one's own position the possibility and necessity of a position which is obscured by what one opposes. Radical democracy ought to involve listening to those whose voices have been drowned out by the very voice of advocacy' (Mowitt 1992: 221). With this, Mowitt cautions us to 'hesitate suspiciously' before Laclau and Mouffe's theory, *precisely because* (among other things) it is a theory, with a particular, limited, limiting, institutional 'reading code' and 'voice of advocacy', which must, in a sense (and this is something that post-Marxism itself would argue about any such institution) constitutively drown out. Accordingly, Mowitt advocates 'textual politics' over 'discourse analysis' because even the avowedly deconstructive political theory of discourse analysis ultimately does not have the requisite deconstructive 'problem' with the institution – for Derrida, '*Deconstruction is an institutional practice for which the concept of the institution remains a problem*' (Derrida 2002: 53) – and therefore with itself *as* institutional practice and institutional *way* of knowing. Post-Marxism sets itself up as if a subject that can be supposed to know, relying on a stable subject-object split – as in: 'out there' is the (political) 'object' which presents itself or is presented by discourse in such a way as it can be 'known' properly by us 'knowing subjects', 'in here', in the academy. In this immediate sense, Laclau and Mouffe's discourse analysis *limits* de-construction, domesticates it, reins it in (or rather, sends it away), and protects itself from it. In Derrida's words, 'being-heard is structurally phenomenal and belongs to an order radically dissimilar to that of the real sound in the world' (Derrida 1974: 63).

Furthermore, as Gary Hall (2002) has argued, what is not often acknowledged in all manner of 'political' analyses is the fundamental *undecidability* of the form, content and limit of the political anyway. (Similarly, Laclau 2005 is all about the different sorts of conceptions of the political. Recall also that Laclau and Mouffe 1985, like innumerable other such books, was also merely the advancement of a different theory of what politics is.) Accordingly, Hall relates the possibility of the undecidability of the political to the various conceptions of what the political has been deemed to be within cultural studies, and explores the ways that these determinations have orientated, or indeed skewed, cultural studies as a politicised practice. This is clearly related to the attention that Mowitt has drawn to the general socio-political significance of the skewing, orientating, organising role that these determinations, concepts, notions, or paradigms and their objects play in intellectual, political, and cultural life – or, that is, disciplinary objects. In Mowitt's sense, Gary Hall's work is involved in the interrogation of the disciplinary object that is the concept 'politics' within desirously 'political' cultural studies. Hall makes this important observation:

> To move away from theory because it is apparently *not political enough* is to subordinate everything to political ends. It is to imply that things are only worth doing if it can be established *in advance* that they will have a practical, political outcome; an outcome which is itself decided *in advance* . . . [However, even analyses that may seem] initially to be the most 'theoretical' of issues may eventually turn out to have more practical and political effects than the most apparently 'political' of political actions and debates . . . (Gary Hall 2002: 5–6)

Gary Hall's argument in favour of hyper-self-reflexive theorisation as a condition of possibility for establishing the form and character of one's own 'conjuncture' is in a sense an almost Laclau and Mouffian answer to Stuart Hall. Indeed Chantal Mouffe argues, like Gary Hall, that:

> As Derrida stresses, without taking a rigorous account of undecidability, it is impossible to think the concepts of political decision and ethical responsibility. Undecidability is not a moment to be traversed or overcome and conflicts of duty are interminable. I can never be completely satisfied that I have made a good choice since a decision in favour of one alternative is always to the detriment of another one. It is in that sense that deconstruction can be said to be 'hyperpoliticizing'. Politicization never ceases because undecidability continues to inhabit the decision. Every consensus appears as a stabilization of something irreducibly unstable and chaotic. Chaos and instability are irreducible, but as Derrida indicates, this is at once a risk and a chance, since continual stability would mean the end of politics and ethics. (Mouffe 1996: 9).

An important critique of this argument will be made by Richard Rorty in the next chapter. However, the point here is that Gary Hall's position concurs with that of Stuart Hall in its insistence on the important role that deconstruction must play in keeping cultural studies self-reflexive and intellectually vital (when speaking of 'theory' Gary Hall basically means 'deconstruction'). Nevertheless, what is not made compellingly or persuasively explicit – in either of the Halls – is precisely the nature and status of any work's 'articulation' with anything else. How is the theoretical work itself to 'polemicize' or be 'polemicized' (Arditi and Valentine 1999)? *How* might a theoretical work 'turn out to have more practical and political effects'? How might this be decided or adjudicated? What is the nature, form, target or modality of its articulation to be? This problematic opacity is shared by post-Marxism. It is addressed by Mowitt, so his arguments should be examined further on the way towards a conclusion in which the post-Marxist theory of *articulation* and Mowitt's thinking on the politics of antidisciplinarity will be combined into a new strategy of intervention.

The Object of the Subject

What all anti-essentialist, post-foundationalist or constructivist thinking (such as that dominant within and characteristic of cultural studies and post-Marxism) has in common is some version of the premise (or axiom) that humans have, in Mowitt's words, a 'deep constitutability' (Mowitt 2002: 87; Laclau 1999). To perceive the contingency of subject formation means to conceive of identity not as innate but as a socio-political 'achievement'. So, the form and 'content' of subjects, as socio-political products, will always (constitutively) be contaminated or supplemented by a context or contingency that means it is undecidable whether subjects could be said to be 'free', and whether 'free decisions' can be made. As deconstructive work regularly points out: any putative 'decision' might always possibly *not* have been a decision (implying as this does a certain 'madness' or *radically* undetermined freedom), as it can only be apprehended retrospectively and could always be interpreted as having been merely a programmed part of a calculable process. Did I, for example, 'decide freely' to write this book, or was my sense of freedom something of a fantasy, given that writing it was something determined or overdetermined by my 'context'? When I or anyone seeks to evaluate the status of an event and to enquire whether it was a free decision or a programmatic inevitability, it might always be possible to construct a narrative or an account that arrives at either decision ('Doing this was decided spontaneously and through free will' or 'Doing this was the inevitable result of the context'). As Hall might say, what are the determining forces at work in this or that conjuncture? Deconstructive reading shows them to be undecidable, and suggests that any decision arrived at is itself the end product of a contingent evaluation, which means that, first, even real events are 'textual' when looked at in any sense; second, it is ultimately impossible to know whether our interpretation is correct (for what is analytically relevant, and what is not?); third, it is impossible to establish what is a free decision and what is overdetermined or pre-programmed; and, fourth, it becomes unclear whether our own act of interpretation is itself a free act, or whether we ourselves are ensnared in a determining structure. (See Chapter 3 for a further discussion of decision.)

Salient here is the way that this discussion connects with the infamous subject-versus-structure problem: the problematic question of agency (Valentine 2003). The various resolutions to the agency-structure conundrum (are subjects totally free or are they totally governed by a structure?) span between positions that claim there is complete structural determination and no consequential subjective freedom, to positions advocating complete aleatory chaos, wherein there is only freedom and no unified determining structure. The position of Laclauian post-Marxism is that the general or universal condition is one of contexts or scenes that are 'relatively structured', more or less fixed, stable, and closed. For, following Derrida, Laclau maintains that contexts will never and can never be *completely* closed or closable (because of an uncontrollable surplus and slippage of meaning, and inevitable dissemination, etc.). So, subjects do necessarily have the delimited propensity to make decisions, but only according to the options that appear contextually possible (Laclau 1996a: 50). In short, Laclau resolves the subject-structure conundrum by inverting and displacing, arguing that *power* is the condition of possibility for freedom; that an absence of power is logically impossible; that power preserves certain freedoms and forms of agencies; that freedom and agency will always-already be limited, in that in its exercise it will come to encounter a limitation and/or come to constitute itself as the exertion of power, and so on (Laclau 1996; 1996a). In post-Marxism, power is seen as *productive and generative*; the positive condition of possibility for subjectivity, limited freedom and praxis (See Critchley 2003; Laclau 1996a; Mowitt 2002).

The reason for introducing this here is not gratuitous, but rather to rearticulate the theoretical with the practical on the way to a fuller consideration of post-Marxist discourse and cultural studies. The Hallian question of the 'determining forces' that determine a conjuncture relies, as has been seen, on Laclauian theory. Post-Marxism is a theory of articulation. But the question to be approached now is how any cultural or political study articulates with anything else. Hall's criticism of Laclau is that in his theory 'there is no reason why anything is or isn't potentially articulatable with anything' (Hall 1996d: 146). Yet, from the current perspective here it appears, rather, that the fundamental challenge for both Hall and Laclau – and any politicised project – is actually the obverse: whether the analysis be theoretical/logical or empirical/historical, for example, what does it articulate with? Does it 'connect' with anything? Does it make 'a difference' at all? And if so, what are the conditions of possibility of such an articulation, in what conjuncture? Theoretical contributions are – or at least assumed to be – valuable, and post-Marxism's theory seems to be satisfyingly complete. But it seems important to note that to construe the complexity of any singular situation or particular instance or example in terms of the metadiscursive categories of hegemony, contingency, subject, structure, context, decision, antagonism, etc., is to impose a manner of analysis that is at once hugely supple (*anything* can be diagnosed as hegemonic and/or undecidable), but also irreducibly problematic too (so, everything is hegemonic/undecidable? So what? Or rather: *and* what? *then* what?). Indeed, such a manner of analysis could also be said to work to shelter that very theoretical perspective itself from the consequences of its own terms: where, why, how, and signifying what *is* this very theory of hegemony to be placed or explained *within* the hegemony it theorises? What is its context, structure, decision? If it is a contingent achievement, as it must be in its own terms, then what 'influenced' it? What supplements it, constitutively, from the outside, at the origin (Derrida 1981; 1998a)? What *hegemon* guides it? In what way does it intervene?

A perspective like Mowitt's, sensitive to the political problem of the paradigm, is invaluable here. This is because this dimension of the general problematic of contingency is otherwise too easily dispensed with. Its reserves could be said to be regularly mined or exploited by intellectuals, but in a way that amounts to a kind of abuse, in the sense that interlocutors tend simply to try to 'refute' or to point out the limitations of one or another kind of knowledge (which is easy to do, as the argument about constitutive contingency entails), only to use this as a point from which to construct *another*, different but equivalent, paradigm of knowledge. But for Mowitt, 'the crucial point is not to challenge disciplinary readings simply by replacing them' (1992: 216). Indeed, to do so is to risk becoming embroiled in academic polemics of the sort that Foucault held in disdain, which as Henry Giroux points out construe intellectual work as 'built upon the model of war and unconditional surrender, designed primarily to eliminate one's opponent', what Chantal Mouffe calls 'the Jacobin model of scholarship (or as Herbert Marcuse aptly put it, "scholarshit")' (Giroux 2000: 14), or the kind of work that Gayatri Spivak argues proceeds by 'mistaking polemic for its own sake for resistance as such' (Spivak 1999: 337).

To pursue such a style of activity is arguably to live in repetition, or to operate entirely within the structure of what Mowitt (1992) calls 'disciplinary power': the institutional production of 'docile' and 'disciplined' subjects. This charge makes most sense in terms of what he calls the 'modern' form of power, a form of power that permeates human subjectivity through the institutional bases of society and which also channels the way that subjectivity is understood, or constructed, as a disciplinary object. He argues that:

> power acquires its status as 'modern' when its productive or positive side emerges . . . [T]his process is inseparable from the advent of disciplinarity, [and] one of the ways to conceive of the 'positivity' of power is in terms of the way experiences of human agency are given epistemic shape, are 'posited' as socially intelligible phenomena . . . [W]hat distinguishes disciplinary power is the way that it participates in what I will call the subjection of human agency, that is, the production and circulation of knowledge that segments, correlates, and thus orders social collectivity around the experiential, but ultimately institutional category of the subject. (Mowitt 1992: 33)

So, Mowitt's argument is that 'the socio-discursive constitution of an object is also, if not primarily, a constitution of subjectivity which devotes itself to the object in order to obscure subjectivity's own grounding in the sociogenesis of objects' (1992: 39). In other words, stability in objective knowledge reciprocates with stability in subjectivity – social stability. Now, Mowitt works through some Girardian (and indeed, implicitly Durkheimian) anthropological formulations to represent community/disciplinary-formation and ultimately subject-formation as involving 'sacralization' (40), with all of the violence, displacements, projections and misrecognitions that this entails, in order to argue for the work of a matrix wherein the internal stability of a group's relation to their (sacred) object at once produces the stability of that external object (and by extension, the stability of discursive 'reality'), as well as being the means of the production of stable disciplined subjectivity as such (26). But what Mowitt is chiefly concerned to draw attention to is the sense in which 'the object of a discipline is not necessarily real', but is rather 'a regulative fiction that nonetheless *really* works to orient research within a particular field – research which may actually lead to interventions in [that which] constitute[s] reality as such' (27). In one respect, then, this is one more way of saying that there is no unmediated knowledge, no unconstructed knowledge (40–1), and so nothing other than 'regulative fictions', or indeed, nothing outside of the text.

But, not all texts are created equal: some are taken seriously; some are not. Experience is segmented in its very constitution, and there are institutions whose texts on whatever sanctioned experience are accorded a certain plausibility or respect in various centres of power and knowledge. This is as much as to say that experience must be sanctioned by an institution *before it 'is' an experience.* This is what Mowitt means when he asserts that it is 'the production and circulation of knowledge that segments, correlates, and thus orders social collectivity around the experiential, but ultimately institutional category of the subject'. Furthermore, he continues: 'the very segmentation of experience that facilitates and requires the coordination of knowledge production contributes immediately to the genesis of an object that is stable precisely to the extent that it is incessantly referred to the diverse, reciprocally legitimating authorities that define the disciplinary field' (35). Experience itself requires institutional legitimation (however metaphorically construed the meaning of 'institutional' is) before it can be a legitimate experience, 'known' as such; and the production of plausible or reliable knowledge is also bound up with the production of legible forms of subjectivity. (This is also why Laclau (2000, 2005) views the contingent inauguration and organisation of any community and its objectivity, norms and values, to be irreducibly *ethical*.) Or, as Mowitt argues, what is 'fundamental' to the very possibility of 'disciplines like sociology or psychology' (i.e., disciplines oriented and ultimately authorised to know about human subjects) is 'a level of social stability that derives from institutions capable of providing the requisite controls'. Such 'knowledge production presupposes a certain saturation of society by disciplinary power': 'There is . . . a certain continuity between the internal organization of knowledge production at the level of academic disciplines and the institutional structure of society' (34–5).

So, Mowitt undertakes a relatively thoroughgoing anatomy of hegemony. It is more detailed an account of the institutional basis of hegemony than one is likely to find in post-Marxist texts themselves, where 'hegemony' is regularly evoked, but mainly as a 'complex unity' or assemblage 'of discourses', and where it ultimately remains expressed quite gesturally and metaphorically, without being specified or broken down in any great detail. It is through his more refined account of hegemony that Mowitt is lead to regard the problem of the intellectual paradigm and the possibility of antidisciplinarity to be acutely political. For him the point is precisely not that agonists and antagonists within disciplinary contexts such as those of academia merely keep knocking old paradigms down and replacing them with different but equivalent ones. Indeed, this reduces academic work to nothing more than a competitive contestation and an ultimately conservative jostling for position within an enduring institutional-political sameness – or an institutional discursive context from whose main workings and constitution (bureaucratic, economic, etc.) such academic jostling remains entirely disengaged and disarticulated. This is to specify the seriousness of the risk that such an orientation of activity will not adequately grasp the mode of its political articulation to any other context, scene or institution. This is why Mowitt is concerned more with the 'micro-political' dimensions of the question of political articulation: if the issue is that of how anything links with anything else, then for Mowitt, this issue should not leap out into the discussion of the macro-political, or 'wider' or indeed 'proper political issues', as if they are simply issues residing 'out there'. The problem remains that of establishing how *this* (each and every 'this' of academic intellectual work) might already be ensnared within a complexly reticulated political context, and how it might thereby seek to make a difference to it, within it, and 'beyond' it. In order to explore further the political ramifications of this Mowittian textual refinement or sophistication of the hegemonic metaphor, it might be helpful to pose explicitly a general question which captures its scope: How does the deconstructive textual micro-political perspective or anti-paradigm relate to or articulate with the macro-political? What is meant by the term 'macro-political' is both the macro-political focus (on the out there) characteristic of the political/discourse analysis of post-Marxism and beyond, and also the 'wider', 'serious', 'pressing issues' 'out there' that are often evoked as the reasons to reject theoretical, textual, deconstructive work in favour of something called 'direct engagement' (whatever this is variously deemed to be).

Deconstruction versus post-Marxism

The textual (anti-)paradigm that Mowitt elaborates problematises every simple claim that 'this is the way things are' and 'this is the necessary relation between things'. Indeed, it is clearly neither simply micropolitical nor simply macropolitical, because it is the demonstration of the imbrication of both conceptual levels before (and the subversion of) their separation into putatively different 'levels'; for such a separation is already a product of the taxonomical, orientating and effective work of a paradigm which differentiates and constructs objects as such. It is in this regard that anything, including the archetypal macropolitical paradigm of Marxism, could be said to be always already in – or in danger of – de- and reconstruction. Anna Marie Smith explains one of the ways that the de- and reconstruction of any such entity occurs. When it comes to making *any* essence-claim about *any* identity, she argues: 'from the original moment in which an essence-claim is made, the essence-claim is already being undone', because, as the very need for the claim itself and the possibility of alternative claims about the putative essence demonstrate, 'there never was/never will be a pure', stable, natural or essential identity to any entity, including such entities as 'Marxism' (Smith 1994: 173). Making any 'essence-claim' is simultaneously to establish or impose an identity and to sew the seeds or initiate the beginning of the deconstruction of that putative essence.

This is one respect in which Marxism, like anything else, is constitutively unstable. As Michael Ryan explains, even a cursory glance at a range of Marxist work and Marxist organisations reveals that 'Marxisms abound' (quoted in Peters 2001: 11). The reason why 'there have always been multiple Marxs' is, in Terrell Carver's words, that the identity will always be constructed differently, so 'each one is a product of a reading strategy'. Marxism is constitutively both possible and yet ultimately impossible by the same token: its contingently constructed character. Every object and identity is constituted through what Carver calls a 'reading strategy', or what we have been calling a paradigm; and 'a reading strategy involves a choice of texts and a biographical frame, philosophical presuppositions about language and meaning, and political purpose – whether acknowledged or not' (Carver, quoted in Peters 2001: 29). Accordingly, micropolitical firstly relates to the macropolitical insofar as the macropolitical could always be said to be determined in this or that way by the putatively micropolitical matter of interpretation. This understanding of the always-constructed character of the signified or supposed referent is the key deconstructive dimension to both the insights of the textual and the post-Marxist discourse paradigm. Indeed, in a slight twist of the 1970s feminist slogan 'the personal is political', it could be argued that the micropolitical is macropolitical.

This observation is, in a strong sense, a key factor linking deconstruction, cultural studies and post-Marxism. However, the name of this relation is also, to echo Derrida, the same as one of its terms. That is to say, what links and separates, equivalates and differentiates cultural studies and post-Marxism are their different relationships to deconstruction. Cultural studies and post-Marxism have different deconstructions. They deconstruct differently. Textual deconstruction differs from discursive deconstruction. And because each deconstructs differently, this causes each to have a different relation to 'Marxism', of course. But, as Peters (2001) is at pains to show, there is no simple disarticulation or opposition between deconstruction and Marxism – even though these two 'approaches' are often held to be opposed to each other. Rather, Peters insists, not only has Derrida often spoken 'of himself as both a communist and a Marxist' (11), but Marxism is always present, in some sense, in the work of all key poststructuralist thinkers: 'postponed or deferred (as in the case of Derrida) or always implicit (as in the case of Deleuze)' (26).

Now, Peters privileges and prioritises Derrida not for gratuitous or simply partisan reasons, but rather to draw attention to deconstruction vis-à-vis the question of Marxism. This is because, along with other work in the continental tradition, 'Derrida's deconstruction [has] changed once and for all how reading should be conceived' (31). This is a change that may still appear to some as being only very trivial or secondary (as in the complaint: of all the important things in the world, what is the big deal about how 'reading' should be conceived?). But it should now be clear why it pertains directly to Marxism as well as to the 'real world' with which political thought is concerned. For, Peters reminds us, the 'traditional order of Marxist texts is not the only possible one' (31); the traditional order and ways (or ordering-ways) that such texts have been read is not the only possible one, nor necessarily the 'correct' one. Reordering makes a difference. Once more citing Carver, he argues that there has been, first, 'a shift in *what* Marx is read; second, a shift in *how* Marx is read; and third, a shift in *why* Marx is read' (31). The problem that deconstruction poses and engages (and the reasons why an explicit reading of Marx was deferred for so long by Derrida), boils down to Derrida's 'search for the *correct protocols* for reading [Marx]' (35). So, despite having deferred a direct engagement with Marx and Marxism, what Derrida eventually came to claim haunts and enlivens deconstruction is, as Peters puts it, 'a certain spirit of Marxism that relates to deconstruction' (37). In *Specters of Marx* (1994), Derrida announces that 'Deconstruction has never had any sense or interest, in my view at least, except as a radicalization, which is to say also *in the tradition* of a certain Marxism, in a certain *spirit of Marxism*' (Derrida quoted in Peters 2001: 37). The sense of what this 'spirit' is or does is according to Peters implicitly shared by Derrida and Deleuze and post-structuralism in general. As he reminds us, Deleuze contended that 'being on the Left' has 'nothing to do with governments'. Rather, 'being on the Left is, first, a phenomenon of perception' (33). This is far from the reduction of politics simply to individual perception, but it is rather to state the constitutive supplementarity or the 'transformational' (35) potentialities of perception, when this is understood as related to the institutional-political context within which perception is constructed, occurs and has effects. This is the significance and political implication of the paradigm, reading strategy, or institution.

In this respect, the key issues arising upon the introduction of deconstruction into political and politicised thinking are the introduction of undecidability into the question of university responsibility, and the problems of determining what proper politics actually is (including determining whether and in what way it might be 'Marxian', if this remains a concern). However, as this work has been arguing, it is important not to make the mistake of thinking that these conceptual problems solely relate to the determination of the object 'to be known' whilst downplaying the ethico-political and institutional (hegemonic) status of the 'knower' and the interventional effects of 'the knowing' (the question of polemicizing articulation). Quite contrary to this, a textual approach insists on the necessity of not subordinating the one dimension to the other, and instead trying to make sense of intervention in terms of an awareness of the institutional basis and operations of society, or of disciplinarity, rather than in terms of what can be called the 'soap-box' conception of intervention. This is to evoke the way that, like any theory or approach, post-Marxism can rather easily make *pronouncements* about what is political and what the political interventions (of others: 'political agencies' or actors, out there) are or should be. Indeed, it is arguable that making such pronouncements amount to the sum total of its aim and aspiration, in one respect. But, the pragmatic question is, in terms of its own theory of discourse and hegemony, where does post-Marxism see itself? What is *its own* pragmatic, political, or interventional status? Is it, in itself, an intervention? Into what? Or is it not interventional at all? Is it simply, as Richard Rorty (1996) deems all theory to be, ultimately merely a form of 'kibitzing' and 'useless onlooking'? To assert this, must one rely on a simple theory (academia) versus practice ('real political engagement') schema, which would fly in the face of the basic tenets of the post-Marxist (and/or) deconstructive (and/or) cultural studies theory of culture and politics as hegemonic. The importance of considering these questions for cultural studies and any politicised intellectual activities should be clear. For this is the question of the way that academics think their own works might intervene. The next chapter more fully and directly engages these questions, on the way to a retheorisation of academic work *as* intervention.

Before turning to these issues, though, a certain controversy that continues to rage between textual approaches and more traditionally political approaches should be addressed. This will be done by looking at the way that the broadly post-Marxist theorist Slavoj Žižek conceives of and treats discourse, politics and textuality. As a stepping stone or segue, it should be noted that the schematic and simplistic but hopefully helpful distinction between 'macropolitical' and 'micropolitical' approaches that this chapter has used to discuss the different orientations and political implications of the textual paradigm and the post-Marxist discourse paradigm, is a distinction that would not be accepted as valid by many kinds of political studies. Indeed, it may be objected to on many grounds, such as through arguments that deny the political character of the cultural, private or personal, or through defining politics proper as being public and chiefly governmental (and solely 'macro'), or by excluding the academic or otherwise merely institutional from the category of the political, and hence from political causality, entirely. In this sense, it is only from the perspective of the more extended understanding of the political – the understanding that as has been seen circulates characteristically within deconstructive, post-Marxist, and cultural studies work – that this doubling and extension of the political, from being something that is solely macro to being something this is both micro and macro could be accepted. Just as 'the personal is political', so is the paradigm and perspective.

As seen earlier, however, the avowedly but problematically 'Marxist' Slavoj Žižek indicates on the one hand that the importance of 'the job of a critical analysis' is to 'discern the hidden *political* process that sustains all [supposedly] "non-" or "pre-political" relationships' (Žižek 2000: 234). But on the other hand, even whilst Žižek acknowledges the important political potential of ideological and intellectual conflicts within hegemony, he nevertheless refuses to follow the logic of the textual paradigm completely. In this sense, Žižek is perhaps *exemplary* of the stance of 'official' post-Marxism, in that he acknowledges the deconstructive insight embraced by cultural studies, but he nevertheless refuses or resists it, preferring instead to give drastically more attention to the perceived 'out there' of the macropolitical 'field' and basically none to the question of his own contingent position. In Žižek one sees a particularly acute post-Marxist acknowledgement and refusal of deconstructive textualism.

This refusal arises because Žižek claims to be *so* concerned with the macropolitical field. And when it comes to the macro-political, according to Žižek, unless one is working towards a total and complete revolutionary transformation (i.e., the mythical global anti-capitalist revolution), then what one is doing is what he calls mere 'interpassivity' (Žižek 2002: 170): chimerical (non)politics, that might or might not change all sorts of *actual* things, but which do not alter any *fundamental* thing – namely, the 'fundamental horizon' of capitalism itself. Thus, the textual paradigm elaborated earlier would indeed constitute for Žižek a complete abdication from politics. As opposed to such allegedly postmodern, deconstructive 'resignation', Žižek instead prefers to regularly and stridently call for revolution (2002, 2000: 101). Nevertheless, what is particularly interesting about his position is that, in being orientated vociferously and avowedly toward the macropolitical world 'out there', he simultaneously identifies and tries to tackle a crisis he perceives to devolve on the very possibility/impossibility of 'Marxism' today, *and* an identical wider crisis that he sees as having arisen throughout the contemporary academic and political intellectual world:

[The] fetishist fixation on the old Marxist-Leninist framework is the exact opposite of the fashionable talk about 'new paradigms', about how we should leave behind old 'zombie-concepts' like working class, and so on . . . [These are] the two complementary ways of avoiding the effort to think the New which is emerging today. The first thing to do here is to cancel this disavowal by fully admitting that this 'authentic' working class simply does not exist. And if we add to this position four further ones, we get a pretty clear picture of the sad predicament of today's Left: the acceptance of the Cultural Wars (feminist, gay, anti-racist, etc., multi-culturalist struggles) as the dominant terrain of emancipatory politics; the purely defensive stance of protecting the achievements of the Welfare State; the naïve belief in cyber-communism (the idea that the new media are directly creating conditions for a new authentic community); and, finally, the Third Way, capitulation itself. Let us just hope that the present anti-globalization movement will introduce a new dimension by, finally, again conceiving of capitalism neither as a solution nor as one of the problems, but as the problem itself. (Žižek 2002: 308)

Thus, for Žižek, the normal, everyday conception of politics as pragmatic and piecemeal, or local and institutional, is in fact chimerical non-politics, or 'interpassivity'. Academic textualism is even worse, to the extent that it does not insist upon the global dimension of 'conceiving of capitalism neither as a solution nor as one of the problems, but as the problem itself'. For Žižek, indeed, only the 'truly global' political act of complete revolution against capitalism would constitute politics proper. Only total global anti-capitalist revolution would be a political intervention. But Žižek believes that he knows why the very idea of macropolitical revolution (and the Marxian call to it) seems so preposterous and untenable in the West today. As he sees it, *any* such call to revolution will always seem self-defeating. This he explains by recourse to an example used by Lacan:

> Lacan developed an opposition between 'knave' and 'fool' as the two intellectual attitudes: the right-wing intellectual is a knave, a conformist who considers the mere existence of the given order as an argument for it, and mocks the Left for its 'utopian' plans, which necessarily lead to catastrophe; while the left-wing intellectual is a fool, a court jester who publicly displays the lie of the existing order, but in a way which suspends the performative efficiency of his speech . . . (Žižek 2000: 324–5)

The proposition that 'anti-establishment' positions might *always* seem foolish is something that deserves attention, no matter what one's political position or intellectual paradigm. As seen earlier, Mowitt's anti-disciplinary textual-political orientation could indeed be said to put little faith in the 'performative efficiency' of such calls to arms. Laclau, too, has confessed to 'smiling at the naïve self-complacence' of Žižek's moments of 'r-r-revolutionary' rhetoric (Laclau 2000: 289; see also Laclau 2004 and 2005). Indeed, it should be asked: if Žižek himself thinks that this knave versus fool situation always obtains, then why does he keep making such 'foolish' calls to macropolitical arms (revolution)? The answer relates to the status and work of the micropolitical within hegemony. For, as Žižek argues in another context – in an evaluation the (then) embryonic public political debate about whether there is ever justification for torture – *any* 'calls to keep an open mind' on the issue [of torture], even and especially when such calls 'do not advocate torture outright, but just introduce it as a legitimate topic of debate, are even more dangerous than an explicit endorsement of torture [because] such legitimization of torture as a topic of debate changes the background of ideological presuppositions and options much more radically than its outright advocacy: it changes the entire field, while, without this change, outright advocacy remains an idiosyncratic view' (Žižek 2002: 239). So, whilst it may at the moment seem idiosyncratic, Žižek sees his task as working to get the issue of revolution back on the 'realistic' political agenda by calling for it to be discussed enough times so that it stops sounding preposterous, starts sounding more legitimate, and as such 'changes the background of ideological presuppositions and options'.

What Žižek both plays and erases, both relies on and rejects, then, is the belief and stake in the university institutions, articulated with publishing and media industries, and the political effectivity of the discursive output of this institutional articulation. Of course, this subscription to hegemonic articulation nevertheless reveals Žižek's view of hegemonic politics to be rather undeconstructed and simplistic. For, even on a fairly elementary level, it is easy to see that in advocating this strategy and orientation what Žižek relies on and yet does not interrogate, in this macro-political argument, is the question of how and why certain voices, words, calls, messages, or events, could ever come to carry or lack anything like political 'force'. Here political intervention is construed as being straightforwardly a matter of speaking and of being heard, whereupon what has been heard is somehow consequentially 'acted upon' in a predictable manner. Whilst this is a crude and undeconstructed notion of articulation, there are however more nuanced and deconstructed versions of it, in which the political is indeed formulated as a matter that is irreducibly one of audibility/intelligibility (Rancière 1999; Arditi and Valentine 1999). Herein, the political has everything to do with *what* anything – any event, signifier, mark, or speech act, etc. – is understood *as*. For, what things are 'understood *as*', the *way* they are understood, is, as Laclau and Mouffe insist, determined by the way articulations are structured within the hegemonic field. And this is again where the macropolitical meets the micropolitical; or, in other words, where the constitutive institutional, interpretive, hermeneutic dimension (traditionally or too easily overlooked, downplayed or deemed secondary), is seen to be primary, orientative and political.

Žižek acknowledges this, but is quick to assert the importance of nevertheless remaining squarely within a crude Marxist formulation of the political. This is because he contends that without a demand for a fundamental and radical revolution, then no matter how 'optimistic' any political discourse may sound, and no matter how transformative it may appear, all political positions which lack a stake in or desire for '*the* revolution' are fundamentally pessimistic. Even in apparently celebratory postmodern positions, or in *any* left, right, or neoliberal, pragmatic or even post-Marxist position, Žižek sees the pessimism of a resigned acceptance that 'capitalism is the only game in town' (Žižek 2000: 95). For Žižek, the macropolitical matter of revolution is *the* matter of the political itself. So, whilst post-Marxists like Laclau and Mouffe may feel that they remain faithful to a Marxist 'spirit' in trying to engender a radical democracy such that its emancipatory force antagonises and infects all relations (including economic ones) and constantly transforms them, Žižek sees Laclau and Mouffe as being unfaithful to Marxism because they are no longer going 'directly' after capitalism. Capitalism remains for Žižek *the* problem, and the 'universal struggle' against 'it', *the* solution. It is because of the fact that there is no one thing that is capitalism, however, because of the fact that capitalism is a complex and multiple discursive arrangement, that Laclau and Mouffe could not agree to oppose 'it'. 'It', capitalism, is not 'one'. Žižek's object of attack is a signifier recruited to try to foreground a spectral logic as being the political problem, and to try to use this signifier as a rallying call to recruit and orientate the efforts of a political constituency. This may not sound too different from Mowitt's call to 'to make education into an openly insurgent practice and break the hold that the vocational or professionally oriented disciplines have had on the commerce between the university and society' (1992: 218), but one can see in Žižek an orientation that exemplifies Mowitt's account of 'the very worst of cases' of post-Marxism: namely, a type of analysis that 'sacrifices the texture of any particular production for a preemptory political evaluation of the cultural work performed by the discourse in which the production was realized' (1992: 18).

So the Mowittian problem with Žižek in this regard is not necessarily with his (macro)political perspective. The problem is with the reductivity of his work to 'preemptory political evaluation'. His conviction that 'university responsibility' demands precisely this kind of political evaluation is bolstered by his holding a belief in what is surely one of the most traditional conceptions of political 'performative efficiency' that there is: namely, the belief in and reliance on the notion of what can be called 'political-will-formation'. Now, despite such an orientation holding fast to the dubious notion of 'intention-ality', and the belief that political intention might directly cause the desired political results of that intention, it might nevertheless be said that the formation of political will is undoubtedly important – whether that be the political will of some universal revolutionary class or of any other kind of hegemonic or forceful agency. But – and even without entering into Laclau and Žižek's ongoing polemic about all of this (Laclau 2000; 2004; 2005; Žižek 2000) – it can be argued that both of them miss the point that should be most important to them: namely, the question of the means or mechanisms by which their own particular message might possibly 'catch on', or make any difference at all, in terms of the things they claim to be working for. The trouble is (and this criticism could be generalised and directed to many academic scenes today) that they *rely* on a largely under-considered conception of the 'intellectual function'. For, put bluntly, what they 'want' is this: Žižek wants to remove the blindfold of 'false conscious-ness', and Laclau wants to transform the hegemonic structure by transforming articulations. Both positions properly demand a utilisa-tion of the intellectual function, or require not just *understanding*, but an ability to 'use' the transmission-, transfer-, relay-, discursive-power-, or communication-mechanisms available to any agency to-day[2] (and, of course, to negotiate the fraught ethics and politics of such an aim). Yet, as has been argued so far, like many academics, they still concern themselves almost entirely with *what* should be said, without considering *how* it might possibly make any difference. Here again, deconstruction seems helpful, in that its inversions, reversals and displacements of focus allow us to see that the 'primary' question of what should be said is actually 'secondary' to that of its discursive status, including who might possibly (be able to) listen and what that listening might amount to.

Any implicit conception of the intellectual function (or whatever else one might choose to call it) as being something like one speaker holding one microphone addressing one assembled and desiring and attentive audience who listen and respond in programmatically pre-dictable ways, is dubious. However, it might not be *as* dubious if we supplement our understanding of this conception with the implica-tions of the post-Marxist theory of hegemony. For, with reference to such a perspective it might be argued that if there is, or to the extent that there is anything like an intellectual function, then it is clear that 'we' do not simply hold the microphone. Holding the microphone would be the non-place of hegemony itself, albeit perhaps most institutionally manifested in and as discourses directly articulated to capital (technoscience, discourses of governmentality, those of managerial performativity or efficiency, etc.). Taking a perspective that acknowledges critical left intellectuals' lack of possession of, 'lack' in the face of, and desire for, the intellectual function enables the overturning, displacement and re-evaluation of what 'university responsibility' may be and what orientations and strategies are conceivable today.[3] For a start, considering the contemporary condition of the left in these terms enables not only the diagnosis of what needs to be revalued, but also to work out what form the left's reconstruction or reorientation could best take if 'performative efficiency' is indeed at least a component of what it wants or needs, as it were, or in the name of the political itself. That is to say that any 'revaluation' requires interruption, or what Derrida calls 'de-railing' (Derrida 1987: 20, 177). It requires interrupting the smooth flow or regular repeating (and repeatability) of what is known and of what is done. For arguably, as writers like Wendy Brown (2001) point out, the left has *itself* been interrupted, unbalanced or wrong-footed, and actually by nothing short of 'the revolution of our times' themselves. This 'crisis' means that something *about the left itself* needs to be interrupted and revalued, *by the left itself*. In what could *intervention* consist?

This talk of 'interruption' suggests that interruption itself should be introduced as topic and a theme to work towards establishing an ethico-political intellectual strategy *of* 'interruption'. Such a strategy would relate to deconstruction and to Marxism, in terms of both the 'spirit' and the 'letter' (albeit promiscuously) of the ethico-political demand for responsible engagement and intervention. For arguably, the battle of the emergence of the political, relates to audibility, to intelligibility; and as such, politics itself could be said to come about solely through and as *interruption* (Rancière 1999: 13, 17). 'Interruption' need not purely be construed in terms of pure positive signification. As Laclau argues, to interrupt even without full coherence '*could be* a first stage in the emergence of a truth which can be affirmed only by breaking with the coherence of the existing discourses' (Laclau 2005: 27). Similarly, Derrida often intimated that the key political strategy of deconstruction is to 'derail' established, sedimented, becoming-invisible institutions of communication, sedimented relay- and referral-systems and mechanisms (Derrida 1987: 20, 177; 2002: 53; Protevi 2001: 20). And Stuart Hall emphasises the double importance of interruption (1996: 268): for him, theory, thinking and analysis must seek to interrupt the established, or the powerful other of the status quo. He views politics *as* interruption (1992: 282), and locates the value of 'Theory' primarily in and as its interruptive capacities, and precisely not in any 'theoretical fluency': comfortable fluency in a theoretical language implies for Hall stability and regularity – hence another dimension of the 'problem' with, or of, Laclau and Mouffe. (In other words, this is the problem of disciplining, of disciplinarity.)

The deconstructive post-Marxist Wendy Brown has called this the problem of how to construct 'politics without banisters' (2001: 91–120), now that what appears lost are all fixed certainties on which to hold and from which to construct ethico-political convictions, as well as anything like a clear and univocal sense of strategy or 'action'.[4] According to Brown, the contemporary conjuncture is one of a condition of great indeterminacy, perhaps a consequence of the intensity of capitalist deconstruction and reconstruction of all that seemed solid and fixed, profaning all that was sacred, melting it into air, up to and including Marxist certainties themselves. Now, for a Marxist or traditional leftist perspective, this capitalist 'deconstruction' is usually to be construed as an ethically, politically and culturally deleterious force, the driving force of which, as has been tirelessly documented, seems simply to be profit. But this simplicity is not unitary (nor self-present), and there appears to be no one locus or ground, but instead multiple mycelia, multiple hydra, multiple causes and effects, multiplying effects that become causes, in an intractable and multiple discursive soufflé.

So, according to Brown, the left cannot but *either* mourn *or* deny the demise of the adequacy of its means of measurement, its universals, yardsticks, certainties, paradigms and purchase. However, if the point remains 'to change it', then especially if what many never wanted to change has changed (Marxist certainties and the very status of Marxism), and if change is still nevertheless desired (the desire for radical/revolutionary emancipatory transformation), then, Brown argues, the modes by which we value, view, and evaluate, cannot stay the same. An 'act', a 'revolution', must change *all* coordinates, including those of its own measurement and evaluation (Žižek 2000: 121–2), and *revaluation* is part and parcel of any 'revolution'. Indeed, the act of *revaluation* is arguably constitutive of change. In this view, an event is an event to the extent that it forces revaluation; and if revaluation is not required, then one might question whether there has really been any change at all. Of course, partial or gradual changes, small pragmatic, progressive stages of improvement, might be the desire. In grieving the apparent demise of a realistic revolutionary imaginary, many have moved from talk of revolution, to talk of pragmatism. But partialism, pragmatism, 'gradualism' and the invocation of 'progress' are, Laclau contends, the first of all utopias (Laclau 2000: 198): they imply that we're *already on track*, and that we *know* what the goal is, in advance of the change. Here politics becomes the banal implementation of a predetermined programme – administration. Partialism, gradualism, or progress, presuppose stability.

So, if Žižek's point about the performative efficiency of speech acts applies to politicised (left) academia as having been knavishly rearticulated as ridiculous and 'utopian' today; if Derrida has a point when he claims that traditionally recognisable forms of politics are becoming obsolete (those of the party and of the nation-state, most blatantly) (Derrida 1994: 84–5, 102–3); if Hardt and Negri have a point in claiming that there is a global 'we' who are all the 'multitude' (we just don't all know it yet); if capitalism and neoliberalism deconstruct, desediment or deterritorialise all that once seemed sacred and solid; if the insights of the contemporary interdisciplinary academic formations, proceeding along deconstructive lines, have any 'force' or suggest any 'law' at all; then it may well be that this very monstrosity is in itself possibly also a bright light, a beacon. For there is certainly something in the proposition that the world is 'in' deconstruction, and this 'something' is certainly not the conclusion that therefore Derridean deconstruction is deleterious. I will not recount the list of wildly different things that deconstruction is febrilely said to exemplify (instead see Derrida 1992a: 206). Rather, it is worth reiterating that what deconstruction insists upon is that no thing is complete in itself, but always only needs supplementing (Derrida 1981: 304). The logic of the supplement is to be found everywhere. This is why it also exerts a force in deeply Marxian and even Leninist injunctions. Maley quotes Lukàcs to argue this point:

> It cannot be too strongly maintained [argues Lukàcs] that the Social-Democrat's ideal should not be the trade-union secretary, but *the tribune of the people*, who is able to react to every manifestation of tyranny and oppression, no matter where it appears, no matter what stratum or class of the people it affects; who is able to generalize all these manifestations and produce a single picture of police violence and capitalist exploitation; who is able to take advantage of every event, however small, in order to set forth *before all* his socialist convictions and his democratic demands, in

order to clarify for *all* and everyone the world-historical significance of the struggle for the emancipation of the proletariat. (Lukàcs, quoted in Maley 2001: 78)

Žižek's rhetorico-political 'fast Leninism' strategy can be seen to be prefigured here. But to aspire 'to set forth *before all*' one's 'socialist convictions' and 'democratic demands' does not simply mean that one will be a Lukàcs or a Žižek. Rather, it might be said that it is through the interruptive reference to *justice* and *responsibility* that revolution, or politics, or that which would be revolutionary about any politics, seeks to occur. Encapsulating this, Benjamin Arditi mines the reserves and unearths the political logic of the famous slogan of the 'events' of May 1968: 'Be Realistic: Demand the Impossible!' (Arditi 2003: 85–9). Arditi reads this demand in terms of the deconstructive insight that states of affairs, institutions, and as Protevi adds, 'sets of positive laws, are deconstructible because they are not justice. Deconstruction is already engaged by this infinite demand of justice . . . Deconstruction also finds its "force, its movement or its motivation" in the "always unsatisfied appeal" to justice . . . Deconstruction is democratic justice, responding to the calls from all others' (Protevi 2001: 69–70). Thus, *justice* is the simultaneously realistic and yet impossible demand of deconstruction. However, it has been asked (Bewes 2001), isn't capitalism itself a most radical form of deconstruction? A valid answer remains: of course, yes, in a way; but capitalism deconstructs institutions because they are not *profit*. To deconstruct that which is not *just*, not *justice* – either not based in justice or producing injustice – is something else. It is a revelatory and always antagonistic process that reveals the injustice of capitalist relations. One difference between deconstruction's sense of justice and Marxism's sense of justice is that a deconstructive understanding of justice asserts that justice can never be assumed to have arrived, because to make such a judgement would be to judge one particular state of affairs to be perfectly just, *which is impossible*, and unjust, in terms of the way this closes down the openness to alterity, to difference, change, and the future. The assumption that the present is just, or that justice is present, is, according to Derrida, always unjust. Any assumption that the just is here is demonstrably a part of the forceful exclusion of change. This is why Protevi calls deconstruction 'democratic justice': it is the interminable effort to listen and try to address and redress injustice. Deconstruction is the revolutionary demand for radical democratic justice, a demand for the impossible which nevertheless 'displays the lie of the existing order', *but in a way which might readily circumvent suspending the performative efficiency of such revolutionary speech*. It will not risk relinquishing this performative force, because it will not declare itself as such.

But what does this mean? In a word: *reading*. This may seem both preposterous and yet disappointing. For, objections to (and misunderstandings of) deconstruction abound. They include: Isn't deconstruction therefore an opposition without opposition – a resigned, mournful, pessimistic abdication from fighting for a radical new world view? Again, it is possible to reply that this is not an abdication from responsibility. For, it is arguably the case that the 'forcefulness' of any demand or claim is substantially reduced, defused, deflated, or derailed when the demand is for something *other*. When the demand seems to come from some *other* place (such as the 'other party', 'the opposition', *the enemy*, or the oppositional 'fools'), or to be infused with *other* values (*their* values, *not our* values, foolish values), it is arguably compromised. Oppositional speech is arguably, as Thomas Docherty puts it, 'always already negated by the structure of the entity which it wishes to oppose', and may actually even amount to 'nothing more than an inoculation of sorts which allows the dominant political power in a social formation further to strengthen itself' (Docherty 1993: 322). But the question still begs an answer: what about constructing utopian visions and calls for otherness, visions of and calls for a different and better (socialist) world? Or: Isn't it only by forming some completely different model that a positive politics and political strategy might be constructed? Again, one can answer, no. This interpretation of 'otherness to come', when metaphysically construed, is often recruited as an argument against deconstruction – in the claim that deconstruction cannot found or propose a positive alternative or oppositional politics. Obviously there is something in this. For *of course* deconstruction can't propose a 'positive' (metaphysical, 'objective') politics. What deconstruction does, though, is show the alterity, the impossibility, the lie, the lack, the inadequacy, at the heart of *any* putative positivity. Alterity does not come from 'over there'. It is produced by the (constitutive impossibility of the) here and now. This is important, both micro- and macro-politically, and this work will return more fully to its strategic implications in what follows. As will become clear, it relates to nothing other than *deconstructive reading* as a force of interruption in *another* context.

The next chapter first examines some apparently very different, indeed apparently diametrically opposed positions on whether and how politicised academic work might in itself be a form of political intervention. The positions taken to be exemplary are those of Richard Rorty, whose 'pragmatism' typifies the anti-theoretical animus within 'engaged' academia, whether left, liberal or otherwise; Slavoj Žižek, who exemplifies the impetus to 'high-theory' as politicised scholarship; Judith Butler, who attempts to negotiate and reconcile these two putative extremes; and Ernesto Laclau whose deconstructive post-Marxism seems to be striving to find a certain 'completion' apparently to be found in an 'articulation' with other paradigms: For, Laclau has at various times explicitly engaged with both the pragmatic Rorty and the high-theoretical Žižek, as if to try to work out precisely what the post-Marxist intervention *itself* consists of. The positions of Rorty, Žižek, Butler and Laclau are taken to be representative of more than one rift and impasse that divides and polarises the academy in general, and post-Marxism and cultural studies in particular, as well as political activism 'proper'. Rorty and Žižek are arguably exemplary cases to be considered when analysing the matter of what political intervention is, and whether and in what sense academic or intellectual work is or could decidedly (or decidably) *be* intervention. This work examines these encounters, with a view to establishing what the post-Marxist construal of its own interventional status may be. For what has yet to be fully established, is the post-Marxist conception of intervention. In the next chapter, we will examine what it is, and see that it is less than complete or adequate, but that it nevertheless holds the kernel of a more adequate and consequential way to retheorise and actualise intervention.

Notes

1. Hall uses the terms text, textual, textuality, etc., interchangeably with and to clarify the properties of the term 'discourse'; for instance when he argues that 'The metaphor of the discursive, of textuality, instantiates a necessary delay, a displacement, which I think is always implied in the concept of culture' (1992: 283–4). That there is a sense of an unproblematic interchangeability between the two terms for Hall suggests of course that he has not undertaken the genealogical analysis of Mowitt (1992), and indeed Hall's tendency to use the terms interchangeably adds further weight to Mowitt's argument overall.
2. In *The Post Card* (1987), Derrida provocatively conceives of this as a complex tele-techno-institutional-'communication' or 'postal' network.

3. Lyotard reminds us that 'radical' work 'is not thrust aside today because it is dangerous or upsetting, but simply because it is a waste of time. It is "good for nothing," it is not good for gaining time. For success is gaining time' (Lyotard 1988: xv).

4. Perhaps the very intelligibility of the question, 'what is left of the left?', indicates that much has been lost, that there may be much to mourn. Indeed, a crisis in the Marxist Left has often been declared, and diagnosed as a consequence of many things: capitalism's triumph, or its default victory by the collapse of all actually-existing alternatives; postmodernist ideological relativism dividing and conquering the left; consumerism and the triumph of irony and irresponsibility; capitalism's deconstruction of all values; Thatcherism, Reaganism, or some other politician-policy-ism; or because of the stupidity of people trading under the name 'left-wing', who have actually sold out to neoliberalism, identity-politics, or whatever. There are ever more diagnoses. Either way, it seems that with the words 'All that is solid melts into air, all that is holy is profaned', Marx and Engels (1967) were just *too* right, also prophesying the evaporation of the traditional political certainties that they themselves established. Many elements of Marxism that were for so many and for so long taken to be axiomatic are now nothing if not contestable, contested, and suspect (Laclau and Mouffe 1985; Brown 2001; Hardt and Negri 2000; Peters 2001). Hardt and Negri agree that today the old political certainties have gone, and add that even that most important of concepts, *exploitation*, 'can no longer be localized and quantified' (2000: 209); something that deals a paralysing blow to left political thought and action. For certainty about exploitation (what, where, how and why it '*is*') formerly set up clear and stable coordinates for establishing what praxis and agency were. But, to Hardt and Negri, our political problem is now actually one of trying to establish 'how to determine the enemy against which to rebel' (211), even before confronting the question of what form rebellion or resistance should properly take. For, if the left has lost a singular, identifiable and determinable enemy because 'we are immersed in a system of power so deep and complex that we can no longer determine specific difference or measure' (211), then precisely *what* properly appropriate praxis should be becomes a tortuously deep and complex matter.

Three – Theory versus Practice

No thing is complete in itself, and it can only be completed by what it lacks. But what each particular thing lacks is infinite; we cannot know in advance what completeness it calls for.

(Jacques Derrida 1981: 304)

Practice versus Theory

What kind of practice is theory? What is the theory of practice? Several key debates, one between Ernesto Laclau, Richard Rorty and Jacques Derrida (1996), a second between Laclau and Slavoj Žižek (1989; 2000), and another between Laclau, Judith Butler and Slavoj Žižek (2000; see also Laclau 2004; 2005), stand as important illuminating and representative encounters that each tellingly illustrate the consequences for scholarship of different answers to the question of university responsibility, or the practice of intellectual work. These encounters can be taken to represent wider tendencies: they stand as clashes between influential examples of key paradigms of cultural/ political study. As we will see, they each have paradigms that are overlapping yet distinct; and that come into disagreement because of apparently slight but nevertheless significant differences in theoretical and practical approaches. These differences derive from the orienting function of different tacit assumptions operative within each paradigm about theory and practice (Derrida 1996: 78). Their effects radiate from the 'merely academic' to the decidedly ethico-political.

These debates are particularly salient because the different theoretical assumptions that they entail can be viewed as exemplary cases of very widely used paradigms. So, although in the following discussion each paradigm is treated in relation to a proper name ('Rorty's paradigm', 'Laclau's paradigm', etc.), it will hopefully be clear that we are nevertheless dealing with examples of very generally occurring paradigmatic conceptions of *what* theory, practice, politics, intervention and university responsibility are widely held to be (however tacitly). In this regard, these debates offer valuable insights into the ways that differing paradigms affect intellectual orientation and work. Of course, these thinkers' paradigms are not simply or exhaustively representative of academic paradigms in every regard. Neither Laclau's, Butler's, Derrida's, Rorty's nor Žižek's work could simply be said to encompass the entire field of cultural and political studies in all its diversity and heterogeneity – even though each thinker may perhaps sometimes imply or state that they do adequately understand all other perspectives, and that their own preferred approach is more adequate than all other alternatives. Such is the academic condition, it seems, that even in the pages of these few published encounters between five intellectuals, each one of them implicitly or explicitly claims to comprehend each of the others' paradigms thoroughly, and yet each often holds entirely different conceptions of each of the others' paradigms! Perhaps such apparently unavoidable parallax can already be taken to illuminate an influential wider tendency. But what is specifically pertinent to this analysis is the proposition that subtending these encounters is a clash of different conceptions of what university responsibility and intervention are held to be, and that the significance of these disagreements extends beyond their own initial contexts, such that the encounters can be said to be bigger than the sum of their parts. In other words, the paradigms to be discerned orientating each of these thinkers' works actually exemplifies something crucial to do with the most familiar manners of conceiving of university responsibility and intervention currently circulating and structuring academic work, throughout political and cultural studies and beyond.

Because of this exemplarity, this chapter will examine in some detail Laclau's encounters with Rortyan pragmatism (1996), Butlerian radical liberalism (2000), and Žižekian high theoreticism (Laclau 1989; 2000; 2004; 2005), in light of the 'textual/deconstructive' argument advanced and developed in the previous chapters, and supplemented here by Derrida's (1996) comments on Laclau's and Rorty's debate about politics and theory, deconstruction and pragmatism. I will argue that what underpins and structures these encounters is the spectre or absent presence of 'intervention', and that what is played out in the encounters is the effort to establish the way that any piece of academic work, theoretical or otherwise, could be said to constitute a practical or effective intervention into the political terrain that it both takes its objects from and takes as its object (as discussed in Chapters 1 and 2). The argument here is that facing up to the demands of this problem constitutes a vital challenge with which all politicised intellectual work should engage. So the chapter examines these exemplary skirmishes between Laclau, Derrida, Butler, Rorty and Žižek with a view to ascertaining what might be learned and unlearned regarding what intervention and university responsibility are deemed to be, in the hope of informing a principled reorientation of cultural studies and discourse analyses in light of this.

What will become clear from the unveiling of the paradigms structuring these works is that a spectre is haunting all of them: the spectre of 'practice'. For, although theory is of course in one sense always already present and at work underpinning and orientating any practice (Godzich 1987: 163; Mowitt 1992; Gilbert 2003: 151), nevertheless, theory is very often construed as being something that is turned to or developed only as an effort to work out how and what to practise, or – more radically – to try to establish what practice should be. If this sounds slightly schematic or simplistic, it should nevertheless be recalled that theory certainly has this status and serves this function for Stuart Hall, at the very least. In Hallian cultural studies, theory is that which is necessary but insufficient: it orientates and might well give insight upon insight, but it is not and cannot be an end, point or purpose in itself. Indeed for Hall, 'the only theory worth having is that which you have to fight off, not that which you speak with profound fluency' (Hall 1996: 265–6). For *the* point and purpose, in Hall's understanding cultural studies, is *intervention* (Hall 1996): some kind of effective political practice. Of course, such an impetus is not the exclusive property of cultural studies. As argued from the outset, Derrida construes deconstruction to be organised by the demand to establish 'university responsibility' and regards this as irreducibly ethico-political in orientation and consequence. Similarly, John Mowitt points out that an equivalent spirit of theoretical 'reevaluation is precisely what . . . motivated the development of "post-Marxism"' (Mowitt 1992: 14–15). In this view, Laclau and Mouffe's theoretical efforts represent a response to their sense of the deficiencies, limits to and problems within extant Marxist theorisations of political practice (Laclau and Mouffe 1985: 1–5). What is significant to a deconstructive reading, however is that in both Hallian cultural studies and Laclauian post-Marxism, theory is simultaneously opposed to *and also* a necessary supplement of practice. This ambivalent double status is even more explicit in the work of Rorty. For the practically-minded, theory is very often widely viewed as what Derrida might once have termed 'a dangerous supplement': something both unwanted but necessary, both 'merely' secondary and supplementary and yet also ineradicably (strangely) 'primary' and necessary; both not enough and yet too much; both digressive and the heart of the matter. (In Derridean terms, this is precisely the plight of the 'supplement' (1974) or 'pharmakon' (1981).)

Accordingly, this chapter will first work to discern and explore this schema; focusing on moments where it arises in and as efforts to explain intellectual/academic work's relation to politics (whether as a supplement or as an 'outside', and so on), and deconstructing this schema. For clearly, *deconstructive* discourse theory cannot seriously be content to operate within the confines of a schema like this, implying as it does the assumption of a stable border (precisely the sort of thing that deconstruction shows to be untenable). However, this chapter will also consider the significance of the curious fact that post-Marxism evidently seems unable to propose any more adequate a way of conceptualising its own work other than within and under the sway of this undeconstructive metaphysical binary. The chapter will primarily focus on post-Marxism, because both Hall and others within cultural studies and Laclau and others within post-Marxism view post-Marxism itself as primarily and exemplarily 'theoretical'. But, the problems that 'political theory' encounters when implicitly or explicitly asked to justify itself in terms of political 'usefulness' are not exclusively those of post-Marxism (Lyotard 1984; Young 1992; Readings 1996). Clearly cultural studies and perhaps any academic intellectual work encounters similar problems in justifying itself, its value and usefulness *as* political or *as* interventional. This chapter is concerned with drawing out the political implication of the recourse to the (all too familiar and facile) theory-practice binary. The reason for this is that justifications of the work, value, status, strategy, orientation and role of intellectual production usually revolve around and hinge on precisely such a binary. This sort of justification of theory as supplement to the practical is highly problematic in the very terms laid out by the post-Marxist discourse paradigm itself. This is because the post-Marxist discourse paradigm demands a complexification of such a putatively simple relation of theory to practice. So, the chapter argues that the very move to discourse theory in post-Marxism and cultural studies was meant to address or redress such simplifications in the first place, so their continuing presence is problematic, to say the least.

So, the chapter explores some exemplary stagings – even if they are ultimately failed stagings – of this problematic in Laclauian theory, and in its encounters with other theoretical paradigms: Rorty's anti-theoretical pragmatist paradigm, Žižek's apparently polar opposite 'high theory' position, and Butler's radicalised form of deconstructive liberalism. Laclauian post-Marxism's encounters with these positions represent key moments at which it has been provoked into responding to requests to account for its status within the political terrain that it theorises. The proposition here is that the significance of this analysis does not exhaust itself in a consideration only of post-Marxism. This 'case study', the discussions explored here, are not to be construed as unique, but rather as representative of wider tendencies. The issues it raises, and the theory-practice problematic it isolates, circulate widely in various forms, particularly in debates about politics, intervention and intellectual activity. It relates to questions of orientation and value, of what should be valued and 'done', and why (Young 1992; Readings 1996; Peters 2001)[1] – and, indeed, of what 'doing' is conceived as.

The problem that post-Marxism keeps encountering and then recoiling from is encapsulated in the observation that to speak of the theoretical implies an opposition to the practical.[2] This has the unfortunate consequence of drumming up a sense that the one is 'mere thinking' (absence) while the other is 'really doing' (presence). This overlooks the *institutional* dimension. A de-contextualised binary and value-hierarchy (devalued 'thinking' versus preferable 'action') is what Martin McQuillan calls 'exemplary of the work of metaphysics itself' (McQuillan 2001: 123), in which 'the trope of the material grounds itself as the trope of tropes' – i.e., as that which seems physically real and present as opposed to that which seems not really present but only speculatively imagined or even invented. Accordingly, 'the material is the concept against which all other concepts must be judged and inevitably be found wanting in contrast' (123). McQuillan moves swiftly on to deconstruct this 'conceptual versus material' binary: 'the material is the metaphysical concept par excellence', he argues, and in what he calls 'traditional' political thinking 'the political might be thought of as exemplary of the work of metaphysics'. This is because its use of the concept of 'the material' works to conceal 'its conceptual status to order a closed political field'. In other words, 'traditional politics', he argues, 'secures the material as a fixed point of departure around which it organizes its conceptual order ("class", "economics", "liberation", etc.). In turn each of these concepts, because they have a defined relation to a fixed point, can seem to acquire fixity themselves, and so translate from a conceptual into a material order' (123).

McQuillan's examination of the metaphysical position serves to reveal that, because 'in a traditional political order, all concepts appear impoverished in contrast to material criteria then the material will occupy a transcendental position in relation to *all* concepts'. In this view, the practical – action that appears to be material or that acts directly on the real stuff of material reality – will always be preferred to the theoretical. McQuillan's rejection of this position, though, hinges entirely on the deconstructive construal of reality as *discursive*, as irreducibly and inextricably both material and conceptual – *institutional* – and hence contingent and political, in precisely a Laclauian sense. McQuillan uses this insight to argue for the *de facto* politicality, consequentiality, and interventionality of deconstruction: 'it follows that all concepts fall within the remit of politics (or at least they cannot escape the field of politics) because they are defined as conceptual in contrast to the material'. He argues, 'Thus, every conceptual encounter, and deconstruction is nothing but conceptual encounters, cannot help but be political' (McQuillan 2001: 123).

This may be so. But the political question remains: even with the world reconceived as discourse, how might intellectual ('conceptual' or 'theoretical') work intervene, in any way that is decidably consequential and adequate to the way that it was desired, hoped or intended? Just saying 'this is important' or 'this is an intervention' does not simply make it so. Richard Rorty throws down this gauntlet when he argues that surely 'the burden is on those who, like Laclau, think [that theory is politically] useful to explain just how and where the utility appears, rather than taking it for granted' (Rorty 1996: 71). This chapter will examine post-Marxist theory's attempts to answer this, arguing along the way that in this regard Laclau's command of the ramifications of his own theory of hegemony is, as it were, less than exhaustive. Ironically, this is because of his imbrication in 'traditional' forms of 'macropolitical' scholarship, an investment that – as will be clarified fully in the conclusion – has limiting consequences for its orientation and, certainly, deployment. (This must not be taken as a 'personal' comment. It is rather a comment on the orienting work of 'tradition' or 'style'.) These problematic limitations are equally, if not more, at work in and on the orientations of Rorty, Butler and Žižek, too. So, once more, the hope is that in light of this analysis, the reasons why and the way in which cultural studies and future works in post-Marxism and other such politicised intellectual work should learn from and thereby take their distances from such orientations, should become clear. The relation of post-Marxism and cultural studies, whilst always possibly implicitly or immanently affiliative, remains nevertheless 'versus' until this reorientation begins. The reorientation will consist of moving away from 'calling for change' and moving into intimate deconstructive interventions into *other* fields and contexts, as will be made clear in the conclusion (Chapter 4).

Theory versus Practice

To begin exploring the post-Marxist response to the question of how intellectual work (as exemplified by 'theory') relates to politics, it will be helpful first to point to two occurrences, at the margins of post-Marxism (and by writers whose work is also influential within cultural studies), of responses organised by very traditional and undeconstructed notions of the relations between intellectual activity (theory) and consequential political interventionality (practice). These are to be found in Slavoj Žižek and Judith Butler. First, let's consider one of Slavoj Žižek's regular justifications of 'high theory':

> It is crucial to emphasize this relevance of 'high theory' for the most concrete political struggle *today*, even when such an engaged intellectual as Noam Chomsky likes to underscore how unimportant theoretical knowledge is for progressive political struggle: of what help is studying great philosophical and social-theoretical texts in today's struggle against the neoliberal model of globalization? Is it not that we are dealing either with obvious facts (which simply have to be made public, as Chomsky is doing in his numerous political texts), or with such an incomprehensible complexity that we cannot understand anything? If we wish to argue against this anti-theoretical temptation, it is not enough to draw attention to numerous theoretical presuppositions about freedom, power and society, which also abound in Chomsky's political texts; what is arguably more important is how, today, perhaps for the first time in the history of humankind, our daily experience (of biogenetics, ecology, cyberspace and Virtual Reality) compels *all* of us to confront basic philosophical issues of the nature of freedom and human identity, and so on. (Žižek 2002: 4)

Here, the value of theory is said to be that *it simply is* practical ('basic' and urgent). Political theory and 'philosophical issues' are said to be simply and straightforwardly part of 'the most concrete political struggle *today*'. Rather than undertaking an examination of the terms constructing the debate, never mind a deconstruction (perhaps akin to McQuillan's), Žižek prefers to justify 'high theory' in the very terms of the polemic that he says is no longer a relevant or valid binary: 'today', theory simply *is* politically practical. (In many ways, this typifies Žižek's inconsistent approach.) What is significant here is that for Žižek the value of theory is *straightforwardly* determined entirely by its rather euphemistic 'relevance' to real and proper political struggle. (Indeed, as will shortly become apparent, Žižek's style of argumentation is basically the same as that of Richard Rorty in this regard.) However, the core problem is that, at the same time as it is identified, the basic problem nevertheless remains unaddressed: Žižek's justification of theory does not answer the question of consequence or relation; or that is, of the very *connection* he so values that would redeem theory and make it become intervention. Žižek does not fully think the nature or structure of intervention, preferring instead merely to assert that we are all compelled 'to confront basic philosophical issues'. He neither says *why* all are compelled to do so, nor what form this takes, nor how any of this might make any difference.

The problem I want to isolate here is that Žižek's construal of the theory versus practice problematic misses what is *most problematic*. The political problem is not actually what he (like Rorty, as will soon be seen) formulates it as and deems it to be. For, it does not simply devolve on *what* intellectuals are supposed to talk about. It does not simply boil down to whether academics and intellectuals should talk about 'theoretical' or 'practical' issues, nor whether they should be talked about 'theoretically' or 'banally', 'philosophically' or 'pragmatically'. Rather, the issue is that of whether and in what way any kind of talking-about might possibly constitute an intervention in any sense into anything – specifically, that which is talked about. Žižek's affirmation of theory operates on the same level of misrecognition or reductivity as Chomsky's (or, jumping ahead again, Rorty's) affirmation of the value of the banal and public exposure of facts. Both positions rest on a faith that either the 'complex theorisation' or the 'obviously intelligible fact' would necessarily make any difference. You could say that the basic political issue to be addressed devolves on the more fundamental problem that, as Stuart Hall puts it, 'it has always been impossible . . . to get anything like an adequate theoretical account of culture's relations and its effects' (Hall 1992: 286). Žižek does not consider anything like this dimension of the question of intervention.

Judith Butler goes further in her consideration of the question of the relation of intellectual production to political 'action' or intervention, or the status of intellectual production for politics. She argues that:

Clearly, the fear of political paralysis is precisely what prompts the anti-theoretical animus in certain activist circles. Paradoxically, such positions require the paralysis of critical reflection in order to avoid the prospect of paralysis on the level of action. In other words, those who fear the retarding effects of theory do not want to think too hard about what it is they are doing, what kind of discourse they are using; for if they think too hard about what it is they are doing, they fear that they will no longer do it. In such instances, is it the fear that thinking will have no end, that it will never cease to coil back upon itself in infinite movements of circularity, and that limitless thinking will then have pre-empted action as the paradigmatic political gesture? If this is the fear, then it seems to rest upon the belief that critical reflection *precedes* political action – that the former sets out the plan for the latter, and the latter somehow follows the blueprint established by the former. In other words, political action would then presuppose that thinking has already happened, that it is finished – that action is precisely not thinking, unthinking, that which happens when thinking has become the past. (Butler 2000: 265).

Of course, Butler's argument does not necessarily *actually* account for the 'anti-theoretical animus in certain activist circles', nor does it necessarily account for the anti-theoretical or anti-intellectual animus within academic circles. Indeed, none of what she asserts is necessarily as clear as she seems to think it is. However, her argument does throw down a challenging gauntlet to anti-intellectualism wherever it may arise in politically engaged circles. But what remains problematic in it is that to the extent that it aspires to be an answer to anti-intellectualism in politicised circles, the logic of Butler's response betrays the fact that at least one of the people who assume 'that critical reflection *precedes* political action . . . and [that] the latter somehow follows the blueprint established by the former' is actually, however unwittingly, Butler herself. For what becomes apparent here is that, to Butler, thinking is always theoretical thinking, different and distinct from, and preceding (or at least other than) action. This is because Butler's very formulations betray an academics-*teach*-while-activists-*do* schema: a straightforwardly undeconstructed theory-practice binary schema. It asserts that on the one hand there is theory while on the other hand there is practice. The invocation of different 'levels' – the level of 'critical reflection' versus the 'level of action' – announces the presence of this undeconstructed metaphysical hierarchy. This is something that the deconstructive understanding of 'institution' radically subverts.

It is vital to note the occurrence of this undeconstructed metaphysical hierarchy at work here, in the argument of this explicitly deconstructive thinker. The fact that it appears and significantly continues to inform or subtend the orientation of an avowedly 'deconstructive' thinker illustrates the important point that, even for the deconstructor, there is no guarantee that one can ever simply or entirely step cleanly out of the holds, sways and traps of metaphysics. In order to clarify and to explore the questions this raises, this chapter will turn to an explicit analysis of salient dimensions of Butler's arguments around and contributions to the thinking of theory, politics and intervention that reflect those of cultural studies and post-Marxism. However, in order to establish more fully the salient context of Butler's interventions in this regard, it is worthwhile to turn first to the question of how the post-Marxism of Laclau and Mouffe (that so influences Butler) itself weighs in on the thinking of this relation. So, first, the important question of how post-Marxist political theory could be said to theorise the politicality of itself, in particular, and of politicised intellectual work in general, should be assessed.

Post-Marxist Theory and Practice

It is possible to establish clearly how post-Marxist theory theorises theory, systems, and structures in general. This is because, in a strong sense, the post-Marxist theory of discourse and hegemony is in effect also a theory of all theory and of all practice. In other words, it is a 'metadiscourse': a discourse about discourse – in this case, implicitly *all* discourses. What it says of the logic of political identity production can therefore be applied to the consideration of any and all structures, systems, descriptions, identities, agencies, contexts, and so forth. Accordingly, in the terms and idiom of post-Marxist discourse, it can be said that, strictly speaking and for 'essential logical reasons', the constitution or institution of any structure, system, identity, or institution, presupposes and is predicated on an initial 'violent' constitutive exclusion (Laclau 2004: 318–19), on the basis of a disjointed or pre-critical cathectic investment (Laclau 2000: 196; 2004: 326; 2005). The positive identity of the system and of the identities constituted by the system are effects established through negation: First, through differential negation 'within' the system (1 is not 2, a is not b, yellow is not red, etc.); and second, through negation of the radically heterogeneous (the outside, the other). Any reinclusion of the constitutively excluded subverts the identity of the instituted or founded identity, showing it to be (or to have been) impossible 'as such'. In post-Marxist discourse theory, a founding exclusion is the condition of possibility for identity as well as systematicity. It is also, by the same token, the condition of their impossibility as such. The exclusions enabling systematicity mean that they would, if reincluded, systematically subvert the possibility of that systematicity. So, the truth of a system or identity is that it is the simulation of a (complete) system or (complete) identity: the positing and imposition of systematicity itself always being strictly bounded and, as such, invented. All internality, such as that of any systematicity or identity, is only possible by the imposition of strictures, boundaries, limits, or demarcations, which work to keep the outside out and the inside in. The excluded 'haunts' the positive identity, antagonises it (Laclau 1996a: 66–8; Butler 2000: 11). As something that has 'necessarily' been excluded, it is also curiously at the heart of the identity from which it has been banished (Derrida 1974: 35). Identity, institution, systematicity, internality, structurality, are always-already only partial, because conditional on an exclusion. Any 'positive identity' is constituted as a repression of the consciousness of its own impossibility (Laclau and Mouffe 1985: 125).

This theory seems to work very well in explaining the political constitution of objects, processes and movements, 'out there'. But the question here is, what if these very insights about systematicity and construction are returned to that theory itself, in the form of the question: what of this logic itself, the 'strict speak' that claims to know all of this; what is the nature of its own lack, or its own constitutive incompletion (Laclau 2004: 325)? What has it excluded to complete itself? For, if, strictly speaking, for essential logical reasons, *all* systematicity, *all* structurality, and the institution of *any* institution, is always already premised on a lack and enabled by an exclusion, and the effacement of a 'constitutive contradiction' or antagonism, then what has the logical system which *knows this* excluded from itself in order to be able to know it? What strictures enable this 'strictly speaking'? What has to be excluded – for essential logical reasons or otherwise – in order to enable a kind of knowledge which says it knows that there *are* 'essential logical reasons'? If this knowledge must exclude, as it itself says it must, then where or how does its own essential partiality betray itself?

Such questions may seem purely academic. But, in post-Marxism, this 'constitutive incompletion' is precisely what precipitates contingency and politicality. However, vis-à-vis the apparent or affected completeness and well-sutured character of the very theory that itself argues that *every* identity comes into existence through a repression of the consciousness of its own impossibility, in relation to a central void, lack and antagonism, then the question of the necessity of *its own* lack – and how to account for its apparent lack of a lack – gains a crucial status. For, the answer to this casts light on post-Marxism's conception of itself qua intervention. The question is: where is its own lack, the very constitutive lack that it itself asserts every such identity or construction must have? The answer is, in its relation to its object; or rather, in the very fact that it persists. This is the index of its lack. In other words, Laclauian post-Marxism can be taken also to exemplify a wider condition, one it shares with cultural studies insofar as it is an entity constitutively desirous of intervention. For both, that is, the constitutive lack relates to intervention. The completion of – completion as – decisive intervention is the desire. Intervention is therefore the lack, in the face of which post-Marxism and cultural studies are 'summoned'. Both come into existence as responses to the ethico-political call for intervention (according to a logic of the call or summons not unrelated to interpellation (Mowitt 2002)). For, the perceived obligation to respond, responsibly, to the demands of the political, in whatever form, is the call to which post-Marxism and cultural studies respond and constitute themselves. It is *because* responsibility, decision, orientation, knowledge, and agency are uncertain that post-Marxism and cultural studies continue. Their condition of possibility is also their condition of impossibility; their drive, aim, goal or object would, if realised, also come to have been something of a death drive. For, to the extent that they could fully intervene and complete themselves, they would, so to speak, cease to (need to) be. Reciprocally put, they would not have (failed or tried to) come into being in this way at all, had they not been 'summoned' in response to a perceived call. In the conclusion (Chapter 4), we will introduce a practical strategy for achieving this goal/demise.

As Žižek once put it on the subject of the relentless driving force of capitalism, and using what he calls 'the standard Derridean terms', this situation is that of the constitutive character of the 'inherent obstacle/antagonism' (Žižek 2001a: 18–19). Cultural studies and post-Marxism's constitutive but ultimately 'impossible' desire is to intervene, *fully*. If they could *fully* intervene (cessation of desire/eradication of lack) they would no longer 'need' to be. Their condition of possibility is, in more than one way, also their condition of impossibility. It is, effectively, their generative frustration. This generative frustration is potentially 'infinite' (Derrida 1981: 304). It is not just that certain interventions might 'fail', and that such failure might be correctable and eradicable. Rather, failure is constitutive insofar as any 'success' begs the question of its adequacy, its rectitude, its responsibility, its effect, etc. 'Success' may be ultimately unquantifiable; but, as will be argued in the following chapter, one index of 'failure' could be said to take the form of *disciplinary* repetition.

Laclau and Mouffe's theory is premised on constitutive incompletion (and it deploys both Derridean and Lacanian thinking on this theme), and it would, indeed, deem this inevitable 'structural failure' to be the only chance for politics and for change (Mouffe 1996: 9). In this sense they are in complete agreement with Derrida (1992; 1992a; 1996): whereas many other paradigms assume that there is and can be discursive closure, neither deconstruction nor post-Marxism do. A peculiar consequence of this perspective, however, is that in arguing that discourses (and identities, institutions and systems) are *not* closed, Laclau's own discourse effectively *becomes* closed, or *seems* complete. Laclau has even said that he believes that the political, discourse and hegemony, are 'perfectly theorized in my work' (Laclau 2004: 322)! In this respect, the possibility that Laclau's theory might be an (or perhaps even *the*) entirely and completely correct and true comprehension of a true property of the human world ('discourse'), seems to contradict that theory's own central principles and tenets.

At this point, it is productive to observe that Jennifer Daryl Slack reads Laclau's argument that 'common sense discourse, *doxa*, is presented as a system of misleading articulations in which concepts do not appear linked by inherent logical relations, but which are bound together simply by connotative or evocative links which custom and opinion have established between them' (Laclau 1977: 7; quoted in Daryl Slack 1996: 119). For Laclau, then, 'articulations are thus the "links between concepts"', and the goal of the logic of the likes of Plato 'is to disarticulate the (misleading) links and to re-articulate their true (or necessary) links. Articulation is at this point then linked to and defined by the rationalist paradigm' (Daryl Slack 1996: 119). Against this logic, Daryl Slack argues that:

> Laclau amends what he takes as this western philosophical move with the insistence that (a) there are no necessary links between concepts, a move that renders all links essentially connotative, and that (b) concepts do not necessarily have links with all others, a move that makes it impossible to construct the totality of a system having begun with one concept, as one could do in a Hegelian system. Consequently, the analysis of any concrete

situation or phenomenon entails the exploration of complex, multiple, and theoretically abstract non-necessary links. (Daryl Slack 1996: 119)

The coherence of Laclauian or any other 'logic', then, is secured by 'essentially connotative' or 'evocative links which custom and opinion have established between them'. The verisimilitude as well as the *logicality* of the logic can only be demonstrated, or be deemed to be apparent, within what Laclau calls 'contextual communitarian orders', and such constructions can only 'show their verisimilitude to people living inside those orders' (Laclau 2000: 85). This leads Laclau to assert 'the constitutive role of the rhetorical in the production of social relations' (Laclau 2004: 312). For Laclau, understanding and 'learning is, to a large extent, a process governed by the same logic as persuasion' and 'persuasion is always, to some extent, a conversion: I *accept* an argument, I am *convinced* that this or that is the case – that subjective moment of acquiescence is essential to persuasion. It is because of that that we can speak of the *force* of *persuasion*' (Laclau 1999: 97). However, Laclau continues:

> what is wrong is to limit oneself to the search for the logical coherence of the text. The work of an author is always a complex discursive universe in which concepts and categories relate and limit each other in their effects in terms of mutual references which most of the time are rhetorical and construct a coherence which is not necessarily a logical one. If persuasion is the creation of the verisimilitude of some conclusions on the basis of the contingent addition of arguments and discursive sequences, 'understanding' an author or a text involves exactly the same: enlarging the system of mutual discursive references on the basis of an ever expanding intertextuality. Lacan used to question the classical idea of understanding, of *Verstehen*, as the reduction of the new to the already known. Metaphor, on the contrary, meant for him creation of new meaningful configurations which indefinitely postponed the arrival to a last meaning. 'Theoretical' learning is, ultimately, the construction of *theoria* through *phronesis*. (Laclau 1999: 97)

For Laclau, then, in being 'logical' and theoretical, and in trying to establish as rigorously as possible what is right, to the extent that one is 'successful', what is also being demonstrated, constructed or conformed to, is a precise ethico-normative community or order. In disproving something or redescribing things, what is transformed is not just an academic argument, but also 'its' community, 'its' context (as was argued in Chapters 1 and 2). This type of knowledge Laclau refers to as 'phronesis' and it is distinguished from 'apodicticity', or certainty. For Laclau, it is because there is nothing outside of discursivity that one cannot have apodictic knowledge of the cultural and political 'discursive terrain'. Knowledge, including theoretical understanding, can only ever be 'phronesis', and ' "Theoretical" learning is, ultimately, the construction of *theoria* through *phronesis*'. This element of a certain inescapable 'unknowability' should not, for Laclau, stop us from trying to establish the logic or logics of the *way* such a terrain works. This is so even if the 'usefulness' or status of such 'knowledge of the logic' is problematic, perhaps by establishing that this 'logic' will never be apodictic, nor of simple pragmatic use in any 'means-end rationality'. (Indeed, Devenney (2004) uses this as an argument in favour of post-Marxism: *because* Laclauian discourse theory deconstructs 'the tenuous logic of determinism' and constitutes a ' "radical" critique of instrumental rationality', therefore it 'disorientates any means-end rationality', argues Devenney (2004: 126).)

For Laclau, the requirement to be logical and as rigorous as possible is an irreducible obligation: for him, the words 'logic' and 'rigour', etc., have the same powerful status as the term 'classical protocols' has for Derrida – functioning as the appeal to the value of *thorough* engagement. However, the appeal to logic, rigour and 'strictly speaking', in post-Marxist discourse can be said to have significantly different effects to the Derridean appeal to interminably 'putting in question', exposing to the 'ordeal of the undecidable', and construing 'classical protocols' through these and similar evocations. Indeed, in this respect Laclau and Mouffe's 'strict' discourse seems quite opposed to Derridean interminable openness (Derrida 1996: 78, 81). In the opening pages of their seminal *Hegemony and Socialist Strategy*, for instance, Laclau and Mouffe assert that in the development of their thinking 'all discursive eclecticism or wavering was excluded from the very start' (1985: 2). For them, in academic intellectual work, all must be logical – always. However, it is possible to justifiably construe this limitation to 'strict' thinking and 'strict' speaking to be something of a *stricture*, with ramifications for what will be deemed legitimate activity. And this could not immediately be construed as fostering 'radical democracy' within the academic context.

As Derrida writes in response to an exchange between Laclau and Rorty on the topics of deconstruction and pragmatism, 'I absolutely refuse a discourse that would assign me a single code, a single language game, a single context, a single situation; and I claim this right not simply out of caprice or because it is to my taste, but for ethical and political reasons' (1996: 81). As such, Laclau's fixation on 'logic' seems problematic vis-à-vis deconstruction. But, what is logic, for Laclau? He answers that:

> by logic I do not mean *formal* logic, not even *dialectical* logic, which, in spite of its widening effects, operates at the same level of generality as the former. By logic I understand something close to its meaning when we speak, for instance, of the logic of kinship, the logic of the market, juridic logic, etc. It means that there is a special grammar governing each sphere of human activity: it determines the objects which it is possible to constitute within that sphere, the relations which are possible between those objects, etc. These are regional logics which, as such, are part of what Lacan would have called the 'Symbolic'. (Laclau 1999: 102)

This expansion of the meaning of 'logic' ultimately robs the Laclauian appeal to it of some of its connotative force. In demanding logic, the questions become 'which sort? Constructed how? Verified how?' The expansion introduces undecidability. Indeed, given this expansion, perhaps to be added to this list should be the 'logic of post-Marxist discourse', a logic which should be distinguished from other 'logics' of academic practice. In terms of this perspective, the 'logic of post-Marxist discourse' would itself clearly be seen to be an *institutional imposition* – and not a necessarily 'logical' one, at that.

According to Åkerstrøm Andersen, Laclau's might be deemed 'an inconsequent and insufficiently defined concept of logic' (Åkerstrøm Andersen 2003: 61). My point, however, is that adjudicating this point in terms of 'logic' is a problematic of a lesser political implication than answering the question of what kind of activity the Laclauian institution of logic *imposes*, *fosters* and *neglects*, or, indeed, *marginalises*, *rejects* or even *forecloses*. This would be a question closer to Derridean deconstruction, and in particular to the political insights provided by its replacement of metaphysical conceptions of 'language' with the politicised notion of 'dissemination', explored in Chapter 1 and 2. Laclau continues:

> But . . . does not the deconstructive supersession of the identitarian logic rob the term 'logic' of some of its force? If the symbolic logic was the only thing there is, [the] objection would be a pertinent one; but there is more, and this more is the crucial aspect as far as 'logic' is concerned. If we speak about the operation of the unconscious, we are no longer speaking about a regional logic but about something universally present, which systematically distorts the workings of the symbolic order. The crucial point is that this distortion is not a random phenomenon but an *orderly* drifting

away: it has itself its own logic. Freud conceived psychoanalytic theory as systematically establishing the grammar of this drifting away. In the case of dreams, for instance, it operated through condensation and displacement. (This shows the absurdity of opposing the use of psychoanalytic categories in social and political analysis on the basis that the latter refer to the social and the former to the individual – this is tantamount to saying that the unconscious is a regional category). The deconstructive movements – the quasi-transcendentals of Derrida . . . – are also orderly forms (logics) of the drifting away from a fully identitarian logic. And . . . tropological movements . . . are another vocabulary describing the same kind of generalised logic . . . (1999: 102)

At this point, and despite the effort to pre-empt precisely this criticism, the expansion of the logic of logic to include so many kinds of tendencies somewhat weakens the imputed academic or rhetorical credentials of the term. Even the effort to anchor it in a 'universal' (the unconscious) does not save it from both the introduction of undecidability ('*which* logic?') and the dampening or weakening of its rhetorico-political 'connotative' force ('This is Logical and hence decisively and decidably right!'). Nor does the expansion save Laclauian 'strictness' from the worrying political implications of valuing and adhering to a *stricture*. For, even though Laclau's expansion arguably potentially infinitely postpones the likelihood that judgements be made of the order 'Because that is not logical therefore it cannot be allowed!', it nevertheless indubitably prioritises the task of uncovering the logic of this or that, and instates such projects as putatively the highest aim of academic intellectual work. This, as was argued in Chapter 2, is a deeply problematic aim, and as can now hopefully be seen clearly, it is problematic not only because it is repetitive and predictable (inevitably leading to the conclusion, 'this is all political, right?'), but also because it is arguably counter-democratic (Mowitt 1992) and even contrary to deconstruction. For, surely, more appropriate than a claim of the universality of 'the unconscious' for Laclauian discourse theory would be a claim of the universality of *dissemination*.

Still on the subject of logic, immediately after the paragraph quoted above, Laclau concludes:

To the same order of generality belongs the logic that I call 'hegemonic'. Its two main movements I have called 'difference' and 'equivalence' (these are, of course, only basic distinctions whose subdivisions would embrace the whole field of the political *tropoi*). This generalisation to the whole of society of the movements governing the political field shows that they are not regional movements but, on the contrary, pervade the ensemble of social (symbolic) relations – as far as the latter are unable to fully suture themselves, to symbolise within their differential systems a real always exceeding them. (Laclau 1999: 102–3)

Clearly, at the end of the day, this logic is precisely not a rationalist or positivist logic of identity and non-contradiction, and is rather a logic enabled by an acknowledgement of the inevitable dissemination of articulation, the inevitability of a 'surplus' (and/or absence) of meaning and the impossibility of permanently fixing the slippage of signification, the constitutive incompletion of any identity, and so on. In this regard, Laclauian 'logic' simply contests the metaphysics of identity (which holds that 'a equals a'), and shows why and how this logic fails. Laclau's position basically maintains that *all* logics also obey the logic of identity and also necessarily fail. The core target of this thinking, then, is any presupposition of discursive closure, in order to demonstrate that discourses don't work in the way that their subjects imagine them to (for example, as in the post-Marxist decon-struction of the essentialisms of 'class'-based political theory); that subjects often don't know they are subjects and don't know that they are in discourse, and therefore don't know that their – and all – discourse fails. The most pertinent 'Laclauian' questions to pose to Laclauian discourse analysis, then, are: *is it logical*? And, if so, which sense of 'logical' is entailed, given that this is so expansive, contingent and even undecidable? In what ways does it *not* work in the way that its own subjects imagine it to (and what does it deem 'working' to be anyway)? And in what ways does it *fail* (what does it set out to achieve)? As proposed throughout, the perspective most adequate to provide a response most consistent with the basic premises of post-Marxist 'discourse' theory itself is to be derived from Derridean deconstruction's rethinking of language and institution as *dissemina-tory* (Chapter 1). Indeed, perhaps the most ethically, politically, theoretically, and practically pertinent points to be made to adherents of the 'discourse approach' of post-Marxism have already been clearly made by Derrida, when he said – to Laclau – that:

the fact that deconstruction is apparently politically neutral allows, on the one hand, a reflection on the nature of the political, and on the other hand, and this is what interests me in deconstruction, a hyper-politicization. Deconstruction is hyper-politicizing in following paths and codes which are clearly not traditional, and I believe it awakens politicization [because] it permits us to think the political and think the democratic by granting us the space necessary in order not to be enclosed in the latter. In order to continue to pose the question of the political, it is necessary to withdraw something from the political and the same thing for democracy, which, of course, makes democracy a very paradoxical concept. (Derrida 1996: 85).

Banal Pragmatism versus High Theory

The dimension of the problems caused by the ambivalent status of 'logic' in post-Marxist theory is for Daryl Slack (1996: 119) to be found in the fact that the contingency of articulations also penetrates and 'impossibilizes' the possibility that 'logical connections' could actually be necessary. This reminds us that the logical connections and relations of Laclau's theory may not be logical. But it also suggests that, because Laclauian theory maintains that articulation is contingent at the same time as it proliferates undecidability, then not only its conclusions but also the 'logic' of its choice of orientation may perhaps both be construed as mistaken. Richard Rorty picks up on this possibility – that post-Marxism's logic and orientation may well be disorientating illogic – in an engagement with Laclau (1996). He does so by pointing out that whenever we have made a decision we should remain 'quite aware that equally rational deliberation might have led us to a different decision' (Rorty 1996: 70).

Now, Rorty's overall position is also important here insofar as it is an exemplary instance of the quite widely held view that politics is intellectually unproblematic and that what needs to be done will always be pretty obvious. Indeed, in this, Rorty's position shares a certain affinity with that of Stuart Hall. That is because, for Hall, it is the examination of the cultural-political historical conjuncture that determines what should be theorised further. Indulging in theory for theory's sake can never really be justified when what is deemed to be important is consequential intervention. (Gary Hall (2002) directly problematises and ultimately rejects this argument, as discussed in Chapters 1 and 2; and problematising the presupposition that one needs to know in advance what something will (allegedly) lead to is cortical to deconstruction, textuality and hegemony.) Indeed, put bluntly, Rorty actually thinks that deconstruction and Laclauian post-Marxism are neither necessary nor sufficient for thinking or for doing politics. Significantly, Rorty thinks this is so specifically because Laclau is too bound up in deconstruction, philosophy and 'high theory'. In a critique that is reminiscent of Stuart Hall's criticisms of post-Marxism discussed in Chapter 2, Rorty argues that Laclau in particular is guilty of an overvaluation of philosophy at the expense of attending to real and pressing ethical and political matters. Again, akin to many often 'anti-theory' thinkers, Rorty relates this to the influence of deconstruction:

> Deconstruction [has not] done much either for the study of literature or for a grasp of our political problems – not because deconstruction is bad philosophy, but because we should not expect too much of philosophy. We should not ask philosophy, of whatever sort, to accomplish tasks for which it is unsuited. Although I have learned a great deal from Laclau's writings, I nevertheless think of him as overestimating Derrida's political utility, and thereby contributing to an unfortunate over-philosophication of leftist political debate. That over-philosophication has helped create, in the universities of the US and Britain (where Derrida's, Laclau's, and Chantal Mouffe's books are very widely admired) a self-involved academic left which has become increasingly irrelevant to substantive political discussion. (Rorty 1996: 69)

These are significant and familiar accusations against 'theory'. As such, it is important to unpack Rorty's position, to work out what rationale (or indeed, what theory) guides these formulations, and what governs or leads Rorty's logic or argument. What first becomes apparent is that the values underpinning these judgements manifest themselves in the form of statements about what is 'too much' and what is 'too little', and about what is implicitly improper versus what is 'just right' or proper. The worldview becomes clear in terms of the operative categories, distinctions, and taxonomies, sometimes declared and at other times left implicit. Specifically, what can be seen in Rorty here can be unravelled as follows: Philosophy, in Rorty's conception (here, at least), is said to be *not related* to politics in the way that deconstruction seems to want it to be. Philosophy is construed as being unable to do the job of politics, conventionally conceived. Rorty's overall argument will come to be that if deconstruction wants to do politics in another way, then it should show that what it wants to do *is* politics. As is well known about his position, Rorty doesn't think that this can be done except as private games of irony. Thus, because deconstruction and post-Marxist discourse theory claim that what they are doing is political, but without explaining how and why convincingly enough, for Rorty, they therefore constitute for him an 'unfortunate over-philosophication' that is deleterious to 'leftist political debate'. Indeed, *any* philosophical component to political debate is held to be an unfortunate inclusion within it, and political debate suffers because of its inclusion. Philosophy is defined as that which is done in philosophy departments, and political 'utility' is conceived as something that cannot be found in over-philosophication, or in over-valuing over-philosophication, or indeed in philosophy departments. Laclau, from whom Rorty has 'learned a great deal', over-philosophises politics, something which has taught Rorty very little about politics – presumably only a lesson in how *not* to do politics (even though this begs the question of whether such a lesson itself might not conceivably have some 'political utility'). The 'over-philosophication of leftist political debate' has done nothing other than help create a self-involved group, movement, or community that talks about politics wrongly and in the wrong place.

One question, however, is why this creation, this 'self-involved' group, might not be deemed political in itself. Indeed, as Derrida replies, 'I hope – and if I can continue to contribute a little to this I will be very content – that the political left in universities in the United States, France and elsewhere, will gain politically by employing deconstruction' (1996: 86). Derrida holds this conviction because, as we have heard, 'the fact that deconstruction is apparently politically neutral allows, on the one hand, a reflection on the nature of the political, and on the other hand, and this is what interests me in deconstruction, a hyper-politicization' (85). But Rorty does not think that any of the parties involved, political or academic, can gain from this. This is because Rorty adheres to a 'commonsense', 'usual view' of politics. Thus, Rorty filters it all through the 'commonsense' anti-intellectual view that the university is not a proper part of the 'real world'. In other words, Rorty explicitly regards academia as *disarticulated* from politics. Hence, this 'self-involved academic left' talking about politics is not properly political because it is exclusively 'inside' the academy, and neither connected to nor in or on the outside (the 'real world, out there'). What is clear here is that Rorty does not rate the production of a minor ('irrelevant') group who think too much about politics, because it's got nothing to do with politics. As well as the problem of location (i.e., that the university, or the philosophy department at least, is the wrong place to be thinking about politics), and of style (i.e., that the 'genre' of philosophy, or deconstruction at least, is the wrong place to look to grasp political problems), it also appears that it is thinking too much, *per se*, that somehow constitutes Rorty's biggest problem, representing for him the biggest detraction from pressing political issues as they should be properly understood.

We 'should not expect too much of philosophy', and apparently because its thinking is not a proper doing, nor is it in the right place or right style. It is 'entirely academic', not political. In Rorty's paradigm, as this 'self-involved academic' group's thinking about politics increases, its 'relevance' to politics decreases.

But what does Rorty mean by 'over-philosophication'? He appears to mean (over-) rigorous or (over-) strenuous conceptual analysis and interrogation of precisely the sorts favoured by Derrida and Laclau. As Rorty sees it:

> Such over-philosophication is evinced when Laclau isolates notions like 'toleration' or 'the political' or 'representation' and then points out that we cannot, simply by thinking about that notion, figure out what to do. Who, except for a few wacky hyperrationalists, ever thought we could? Who takes seriously the idea that an idea, or notion, or principle, could contain the criteria of its own correct application? (Rorty 1996: 69)

Now, almost as an aside – but an aside that does answer Rorty's (rhetorical) question – it could be suggested that among the people who might well think that 'an idea, or notion, or principle, could contain the criteria of its own correct application' might be politicians themselves, or the most standard political discourses. For, standard political discourse regularly relies on the invocation, activation and circulation of supposedly self-evident or supposedly transparently understood but highly dubious persuasive rhetorical players (like 'toleration', for instance, or 'terrorism'), as if assuming that the notions themselves radiate their own correct interpretation and application. (For Laclau, of course, this is precisely what regularly happens with such terms and 'concepts': they are tendentiously reiterated in order to further a particular – always irreducibly populist – cause (1985; 2005). For Laclau this is definitional of politics.)

Indeed, it is, repeatedly, something about the *thinking about* all of this with which Rorty has the biggest problem. This appears to be because, for Rorty, politics is held to be straightforward, obvious, banal, and, basically, simple. This is why Rorty disqualifies what he sees to be Laclau's hyper-academicism from politics and institutes 'commonsense' and the supposedly unphilosophical (the 'pragmatic'), as being more political precisely because they are less academic. However, consistent with this anti-intellectualism, Rorty even considers his own pragmatist approach to be of no real interventional use to politics, precisely because it is just another academic approach. For Rorty, the discourse of politics is that of public debate. But the

paradox here is that, at least to Rorty's mind, his academic pragmatism nevertheless contains the correct understanding of politics, and it
knows (in advance) what political discourse should be like. So, Rorty's
is a 'theoretically anti-theoretical' metadiscourse which is forced to
disavow its own status as such. This is because, to be consistent,
Rorty's approach must contradict itself. In other words, it is inconsistent. Its intellectual position on the question of politics is paradoxically anti-intellectual, in the name of denying that academics are
political when they are academic, that politics is academic, and that
academia is political. Deconstruction, on the other hand, is concerned
to show that academic knowledge cannot be bracketed off from
politics in practice, for practical reasons: in deconstruction, knowledge not only 'publicises', in the Kantian sense (Derrida 1992; 2001),
but it is institutional and therefore political in the Gramscian sense.
Furthermore, Derrida also maintains the ethico-political importance
of 'the necessity of posing transcendental questions in order not to be
held within the fragility of an incompetent empiricist discourse' (81).
The necessity of this sense of the philosophical for thinking politics
devolves on the importance, for Derrida of 'following paths and codes
which are clearly not traditional', which 'permits us to think the
political and think the democratic by granting us the space necessary
in order not to be enclosed' (85) by conventions and strictures that
might 'repress' (80) certain questions, the exploration of which *may*
turn out to be institutionally and politically consequential.

However, for Derrida, one cannot be content to presume that
philosophy itself is simply a priori enabling. Indeed, versus institutional philosophy he asserts the importance of literature, observing
that 'literature is the right in principle to say anything, and it is to the
great advantage of literature that it is an operation at once political,
democratic and *philosophical*, to the extent that literature allows one
to pose questions that are often repressed in a philosophical context'
(80). Derrida's deployment of the category of literature here is
strategic. For literature, as he points out in a move that undercuts
Rorty's operative orienting distinction between the private (non-
political) and the public (political), 'is a public institution of recent
invention, with a comparatively short history, governed by all sorts of
conventions connected to the evolution of law, which allows, in
principle, anything to be said. Thus, what defines literature as such,
within a certain European history, is profoundly connected with a
revolution in law and politics: the principled authorization that anything can be said publicly' (80). Literature is not a natural or inevitable

phenomenon or property of the world. It is a contingent *institution*, at once public, private, philosophical, political, and more. Against all simplifying taxonomies, Derridean deconstruction proposes the constitutive politicality of institution and its productive role in the formation of both objectivity and subjectivity (Chapters 1 and 2; Mowitt 1992; Weber 1987). Indeed, Derrida asserts:

> All that a deconstructive point of view tries to show, is that since convention, institutions and consensus are stabilizations (sometimes stabilizations of great duration, sometimes micro-stabilizations), this means that they are stabilizations of something essentially unstable and chaotic. Thus it becomes necessary to stabilize precisely because stability is not natural; it is because there is instability that stabilization becomes necessary; it is because there is chaos that there is a need for stability. Now, this chaos and instability, which is fundamental, founding and irreducible, is at once naturally the worst against which we struggle with laws, rules, conventions, politics and provisional hegemony, but at the same time it is a chance, a chance to change, to destabilize. If there were continual stability, there would be no need for politics, and it is to the extent that stability is not natural, essential or substantial, that politics exists and ethics is possible. Chaos is at once a risk and a chance, and it is here that the possible and the impossible cross each other. (1996: 84)

Whilst Rorty may well agree with (at least the first half of) what Derrida says here, he disagrees with the necessity or political efficacy of saying (at least the second half of) it. Nevertheless, Rorty himself continues to talk politics and philosophy in a still academic manner in an academic context, while denying the political relevance or validity of any of it. (In the next paragraph, Rorty makes declarations about the mistakes made on the topic of politics by Kierkegaard, the Vienna Circle, rationalism and existentialism. These are declarations that rely on his philosophical interpretation of the political.) Knowing enough about philosophy to be able to think and speak about politics, Rorty argues that:

> Granted that decision is not deliberation, it seems to me misleading to say, with Derrida and Laclau, that 'decision always *interrupts* deliberation'. That suggests a picture of Will swooping down and taking matters out of Reason's hands. It is more plausible to describe decision as we normally do, as the *outcome* of deliberation – even when we are quite aware that equally rational deliberation might have led us to a different decision. Wittgenstein has taught us that the fact that anything can be made out to be in conformity with a rule does not mean that rules are useless, nor that decisions cannot be made in conformity with them. (70)

Here, Rorty is responding to Laclau's account of 'the logic of the decision' – a central category for Laclau. Indeed, for Laclau, 'the subject is merely the distance between the undecidable structure and the decision. And analysis of the exact dimensions of any decision reached on an undecidable terrain is the central task of a theory of politics, a theory which has to show the contingent "origins" of all objectivity' (Laclau 1989: xv). For Laclau, the theory of 'decision' is also the theory of subjective agency and/within hegemony. As he argues, any decision, if it is a *free* decision, 'cannot be *ultimately* grounded in anything external to itself' in order for it to *be* a decision and not part of a 'calculable programme' (Laclau 1996: 52). This peculiar 'logic' is the correct understanding of 'decision' for Laclau because, in order *actually to be* a decision, an apparent 'choice' must be entirely free, and not determined by anything else. In Derrida's words, 'If one knows, and if it is a subject that knows who and what, then the decision is simply the application of a law' (1996: 84).

Laclau's thinking on the decision is clearly influenced by Derrida, who has emphasised that it is always undecidable whether or not a decision has ever taken place (as discussed in Chapter 2). This undecidability arises precisely because it is equally possible to represent something that seems like a decision either as having been a *completely* free 'moment of madness', of leaping into the unknown, or, on the other hand, a totally unfree and structurally determined part of a 'calculable programme'. Laclau is interested in the way that thinking decision helps him to theorise questions of agency, freedom or determination, *and* power. For, he ties decision (freedom) to the issue of power and hegemony. Indeed, to Laclau, decision itself must *be* a power – a productive and repressive power: both productive of a new state of affairs and the 'repression of possibilities which are not actualized'. Laclau deems decision to be a repression or exclusion that is 'at the same time, the exercise of my power and the exercise of my freedom' (52). Moreover, Laclau implicates the thinking of decision in the theory of the production or invention of the subject, and ties this to irreducibly institutional ('structural') contexts, insofar as the subject that takes important, 'constitutive' decisions about itself is in a sense the product of such decisions. Power, for Laclau, is 'what makes freedom possible' (52). It is also what makes freedom an impossible concept, 'in itself'. For the exercise of power becomes the very condition of freedom (52). Derrida usually largely agrees with Laclau's thinking, but on this point he supplements Laclau's theory with a number of caveats:

I would like to come back to what Ernesto Laclau said about the subject and the decision. The question here is whether it is through the decision that one becomes a subject who decides something. At the risk of appearing provocative, I would say that once one poses the question in that form one imagines that the who and the what of the subject can be determined in advance, then there is no decision. In other words, the decision, if there is such a thing, must neutralize if not render impossible in advance the who and the what. If one knows, and if it is a subject that knows who and what, then the decision is simply the application of a law. In other words, if there is a decision, it presupposes that the subject of the decision does not yet exist and neither does the object. Thus with regard to the subject and the object, there will never be a decision. I think this summarizes a little what Ernesto Laclau proposed when he said that the decision presupposes identification, that is to say that the subject does not exist prior to the decision but when I decide I invent the subject. Every time I decide, if a decision is possible, I invent the who, and I decide who decides what; at this moment the question is not the who or the what but rather that of the decision, if there is such a thing. Thus, I agree that identification is indispensable, but this is also a process of disidentification, because if the decision is identification then the decision also destroys itself. (Derrida 1996: 84)

Rorty does not buy any of this. Or rather, he does not see its point, purpose, or political utility. On the contrary, 'It is more plausible' for Rorty (the question of the determination of plausibility, and the stakes of this, are absent), 'to describe decision as we normally do': *we who are normal*. With this, much of Rorty's paradigm becomes clearer still: it is not concerned to consider the constitution of normality until this becomes posed or present on the public political arena and agenda. Thus, the Laclauian problematic of the interimplication of objectivity, values, and the ethical character of a community (2000; 2004; 2005) is of no interest to Rorty as long as it remains merely academic. The problem is, though, that Rorty's position denounces in advance the 'utility' of engaging in such 'over-philosophical' discourse, even though it is immanently political. As shall become more apparent, this *passive* schema of what constitutes legitimate political considerations hampers Rortyan thinking through and through, constrains it to denial, rejection and refusal after denial, rejection and refusal, and ultimately makes it seem not only anti-intellectual but also fundamentally schizophrenic and clearly prohibitive as an institutional academic paradigm. Rorty's position would deny the 'right' that Derrida claims not to be limited to one mode and perspective, and it denies hegemony or the place of knowledge within it. In this paradigm, the object and scope of political inquiry is strictly demarcated and policed, and the range of legitimate political questions is rigorously reined in.

Thus, it is on the basis of an appeal to the claim of normality that Rorty can also see, as he puts it, 'little resemblance between taking a decision and (in Laclau's phrase) "impersonating God", if only because we do the former, but not the latter, dozens of times a day'. Furthermore, Rorty does not 'see that the content of a decision has, as Laclau puts it, "the function of embodying the absent fullness of the subject" '. Indeed, all that Rorty says he *can* see is 'that it might be so described if one were interested in constructing a philosophical or psychoanalytic theory of selfhood in terms of a dialectic of presence and absence. But I doubt that such a theory could be of any help in thinking about politics'. In other words, Rorty cannot see any connection between a theory of the subject and politics, and in fact he can only see the 'worth' of philosophical-theoretical thinking by locating it solely within, or reducing it to, the institutional context of academic case studies situated entirely within the cloistered privacy of academic institutions. Quite opposed to this divided vision of academic versus political space, deconstruction (like, but more radically than mainstream post-Marxist theory) explicitly proposes the ineradicability of the political dimension to all institution (Weber 1987; Godzich 1987; Derrida 1992; Mowitt 1992). Laclau, too, can of course see an indelible connection between the theoretical or philosophical question of 'decision' (freedom versus structure) and, at one and the same time, the question of the subject and the institutional hegemonic terrain of culture and politics. In Laclau's view, in fact, the point is to understand that everything becomes:

> a hegemonic battlefield between a plurality of possible decisions. This does not mean that any time everything that is logically possible becomes, automatically, an actual political possibility. There are inchoated possibilities which are going to be blocked, not because of any logical restriction, but as a result of the historical contexts in which the representative institutions operate. (1996: 50)

In terms of Laclau's paradigm, it always remains centrally important to be logical, and to engage in the rigours of theoretical explorations of ontological conditions. In terms of Rorty's paradigm, though, the Laclauian decision to pursue these issues is, politically-speaking, regarded as a bad one. For Rorty, there are enough 'obvious' problems to deal with without getting involved in the fundamentals of ontology or preoccupied with their mirror opposite, the lack of ontological fundamentals. However, surely even the most pragmatic, practical, or untheoretical of positions might hesitate in the face of Rorty's doubt that 'such a theory could be of any help in thinking about politics'. This is because this claim amounts basically to a doubt that theorising 'about politics' could be any help in 'thinking about politics', and ultimately therefore to a doubt that *thinking* could be any help in *thinking*. Rorty seems to be claiming here that he does not even endorse thinking, at least philosophically, about politics. His claim is that real politics and academia are disarticulated.

What is jarring here is that for a thinker who engages intellectually with questions of the political and cultural forces and consequences of descriptions and redescriptions, Rorty seems peculiarly hostile to Laclau's favoured kind of genre or language game. This is so to such an extent that he seems led to (mis)construe Laclau's argumentation about the constitutive character of representation – that, first of all, there's no getting outside of, away from or beyond representation – and of the ethico-political implications of this: namely, the inevitability that every representation will be biased, limited, susceptible to redescription or re-articulation, and that 'the role of the representative cannot be neutral, and . . . will contribute something to the identities of those he represents' (Laclau 1996: 49). For Laclau, *every* representation (and *every kind* of representation) is irreducibly political: 'the process of representation itself creates retroactively the entity to be represented' (Laclau 2000: 66). Given Rorty's own involvement in questions of the consequentiality of representation or redescription, it is surprising when he flatly rejects all of this. However, Rorty prefers to maintain that there are 'normal' versus evidently 'wacky' representations; there are proper commonsensical ways of looking at things and there are silly irrelevant ways. According to him:

> To be a bit more concrete, consider Laclau's example of political representation. I see the election of representatives to govern a population which is too large, or too spread out, to get together in a town meeting as a sensible practical expedient. Every polity that resorts to this expedient is aware that the decisions taken by the representatives may not be those which would have been taken by a gathering of the entire citizenry. But I do not see that this situation is clarified by the claim that 'the relation of representation will be, for essential logical reasons . . . constitutively impure'. (70)

Leaving aside the presumptions about society that Rorty demonstrates ('citizenry', 'election'), and before getting to the crux of the problem that Rorty has with Laclau, it is helpful to note the appearance here of clearly a rhetorical effort to convey a 'reality-effect': that is to say, to be 'a bit more concrete', *there is nothing 'concrete' here*. This is entirely hypothetical, fantastical even. 'Concrete' – the evocation of the material – appears here and functions as the appeal to external reality, the hard stuff, the proper stuff – the appeal that here we are *in* it, dealing with *it*, no longer just in theory, but actually in reality, engaging with it. This appeal occurs because if this weren't concrete then it would be only theory. It is the 'believe me' appeal extraordinaire, the appeal to the 'trope of tropes', material reality, the 'concrete'. There is also another kind of appeal: this time not to the putative material of reality, but to the as-if-sensible stuff of values, or 'gradability': that is, to the idea that things can unequivocally be value-graded on a scale, from too much to too little, via the just right. However, Rorty makes this appeal before having established whether *any* of this can even *be* at all, never mind whether it can be graded. This use of gradability ('too . . .') both defers the question of whether and in what way such a thing can be at all, at the same time as it activates or produces a norm, universal, and/or phantasy about what is normal, proper, present and correct. Here, for instance, we are told the hypothetical 'original' population is *too* large or *too* spread out to be governed in a fully self-present manner. One question might be that of what sized population would ever be *not* too large or too small or too spread out as to be able to sidestep the constitutive operations of 'representation'? Moreover, in whose or which terms and to what end is the 'too' working to persuade us that something is indeed too much or too little? Rorty contests all of Laclau's points – and all of this 'useless' Theory – by reference to 'the usual view'; as if there *is* a 'usual view' that is not political, and as if such a usual view must therefore be right, responsible and correct. Furthermore, though, even this invocation of 'the usual view' is not simply a statement of incontestable fact (for *whose* view is it?), but is rather always-already a projection-construction, at least as 'un-concrete' as even the most theoretical view. As well as being a tendentious *assertion*, it is also something that is enabled by and working for a specific universal or norm that is taken as read, that goes without saying here, and that accordingly remains exempt from scrutiny. Rorty presents many things as if being natural, 'sensible', or as if being inevitable. Democracy, for instance, is represented as merely 'a sensible practical expedient', rather than as a contingent achievement, a contingent arrangement, fought for and established, in various ways. Rather, 'the election of representatives to govern a population' is simply 'a sensible practical expedient'.

Rorty's pragmatic position is one which holds that because everything is conventional, there is no rational reason to change it; there is no ratio of conventions; politics is a series of conventions; but pointing this out doesn't change the conventions. So to be pragmatic you simply have to understand how the conventions work (this is the position of the Lacanian 'knave', in Žižek's terms (Žižek 2000: 324–5): See Chapter 2). Pointing out that conventions have no grounds doesn't undermine conventions. Convention is all there is. So theory is both unnecessary and pointless (although, soon Rorty suggests that it is often 'handy' and 'helpful'). Specifically, it is Laclau's 'abstraction' that Rorty has most distaste for: what he calls the ever-higher abstraction of Laclau's work. (To be polemical: if what Rorty dislikes is ever-higher 'abstraction', what he evidently enjoys is ever-cruder reduction and simplification.) The move to higher abstraction equals, for Rorty, a drifting away from the real. 'Reality' is therefore that which we are in, closer to, or more connected with when we use banal, everyday, commonplace language. And for Rorty, even the theme of language is to be understood in a banal, reductive and simplistic manner. The question of language that he chooses to formulate is that of 'high' versus 'low' language:

> I have nothing against higher levels of abstraction. They often come in handy. But I think that the pressure to rise to a higher level of abstraction should, so to speak, come from below. Locally useful abstractions ought to emerge out of local and banal political deliberations. They should not be purveyed ready-made by philosophers, who tend to take the jargon of their own discipline too seriously. Unless you were already familiar with Kant's and Hegel's use of *Grund*, it would never occur to you to try to 'ground the concept [of tolerance] in itself' or to ground it in 'a norm or content different from itself'.

The higher/lower figure in this anti-theoretical argument combines with the too much/not enough. The 'just right' has not specified, until now, where the proper order of things can be seen: influence should properly come from below – 'so to speak', from the ground (but *not* the *Grund*), or the concrete of the street, and *not* the pages of a book. Rorty has 'nothing against higher levels of abstraction', though presumably he must still 'doubt that such a theory could be of any help in thinking about politics', even though they 'often come in handy'. The 'pressure to rise' should come to hand 'from below'. 'Locally useful abstractions ought to emerge out of local and banal political deliberations'. Everything is split up into distinct localities, allegedly unsynthesised by any universal, save the common sense 'norm' of usefulness, the pragmatic and the practical, which should just be universally accepted. Philosophers should not tell us about any of this, because they 'tend to take the jargon of their own discipline too seriously'. Because they take their own discourse too seriously, they should not purvey ready-made abstractions. They should acknowledge their own ministrations for what they are: just philosophy 'playing with itself' and not 'doing' anything. Because it is 'too much' *therefore* it is 'too little'; because it comes too soon or unasked-for, therefore it is too much *and* not enough. (This is the structure of the (masturbatory) supplement as Derrida (1974: 141–64) finds it in Rousseau.) However, if universalising abstractions are bad, universalising analogies on the other hand are evidently acceptable; for Rorty continues:

> Consider an analogy. Although some mathematics is obviously very useful to engineers, there is a lot of mathematics that isn't. Mathematics outruns engineering pretty quickly, and starts playing with itself. Philosophy, we might say, outruns politics ('social engineering', as it is sometimes called) pretty quickly, and also starts playing with itself . . . I suspect the notion of 'condition of possibility and impossibility' is as useless to political deliberation as Cantorean diagonalization is to civil engineers. Surely the burden is on those who, like Laclau, think the former useful to explain just how and where the utility appears, rather than taking it for granted? (71)

So, in this analogy, mathematicians are to engineers what philosophers are to politics. The binary is both higher to lower and also, in a connotative twist that will not surprise readers of Derrida's essay on Rousseau ('. . . that dangerous supplement . . .' (1974)), wankers to workers. Disconnected theoretical speculation, like unproductive, unconnected masturbation, is bad, *because* it is both too much and disconnected and unproductive. Abstraction, like theoretical mathematics, should be explicitly orientated towards the real and present state of affairs, so to speak, as it is constructed on the ('concrete') street. It should all come as a response to the pressure from the other, the real, the base, the concrete, out there. But the lower, 'doing', others, who can't keep up with unconnected theorists, but who are better than them because they 'do', are nevertheless trying to catch up. This analogy is out of joint; out of step with itself. Rorty continues:

> It is of course true that engineering is always catching up with mathematics
> – using mathematical concepts in desperate earnest which had been

dreamed up just for fun, and with no thought of being applied to anything. Transcendental numbers were once of no interest [to] engineers, but they are now. So how can we tell in advance whether or not transcendental conditions will be of interest to the electorate, their representatives, and onlooking kibitzers (like Laclau and me) on the political process? (71–2)

The breathtaking reductivity of this picture of academia and industry that Rorty is sketching might of course be justifiable on the grounds of trying to be clear. But it is far from clear, not least because Rorty invalidates his own argument. If you don't know the outcome in advance then how can you say what can't happen? In addition, political philosophers like Laclau, the equivalent of theoretical mathematicians, go about being *too* serious 'just for fun'. The earnest engineers, who look up to the mathematicians and chase after them, however, are analogous to 'the electorate' *and* to 'onlooking kibitzers' as well as the properly political 'representatives'. The engineers and electorate (and kibitzers?), and so on, look upwards at the dazzling productions of their superior, unconnected, playful wankers (theorists, of both kinds) and try to catch up with them and use their (unconnected: 'disseminational') productions for practical (connected: 'inseminational') purposes. The mathematicians in Rorty's analogy, however, unlike the political theorists like Laclau (and Derrida), have been under no obligation to take 'the burden' of explaining why they think that the undecidable, possibly unconnected wank that they produce just for fun is useful in terms of already-existing engineering. But, on the other face of the analogy, the burden of having to explain utility *should* be on the shoulders of the political theorists or politicised philosophers. So, there is a good 'high' (mathematical mind-wank) and a bad 'high' (over-philosophical mind-wank). Low is unequivocally good (engineering, proper politics: the proper hard stuff, the concrete material of metaphysical reality, or rather, tropology). Some kinds of intellectual 'playing with itself' in masturbatory distraction/abstraction can be acceptable – *sometimes*, and only in *some places* (such as in maths). For, Rorty asks, 'how can we tell in advance whether or not transcendental conditions will be of interest to the electorate, their representatives, and onlooking kibitzers (like Laclau and me) on the political process?'

We cannot, of course. Still, we should notice that the demand for more information about transcendental numbers, information which turned out to be purveyable by mathematicians in ready-made form, emerged from below, as engineers became more ambitious and courageous. The mathematicians were not in a position to predict the utility which their inventions turned out to have. Nor did they have the skills and information required to predict when and how a demand for their products might emerge. (72)

With this Rorty might seem to be arguing against himself, in that it now seems that one might be able to justify, for example, Laclauian unconnected theoretical speculation, on the basis of the possibility that it *might* 'come in handy' politically, if and when 'the electorate, their representatives, and onlooking kibitzers' become 'more ambitious and courageous'. But this is not so. For what Rorty is seeking to do is to displace the value of any innovation from what this account might deem to be the innovators themselves (the disconnected theoretical onanists who produce too much high and abstract and always-possibly-useless stuff too soon), so that it can only ever have value afterwards, if and when connected to the 'demand for more information'. The paradox seems to be that, because any theory may get too far ahead, too abstract, too fast, or rather, too unconnected, then therefore it should not be done, even though it also should, because as hyper-theoretical mathematics turned out to be for engineers, it is good when the over-serious fun stuff is 'purveyable' in 'ready-made form' for the proper, when it is wanted or needed for *doing real stuff*.

This is only paradoxical in terms of the analogy's equation of (high) mathematicians with (high) theorists like Laclau; until, that is, one realises that (bad/high) Laclau is not *exactly* like (good/high) mathematicians. The former is devalued compared to the latter because in the high theory of Laclau there is no clear and simple connection or translation of his 'abstractions' into real political contexts. Laclauian mind-wank has no clear application – no 'social engineers'. However, this is where Rorty's analogy really does start to spin, dizzyingly, because only three paragraphs earlier, he declares that abstract political ideas 'should not be purveyed ready-made by philosophers' – implicitly, even if there were 'social engineers' ready to incorporate them into politics. Moreover, in Rorty there is no appeal that the electorate, their representatives, or kibitzing onlookers of any sort *should* become 'more ambitious and courageous', like the engineers allegedly 'did'. No. On the contrary, theorists should calm down and be banal. Presumably they should not try to solicit, recruit, or indeed try to 'conceive', grow or engineer their own 'engineers' in their own laboratories, either. What is certain, here, is that philosophers should stop talking about politics. It is not *just* that 'mathematicians [are] not in a position to predict the utility' of any 'inventions'; it is rather that philosophers should not be 'inventing' at all, unless there is a pressure or a demand 'from below'. For Rorty, everything can only properly be solved only when supply meets demand, and when everything is synthesised, in 'utility', as in the encounter between the theorists' wank and the 'lower' more 'hands on' lot, in the *demos* (or *domos*), who can 'produce' something 'real' from the exchange – and the exchange Rorty uses to explain all of this is an exchange of fluids: abstract maths becomes 'fluid' in the next paragraph (Thus, the structure or Rorty's critique of theory is identical to that which Derrida discerns in Rousseau's rejection of masturbation and preference for sex):

> Fans of Cantor's diagonalization method did not assume that there *should* be such a demand (from, for example, people trying to forestall flash flooding). Hegelians of both the left and right, however, have assumed that certain notions – notions which will remain pretty much unintelligible unless one has read some Hegel – *should* be found useful (by, for example, people trying to forestall dictatorship). (Rorty 1996: 72)

It turns out that the sin of political philosophy (or the sin of 'Hegelians') is a sin of presumption, of assuming that their notions *should* 'be found useful', by someone else, somewhere else. Basically, of course, Rorty is saying that philosophy *should* be discrete (private) about what it does (which suggests that his admonition of Laclau might be because secretly Rorty buys into the philosophical illusion that philosophy *is* a subversive and dangerous activity). To stick to the structure of Rorty's analogy, then: political theorists have assumed a market or an intercourse or an intervention 'to come', which may never come of its own accord, and which they should not assume is going to come. So, in banal terms, the fundamental political and intellectual error of theorists, deconstructionists and/or political philosophers is that they 'fancy themselves'. This is why Rorty disapproves of the over-philosophical 'self-involved academic left': it is narcissistic, aloof, conceited, and (what is inestimably worse) *fundamentally disconnected*. Rorty has an irreducibly ambivalent relation to 'connection', then. He effectively argues that theory both should and should not try to connect.

Ultimately, then, it is precisely because Laclau proceeds as if he actually thinks he *is* exactly like a mathematician or other such potentially worthwhile theoretician that Rorty has a problem with his 'over-philosophication'. Rorty in effect believes that the Laclauian over-philosophication of the political is at once irrelevant *to* politics and nevertheless also strangely irresponsible *in the face of* politics. He should both *not* try to connect *and* should try to connect *differently*. Rorty's own convictions – that in the face of political questions, issues and problems, one need only 'muddle through' in a 'pragmatic', 'piecemeal' manner; that philosophy has no use, and that theory is 'unrelated' or not connected – are of course banal and facile, and yet they remain strangely relevant. For, to Rorty too, as with Laclau, *everything depends on the question of connection* – of how 'this' relates to, acts upon and is acted upon by 'that'. This means that despite or even because of his refusal of Laclauian political theory, Rorty's challenge to Laclau, then, is actually to *finish* thinking the political – specifically to clearly express its mode of articulation and efficacy. This is what Rorty accuses Laclau of being unable to do. It is also the very thing that Rorty too is unable to do. As we will see in the conclusion, this all hinges on *articulation*, but in a sense that has yet to be fully or widely developed in post-Marxism, cultural studies, and beyond.

The (Dis)Articulation of Theory and Practice

As Stuart Hall said of the problem of the impossibility of arriving at 'anything like an adequate theoretical account of culture's relations and its effects' in cultural studies (Hall 1992: 286), so it can be said of the problem of post-Marxism. It might be expressed like this: if it is known that the post-Marxist 'account of culture's relations and its effects' is one of the regularity in dispersion of articulations stabilising and destabilising hegemonic arrangements, then what does post-Marxism think the stabilising and destabilising effects *of itself* will be? What does it see its own 'relations and its effects' to be? In what relation is this or any such theory with any other practice? The problematic character of post-Marxism's lack of attention to this is signalled by Rorty. Other than in evocations of structures, relations and effects, post-Marxist discourse theory does not consider *itself as discourse*, or as being *in* discourse. It does not reflect on the politicality *of itself*. It doesn't directly address the impact of itself as politically consequential intervention. Indeed, it almost exclusively views itself as politicised political theory, without expanding on the specificities of its political character. Of course, in terms of the propositions of the post-Marxist discourse paradigm, arguably no institutionally extant and discursively circulating 'theory' is going to be 'merely academic'.

When analysed and evaluated through the post-Marxist paradigm itself – namely, when evaluated in terms of its own theorisation of politics – the question becomes that of the status that post-Marxism attributes to theory. This is the same as asking how post-Marxism assesses its own intervention.

When one surveys post-Marxist texts for moments of engagement with the problematic question of the status, place, and work of theory in terms of the question of political intervention, it is actually in Laclau's brief preface to Slavoj Žižek's book, *The Sublime Object of Ideology* (1989), that one finds a key moment wherein Laclau is very keen to consider theory *as* political intervention. Indeed, this preface is particularly telling, because as Ian Parker points out, 'It is clear from Laclau's preface to the book that he hoped Žižek would be recruited, if only temporarily, to a political project of post-Marxist "radical democracy" which would solve the crisis of left politics by blending aspects of post-structuralism with pragmatism' (Parker 2004: 3). If Laclau's interest in Žižek relates to an effort to 'solve the crisis of left politics by blending aspects of post-structuralism with pragmatism', then in this preface, Laclau should be read as not simply merely introducing another object, someone else's project, or some practice entirely unrelated to his own. Rather, he should be construed as in a way also representing his own project, offering an account of the consequentiality of his own theory. Throughout the preface there are repeated and strong references to his own project, and therefore signs of his own apperception and investments. There is also a sense that Laclau feels this to be the beginning of a new and exciting collaboration. Žižek, too, thanks Laclau and Mouffe in his acknowledgements to *The Sublime Object of Ideology* for the way that their book *Hegemony and Socialist Strategy* (1985) 'orientated' his own approach (Žižek 1989: xvi). So, this putatively minor text might actually reveal a lot about post-Marxism's theorisation of or hopes about itself as intervention. Indeed, Laclau begins and orientates the entire preface in terms of a consideration of the importance of 'theory'. It begins:

> Like all great intellectual traditions, Lacanian psychoanalytic theory has shed light in a number of directions. Such illuminating effects have tended to present it as a source of diffuse inspiration feeding highly differentiated intellectual currents, rather than a closed and systematic theoretical corpus. The reception given to Lacan has thus varied from country to country; each set of circumstances has emphasized different aspects of a theoretical body of work which had itself undergone considerable transformation over a long period of time. (Laclau 1989: ix)

A closer look at these words reveals that the opening statement tries to pass itself off as a (constative) statement of fact, whilst (performatively) imposing the reality-effect of what it seems simply to state, as if it all were self-evident. Opening with an analogy ('like'), the statement actually next introduces an equation between two unknowns. We are told that the two referents are equivalent: 'Lacanian psychoanalytic theory' and 'all great intellectual traditions' are presented as equivalent, insofar as they have all 'shed light in a number of directions'. Therefore: theory sheds light. This is its 'impact'. Now, Lacanian theory exists differently 'from country to country'. The effects of this are differences in reception. In certain countries, it is 'a source of diffuse inspiration': 'the professional training of psychoanalysts has been the most important aspect of this' (Laclau 1989: ix). In other countries, the 'impact' is in 'literature, philosophy, film theory, and so on'; and elsewhere, in the 'literature-cinema-feminism triangle'. In addition to 'these national variants we must also add a differentiation in terms of the diverse interpretations of the Lacanian corpus, as well as the various attempts to articulate this with other theoretical approaches' (x). Theory impacts on practice primarily as practice. In this case, some practices are tangibly very practical (the professional training of psychoanalysts), while some remain very theoretical (philosophy, film theory, and so on). The border between theory and practice is clearly unstable. However, what deserves to be emphasised here is a difficulty, or circularity, that soon becomes manifest. Throughout the preface, the expression 'theoretical approaches' is repeatedly used ambiguously; simultaneously intransitively, as a gerund, and as 'the object' itself. Effectively, that is, the expression 'theoretical approaches' seems to announce but also actually evades the question of precisely what a theoretical approach is approaching and why. Actually, nowhere in this text is the question of what we are approaching theoretically and why we are approaching it really made all that explicit, although Laclau does eventually come to mention 'the problems of a radical democracy' (xi). Theoretical approach remains simultaneously entity, field and object/ive. Indeed, rather than getting closer to specifying an object, it all divides and doubles: Theoretical approaches are theoretical approaches to theoretical approaches, within fields of theoretical approaches. The question of 'why approach theoretically?' is absent. Nevertheless, what Laclau finds important in the 'approach' of Žižek and the Slovenian School is this:

the Slovenian Lacanian school, to which this book by Žižek belongs, possesses highly original features. In contrast with the Latin and Anglo-Saxon world, Lacanian categories have been used in a reflection which is essentially *philosophical* and *political*. And while the Slovenian theoreticians make some effort to extend their analysis to the domain of literature and film, the clinical dimension is totally absent. Two main features characterize this school: The first is its insistent reference to the ideological-political field: its description and theorization of the fundamental mechanisms of ideology (identification, the role of the master signifier, ideological fantasy); its attempts to define the specificity of 'totalitarianism' and its different variants (Stalinism, fascism), and to outline the main characteristics of radical democratic struggles in Eastern European societies. The Lacanian notion of the *point de capiton* is conceived as the fundamental ideological operation; 'fantasy' becomes an imaginary scenario concealing the fundamental split or 'antagonism' around which the social field is structured; 'identification' is seen as the process through which the ideological field is constituted; enjoyment, or *jouissance* enables us to understand the logic of exclusion operating in discourses such as racism. The second distinctive feature of the Slovenian school is the use of Lacanian categories in the analysis of classical philosophical texts . . . (x)

For present purposes, what is most notable within this passage relates to the status of theory, practice, politics, and philosophy. This theory is 'essentially *philosophical* and *political*'. It has no interest in perhaps the most literal interpretation of what the practical application of Lacanian theory would be ('the clinical dimension is totally absent'). Instead, this is a philosophical practice that 'is' political *because* it makes 'insistent reference to the ideological-political field'. Ultimately, however, this means that 'the political' has a double status: it is both the object out there to be studied ('the ideological-political field'), and the aim of the studying (which is not merely philosophical, but actually *is* 'essentially *philosophical* and *political*'). The double status of the political is this: on the one hand, there is the ideological-political (object); on the other hand, there is the philosophical-political (subject). The *object* is ideological; the *subject* is philosophical. The thing that prevents this activity from being merely ideological is the philosophical. So, the schema here is one in which the guarantee against the infection of one's position by ideological contamination is the philosophical. It is the philosophical that prevents the parasitic ideological-political from contaminating the intellectual activity. This is an undeconstructed (presumed, imposed) border, that is, of course, ultimately less secure or even tenable than is here implied. Such a schema seems dubious not least in deconstructive terms wherein such a boundary between the ideological and the philosophical must be always already transgressed and can only maintained by imposing conventions of propriety, by maintaining exclusions, and by policing the boundary. Throughout the Preface, Laclau does not move to interrogate further the problematics introduced and problems harboured by such manoeuvres as these.

Judith Butler has directly posed questions to Laclau about the problems of relation, articulation, 'impact' or intervention, identification, institutional context, and orientation. These bear directly on this discussion. For in her engagement with Laclau (as well as with Žižek) in *Contingency, Hegemony, Universality* (2000), Butler tries to remain attentive to questions of the institutional context of and the institutional conditions of possibility for intervention. In her contributions to this debate, Butler urges academics always to interrogate themselves about the *point* of what they even *think* they are doing, whenever they do anything. Accordingly, a question she puts to Laclau is that of identification (Butler 2000: 266): With what are the academics involved in politicised 'projects' to identify, and what do such identifications and investments mobilise, and avoid? Butler poses this as being a question of 'why our collective interests are so difficult to know – or, indeed, to remember' (2000: 149–50).

Here, Butler can be read as posing a similar question about 'theory' as that posed to Laclauian post-Marxism by Stuart Hall and Daryl Slack. As Daryl Slack formulates it, the problem is that 'in theorizing the space by highlighting the role of the discursive in the process of articulation, Laclau foregrounds a theoretical position that has an interesting – even ironic – backgrounding effect on the very politics that played such a crucial role in Laclau's work to begin with' (Daryl Slack 1996: 120). Accordingly, says Hall, what comes to matter in the Laclauian paradigm are 'positionalities but never positions' (Hall 1996d: 146). In such a reading, Laclau's political discourse analysis has in a sense 'forgotten' its politics: its investments have changed, from those of a political position to an identification with a certain 'philosophical' conception of the logical. Therefore, Butler's concern with the problematic situation wherein 'those who are oppressed by certain operations of power also come to be invested in that oppression [and whose] very self-definition becomes bound up with the terms by which they are regulated, marginalized, or erased from the sphere of cultural life' (149), can be read as being pertinent here. For at issue is the problem of overidentification with one's discipline, coupled with under-theorisation of one's project or *raison d'être*.

In terms of post-Marxist political theory, such 'domestication' (149–50) of potential antagonism would be an exemplary instance of the operation of hegemony. Butler suggests that subjects are constitutively compromised not least because all identity-establishment is bound up with the question 'of self-preservation'. Institutional establishment, development or self-preservation arguably *oblige* a kind of amnesia: repressing what was 'wanted' or 'declared' before and in the process of coming to establish an institutional identity or presence (this is similar to Derrida's sense of the 'violence of forgetting' (1974: 37)).[3] In other words, Butler is keen to emphasise the ethico-political relevance and salience of the observation that all subjects, including academic subjects, are performatively produced in and as the expression of an institutional field (Butler 2000: 26–7; Mowitt 1992; and as was argued following Derrida (1981) in Chapter 1, above). 'Power emerges in and as the formation of the subject' (154), she points out. In the light of this perspective, the specific academic example that Butler is most concerned with is the work of Žižek, and the problematic way that Žižek orientates and executes his work. But the points she makes about Žižek's work deserve to be applied to any cultural study. For, her problem is that the *way* academics know and teach about the real phenomenal world of things (encapsulated in examples) tends to overlook the fact that the motivated selection and tendential reading of examples also reciprocally 'proves' the theory that 'uses' them (26). As she argues, too often 'theory is articulated on its self-sufficiency, and then shifts register only for the pedagogical purpose of illustrating an already accomplished truth' (26–7). But who does any answer satisfy, and why? She asks: 'Are we using the categories to understand the phenomena, or marshalling the phenomena to shore up the categories "in the name of the Father", if you will?' (153; see also Derrida 1998: 39). The criticism here is that in speaking from the position of as if already having found the universal logic, then the 'knowledge' enabled by theory becomes recognition, reconfirmation. Of any theoretical knowledge, though, Butler asks, 'who posits [its] original and final ineffability', and what does 'such a positing achieve . . . and at what expense' (145)? What does theory *do*?

For Butler, the point of theory is not about the knowing, *per se*. Indeed, in a deconstructive mood, Butler argues that any actual knowledge ever produced *must* always be questioned. This is because Butler's attention to knowledge is orientated by the belief that, whatever else is being done, intellectuals should keep one eye firmly focused on the theme of power and the co-implication of ways of knowing with the institutional field of power/knowledge (Butler 2000: 28). Butler claims that what is most important is 'radical interrogation', because:

> The commitment to radical interrogation means that there is no moment in which politics requires the cessation of theory, for that would be the moment in which politics posits certain premises as off-limits to interrogation – indeed, where it actively embraces the dogmatic as the condition of its own possibility. This would also be the moment in which such a politics sacrifices its claim to be critical, insisting on its own self-paralysis, paradoxically, as the condition of its own forward movement. (264)

As Mark Devenney has expressed it, in theories such as this, the only really justifiable identification is with *contingency*. According to Devenney, deconstruction, post-Marxism and all anti-essentialist cultural and political theory:

> sanctions contingency as necessarily and, ironically, not contingent. This recognition entails (social) identification with radical contingency and the insistence that all political decisions require justification. A properly ethical decision does *not* rely on any principles or laws which precede it. This has the slightly bizarre consequence that a properly ethical decision would be taken by a wholly indeterminate subject, independent of all social practice. Given that such an ideal of subjectivity is precisely what post-structuralist thought rejects, this ideal of sovereign decision-making requires revising. It returns us to the condition of possibility for autonomous action *and* the condition of its impossibility. Sovereign decisions cannot be taken but they must be taken. It is this structure of indeterminacy that opens a realm of freedom in which subjects can begin to question the laws given to them and recognise that the following of a law presupposes the taking of a decision every time the law is followed. (Devenney 2002: 190–1)

Devenney argues that 'identification with an ultimate contingency implies that the ethical, as an impossible ideal, should be contrasted with any particular normative order which attempts to achieve that ideal' (Devenney 2002: 191). This encapsulates something that Butler regards as politically salient because 'at stake here is the exclusionary function of certain *norms* of universality which, in a way, transcend the cultural locations from which they emerge' (39). Butler's concern, expressed in our terms, is that post-Marxism is disciplinary and therefore, in Devenney's words, 'conservative' and motivated to 'police institutional boundaries in defining appropriate objects of study, in authorising methodological principles and in legitimising accredited subjects as their agents' (Devenney 2002: 176). Indeed, one of her principal worries is about any limitation or restriction being placed on theory. She argues that:

> the feared prospect of a full co-optation by existing institutions of power keep many a critical intellectual from engaging in activist politics. The fear is that one will have to accept certain notions which one wants to subject to critical scrutiny. Can one embrace the notion of 'rights' even as the discourse tends to localize and obscure the broader workings of power, even as it often involves accepting certain premises of humanism that a critical perspective would question? Can one accept the very postulate of 'universality', so central to the rhetoric of democratic claims to enfranch-isement? The demand for 'inclusion' when the very constitution of the polity ought to be brought into question? Can one call into question the way in which the political field is organized, and have such a questioning accepted as part of the process of self-reflection that is central to a radical democratic enterprise? Conversely, can a critical intellectual use the very terms that she subjects to criticism, accepting the pre-theoretical force of their deployment in contexts where they are urgently needed? (Butler 2000: 159)

This argument is unfortunately again organised by the problematic theory versus practice dichotomy discerned at the beginning of this chapter. In it, the role of the 'critical intellectual' is to interrogate radically, and thereafter to try to 'have such a questioning accepted as part of the process' of politics, and possibly or possibly not thereupon to 'use the very terms that she subjects to criticism, accepting the pre-theoretical force of their deployment in contexts where they are urgently needed'. The problem, though, is again that the most pro-blematic questions of intervention are precisely what are most ob-scured in this passage. This is the same problem that we saw in Žižek at the start of this chapter. For what is 'engaging', and what is 'deployment'? What is 'pre-theoretical force', and how does one establish, enter and engage within 'contexts' where something as yet to be established is 'urgently needed'? In short, what is intervention for Butler? Again, it seems clear that her entire argument and orienta-tion here is organised by an undeconstructed theory versus practice schema, organised also by an us-and-them, here and there, inside and outside set of binaries. Like Rorty, for Butler:

It seems important to be able to move as intellectuals between the kinds of questions that predominate these pages, in which the conditions of possibility for the political are debated, and the struggles that constitute the present life of hegemonic struggle: the development and universalization of new social movements, the concrete workings of coalitional efforts and, especially, those alliances that tend to cross-cut identitarian politics. (159)

For Butler, the really important task of the intellectual is to try to make arguments as *persuasively* as possible (165). However, this assertion (that we've got to argue *for* things) contradicts her cautionary warning about *any* theory that claims to *know with certainty* (because, as has been seen, she worries about the exclusionary effects of any such certainty). It also jars with her massively problematic claim that one needs to know 'how . . . it become[s] possible to keep an open and politically efficacious conflict of interpretations alive' (161). (The Rorty-esque premises that (a) everyone already knows what a *politically efficacious* conflict of interpretations is, (b) that we *already have* such a situation, and that all anyone need to do is (c) try to 'keep' it open, seem *very* difficult to subscribe to.) For what really remains at issue here, and precisely what Butler does not address or reduces to euphemistic allusive evocation, is the question of what any 'effects' (inclusionary, exclusionary, or otherwise) *are* or might ever be. In other words, the question remains: whether committed to 'radical interrogation' or whether committed to speaking or persuading of the univocal or universal 'truth', what are the relations and effects of such activity? What difference does it make? Where and how?

Knaves versus Fools

Despite the problems of what appears to be a straightforwardly journalistic impetus in Judith Butler, she does spend some time thinking about the issue of the 'performative efficiency' or interventionality of academic discourse. Her argument is somewhat divided between, on the one hand, gesturing to the complexity of the institutional and hegemonic production of subjectivity (154) and the possible transformative or subversive power of (re)iterative performativity, and on the other hand a theory versus practice schema and a simple faith in the efficacy of public political debate. This framework enables Butler to perform according to the norms that she imagines she has created for herself in order to feel like an autonomous Kantian self-legislator. But she avows the importance of 'articulation' as key to politics within hegemony, yet then reduces the understanding of articulation until it comes to refer only to the conscious intentions of political actors. This is at the cost of remaining attentive to the deconstructive problematisation of the limits of consciousness (*dissemination*). The problem with this is, of course, that although subjects may well be performatively produced within contexts that they can thereafter or reciprocally alter (again performatively), this cannot really be reduced to the work of conscious intention, either on the part of the 'context' or on the part of the 'subject'. Indeed, it is precisely this tendency to reduce discourse analysis to political consciousness analysis that Mowitt problematises, by asking, 'why should we reconceive the social as discourse if, in the final analysis, we are only really interested in the consciousness motivating agents' (Mowitt 1992: 17)? What falls by the wayside is attention to the institutional production of articulation.

A post-Marxist discourse analysis-based critique of Butler's paradigm could begin by noting such aspects of Butler's position as the theory versus practice dichotomy, the simplification of 'articulation' to conscious intention, and the interpretation of intervention as a faith in the political efficacy of public debate (Butler 2000: 162–9). Such a critique need perhaps only pay attention to the question of *institution* within culture and politics to begin to transform the terms of the debate, and to show that it is because Butler does not do so that her work hits a certain dead end, moves away from deconstruction and discourse analysis, and reverts to liberal hope in public debate. The value of Butler's position – exactly like the value of Rorty's position – consists in its ability to construe such 'high theory' as that of Laclau and Žižek as problematic because it does not seem even to care or think about *how* it might be articulated to or constituted *as* politics or political intervention. Like Rorty, perhaps Butler's most valuable contribution consists of the observation that surely 'it will not do simply to say that all these concrete struggles exemplify something more profound, and that our task is to dwell in that profundity' (161). This is a very important matter, and Butler, like Rorty, suggests that Žižek, like Laclau, has failed to address it.

Žižek, on the contrary, seems quite confident that he has *settled* the problem of intervention, and that he does so far more satisfactorily than either Butler or Laclau. This is because, for Žižek, Laclau and Butler risk being what he calls 'knaves':

Lacan developed an opposition between 'knave' and 'fool' as the two intellectual attitudes: the right-wing intellectual is a knave, a conformist who considers the mere existence of the given order as an argument for it, and mocks the Left for its 'utopian' plans, which necessarily lead to catastrophe; while the left-wing intellectual is a fool, a court jester who publicly displays the lie of the existing order, but in a way which suspends the performative efficiency of his speech. In the years after the fall of Socialism, the knave was a neoconservative advocate of the free market who cruelly rejected all forms of social solidarity as counterproductive sentimentalism; while the fool was a deconstructive cultural critic who, by means of his ludic procedures destined to 'subvert' the existing order, actually served as its supplement.

Today, however, the relationship between the couple knave-fool and the political opposition Right/Left is more and more the inversion of the standard figures of Rightist knave and Leftist fool: are not the Third Way theoreticians ultimately today's *knaves*, figures who preach cynical resignation, that is, the necessary failure of every attempt actually to change something in the basic functioning of global capitalism? And are not the conservative *fools* . . . far more attractive? Today, in the face of this Leftist knavery, it is more important than ever to *hold this utopian place of the global alternative open*, even if it remains empty, living on borrowed time, awaiting the content to fill it.

. . . It is my contention that Laclau and Mouffe's 'radical democracy' comes all too close to merely 'radicalizing' this liberal democratic imaginary, while remaining within its horizon . . . This means that the Left has a choice today: either it accepts the predominant liberal democratic horizon (democracy, human rights and freedoms . . .), and engages in a hegemonic battle *within* it, *or it risks the opposite gesture of refusing its very terms, of flatly rejecting today's liberal blackmail that courting any prospect of radical change paves the way for totalitarianism.* It is my firm conviction, my politico-existential premiss, that the old '68 motto *Soyons réalistes, demandons l'impossible!* still holds: it is the advocates of changes and resignifications within the liberal-democratic horizon who are the true utopians in their belief that their efforts will amount to anything more than the cosmetic surgery that will give us capitalism with a human face. (Žižek 2000: 324–6)

For Žižek, intervention is a total, voluntaristic, subjective, radical 'act'; an act which (as he frequently puts it) 'changes the very coordinates' of the situation and indeed of *what* 'reality' and truth, etc., are deemed to be. Now, questions are attracted to this assertion like flies to manure. What, it might be asked, is the difference between what Butler means by the power of the 'performative' and Žižek's notion of the 'act'? For Butler, 'the theory of performativity is not far from the theory of hegemony in this respect: both emphasize the way in which the social world is made – and new social possibilities emerge – at various levels of social action through a collaborative relation with power' (Butler 2000: 14). Laclau agrees with this affinity between Butler's notion of performativity and the logic of hegemonic trans-formations (Laclau 2000: 188–9), adding that Butler's belief in the political possibilities and of 'parodic performances' and the Derridean notion of 'iteration' (from which Butler draws heavily) both, like hegemonic logic, 'presuppose the possibility of this bending or trans-formation. Without this possibility, hegemonic displacements would be impossible' (Laclau 2000: 284). For Žižek, however, this is very different to his theorisation of the 'act'. The act does not *modify* an existing reality; in a sense it *produces* the reality that it transforms: that is, through a rejection or denial of any given 'dominant view' which presents itself as the correct or true view, the act entails the affirmation that an 'utterly different' situation is the 'real' one.

So Žižek's dispute with his bugbears, 'postmodernist relativist deconstructionist cultural studies' and 'Third Culture' ideologues, devolves on the existence or status of 'reality'. One often hears it alleged that postmodernists deny the existence of reality, and maintain that everything is merely signification or simulation; while common-sensical realists of all colours of positivism and empiricism are said to maintain that there is obviously and of course a single reality. Of course, each position falls into the trap of the other. Walsh (2002) argues that one benefit of Žižek's thinking is that instead of 'this binary opposition, the work of Žižek suggests a tripartite system (the "impossible" Real, reality as an attempt to symbolize the Real, and renderings of reality such as fiction and film)' (Walsh 2002: 395–6). To Žižek, 'deconstructionism' (etc.) and positivism have symmetrical, structurally identical, constitutive refusals and enabling prohibitions, and are, basically, each other's symptoms, the index of each other's blindness. In contrast, Žižek construes his own position as circum-venting all of the problems of both of these rivalrous (false) alter-natives. Thus, he can concede that positivist approaches do have a point – which is that 'one cannot postpone the *ontological* question *ad infinitum*' (Žižek 2001: 204) – but he can also concede that so do deconstructionist cultural studies approaches – namely that 'our grasping is always refracted, "mediated", by a decentred otherness'. He is able to concede both positions, and to diagnose them as symptomatic of a problem, because he has a 'different' model of ontology, reality, politics and truth. This is the politics of the 'act': the individual, voluntarist intervention that 'changes the very coordinates' of the situation, of *what* 'reality' and truth, etc., are deemed to be. As he explains: '*the very notion of what "reality" (or "actually to exist") means, of what "counts" as reality,* [always changes], so that we cannot simply presuppose a neutral external measure' (2001: 221–2).

This is how Žižek can know 'the truth': because the act invents it, 'changes the coordinates'. Needless to say, this is a very paradoxical theorisation. However, even as it causes problems, it also solves them. For it simultaneously obliges and also enables Žižek to negotiate fiendish paradoxes, stunning aporias and outrageous contradictions – very much like the cartoon character, Wile E. Coyote, running off a cliff, in *Road Runner* – but perfected. For, when the Coyote runs off a cliff in *Road Runner* and continues on and out through thin air, he continues as if on solid ground until such a time as he notices the absence of ground, and the impossibility of his situation, whereupon he looks forlornly and resignedly to camera, and falls. Žižek, however, will not fall. This is not because he doesn't know that he's running through thin air in the absence of any ground, but rather because he knows precisely that *this is all an act*. You don't *need* to look down from these dizzy heights. There is no ground, just as in the film, *The Matrix*, 'there is no spoon'. Žižek's ultimate faith is in the capacity of what he calls the act to change the coordinates of socio-political reality. To act is to intervene, to change the coordinates of, the notions of this 'reality' that is necessarily not 'the real', and as such, is ontopolitical, changeable. For Žižek, in order best to do this, one must first refuse to accept the apparently real and true coordinates offered by the dominant hegemonic order – even if that refusal seems to be an impossible act (in both senses of the word 'act' – both interventional event and performance). Everything about Žižek's conceptual edifice is an act. But he knows that, and knows that it doesn't make any difference that there is no ground. In *The Matrix*, Neo first needs to know that 'there is no spoon' in order to be able to bend the spoon.

There is therefore, in Žižek, a peculiar relation of theory and practice. Indeed, the most urgent practice for him seems to be hyper-theoretical: he is always in a hurry to get to what he calls the 'properly transcendental-hermeneutical level' (Žižek 2001: 221) of metadiscursive philosophising, diagnosing, and prognosticating. Žižek does this in order to affect the pose or position of as if being able to see and speak the truth about reality. So, one might well ask, what is 'ultimately' to be seen from these dizzy heights? Žižek recruits all of his preferred ingredients (from philosophy and psychoanalysis) and sets them to the task of elaborating his perspective on the political. The proper political perspective, according to Žižek, is pointedly *not* that of 'today's twin brothers of deconstructionist sophistry and New Age obscurantism' (1998: 1,007), nor is it 'capitulation itself' (2002: 308), or the position of 'the Third Way' ideologues, like Giddens or Beck. Such positions, according to him, *cannot see* the political truth and cannot act to change it because they are resigned to it and operate blindly within it. In this, the 'dominant' positions are all the same. As already seen, Žižek explicitly diagnoses a profound solidarity between deconstruction and cultural studies – invoking a beast that he calls 'postmodernist-' or 'deconstructionist cultural studies', an entity he deems to be at the vanguard of 'political correctness'. 'Political correctness', for him, is an aspect of neoliberalism, or sheer ideology, the 'obscene, disavowed' truth of which is a fundamental *intolerance* towards every *actual* or *significant* difference. This dominant neoliberal hegemony is intolerant of anything that cannot be recuperated by and for the banal, facile, saccharine, anodyne, and cynical position of the ideological ideals of apathetic consumption and complete identification with and capitulation to the market. For Žižek, therefore, anything that is not *explicitly and vociferously* opposed to capitalism is itself a promulgator of what he calls 'interpassivity' (2002: 170): chimerical (non-) politics that might change all sorts of *actual* things but without altering any *fundamental* thing – i.e., the 'fundamental horizon', systemic- or epistemic-architecture of capitalism itself. Thus, Žižek discerns equivalence and tacit solidarity between Derrida, Butler, Rorty, 'politically correct postmodern deconstructionist cultural studies', and political movements of virtually *any* kind, whether identity-, gender-, sex-, race- or ecology-based (2002: 308) – except vociferously anti-capitalist ones. Their fundamental solidarity, he claims, is a 'resigned and cynical' agreement that capitalism is 'the only game in town' (2000: 95). His point is that deconstruction, cultural studies, and so on, *cannot* see the changeless backdrop to their own activity: capitalism, the horizon *within which* all actually-existing politics drone on, whilst always avoiding '*the* problem itself'.

So, Žižek wants 'direct' political/interventional action. But in Žižek's paradigm, that which is commonly called 'direct action' is not *really* 'direct', because it is 'misdirected' – *unless* its target is 'systemic', or, in other words, unless it is rhetorico-politically organised as 'anti-capitalist' (2002: 308). The worst offender against politics and truth in all of this is said to be postmodernism, or the myth directly generated by 'the dynamic, rootless postindustrial society' (2001a: 11). The worst manifestation of this mythological misrecognition is what he interchangeably calls 'Western Buddhism' or 'Taoism' (2001a: 12, 13). These belief systems, he claims, 'perfectly fit' the *'fetishist* mode of ideology of our allegedly "post-ideological" era' (2001a: 13), as they enable 'you to participate fully in the frantic pace of the capitalist game while sustaining the perception that you are not really in it, that you are well aware how worthless this spectacle is' (2001a: 15). Against all of what he sees as sophistry and delusion, Žižek sees himself as authentically Hegelian, authentically Lacanian and authentically Marxian. This complex combination is why Žižek often seems so difficult to read or make sense of. However, through this putative complexity, what nevertheless remains crystal clear is that everything in Žižek is – ultimately, fundamentally, and precisely – overdetermined by a sedulous refusal to get over the most pessimistic moments in Adorno and Horkheimer. That is to say, Žižek's *entire* perspective is reducible to a bleak, resigned and pessimistic reading of 'The Culture Industry: Enlightenment as Mass Deception' (1972), plus a complex, ostensibly 'classical' tangle of Hegelian and Lacanian terms.

Needless to say, there are many problems with all of this, particularly in terms of this conception of political 'agency'. For, first one might note that Žižek's ensnarement in a hyper-Adornian, meta-Debordian, or ultra-Baudrillardian belief in the totality of the structuring, determining 'horizon' (of the capitalist system) makes him portray 'neoliberalism' as the total and universal backdrop against or within which things *appear* to change but fundamentally remain the same. This perspective, then, utterly contradicts the post-Marxist theory of hegemony. It also consigns 'neoliberalism' to function as a signifier of the limit of his thought, which prevents him from being able to treat 'neoliberalism' as a historically real, deliberately implemented geopolitical economic 'experiment' of ongoing, piecemeal, pragmatic, legislative violence. Ironically, however, the anti-globalisation movement(s) that he often feels inclined to ridicule can themselves quite easily construe neoliberalism as a project that is politically contestable (Kingsnorth 2003), rather than being the *fait accompli* it often appears to be for Žižek. As such, Žižek's 'politicised' perspective, then, actually appears to *renounce* politics, and to reject anything like a dialectical or material approach to history.[4] Indeed it seems to be exactly the kind of postmodern bricolage that he otherwise decries. And, just like his claims that the fundamental truth of sexuality does not consist in the encounter between two bodies, but rather in the imaginary fantasy of the lone masturbator (2001a: 24), so he seems to deem politics and political intervention to consist in a kind of sub-Derridean 'teleieopoetic' conjuration of and with spectres;[5] or rather, the mobilisation of signifiers against signifiers Thus, his entire interventional strategy consists in opposing 'anti-capitalism' (good) to 'capitalism' (bad).

Nevertheless, this is not actually the shortcoming within Žižek's conceptual architecture that it might at first appear to be. That is: it isn't something that Žižek hasn't noticed. It is rather Žižek's *wager*, Žižek's *decision*, Žižek's *act*. For, it is indeed the case that, with Žižek, 'everything is the opposite of what it seems'. Thus, in his paradigm, the contradictions don't matter, the aporias don't matter, even the facts don't matter. What matters is the conviction, the spirit, the belief, the name, the act. (Unfortunately, from any other kind of 'Marxist' perspective (and Žižek stakes a key claim in being thoroughly Marxist), this could be said to add up to Žižek not being able to grasp the objective tendencies of capitalism and 'class' or hegemonic struggle.)

Arguably, this accounts for the oscillation in Žižek between sometimes holding the view that academic words in themselves can equal political intervention (theory *equals* practice) and at other times viewing proper political intervention as being something that can only take place physically, out there, in the real world (theory *versus* practice). This oscillation relates to the 'act'. For Žižek, *anything, anywhere*, can be a political intervention, as long as it 'changes the coordinates', or alters the architecture of ontology, epistemology, and organisation. Thus, even the most academic or theoretical production can be a political intervention, for him, as long as it changes the 'structural principle of society' (2000: 93). Of course, this seems somewhat at odds with his simultaneous conviction that the only true or proper politics is class politics – a theme that he returns to repeatedly (unless, of course, it is only that 'working class' academics can intervene politically!). So there is a vacillation in Žižek between sometimes arguing that only class politics (qua universal anti-capitalist revolution) is politics proper, and at other times arguing that any individual's 'act' can be political. There appears to be no real way to reconcile these two contrary conceptions of political intervention, particularly insofar as, for Žižek, the authentic subjective act would be that of changing the coordinates by 'striking at oneself' during conflict with another, by conceding their point completely. For this would mean that the authentic political act of the working class would be to concede the neoliberalist point that there is indeed no class war any more, no class antagonism, and indeed, no class politics. (However, there is another possible reading of 'striking at the self' that can be mobilised in a much more pragmatic interventional strategy of inter-disciplinary articulation; which will be discussed in the concluding chapter.) Nevertheless, Žižek insists that class antagonism *is* the fundamental political antagonism (2000: 98), despite all of the pro-blems and contradictions that this would seem to usher in (Parker 2004). But he does so, presumably in order to try to affect the 'act' of 'changing the coordinates' of dominant political discourses:

> an authentic act is not simply external with regard to the hegemonic symbolic field disturbed by it: an act is an act only *with regard to* some symbolic field, as an intervention into it. That is to say: a symbolic field is always and by definition in itself 'decentred', structured around a central void/impossibility . . . and an act disturbs the symbolic field into which it intervenes not out of nowhere, but precisely *from the standpoint of this inherent impossibility, stumbling block, which is its hidden, disavowed structuring principle*. (2000: 125)

Žižek's discourse could be said, then, to doubly and duplicitously use and abuse 'logic', and to have determined that intervention simply equals shouting 'down with capitalism' as loudly as possible. His work is a postmodern 'bricolage'; a tendential deployment of 'logic' for rhetorico-political effect; a contribution to ideological phantasy masquerading as objectively revealing 'false consciousness'; and emi-nently traditional yet spectacular sophistry. As such, the effect of Žižek's work is perhaps an exemplary example of a 'power [that] can reproduce itself only . . . by relying on the obscene disavowed rules and practices that are in conflict with its public norms' (2000: 218).

However, this *perhaps* makes it nevertheless extremely worthwhile, in that, by virtue of the very problems themselves, discerning them might enable us, as Žižek puts it, to 'perceive the "repressed" potential of the observed constellation' (248). Similarly, perhaps Žižek is indeed right when he suggests that taking all such work 'at its (public) word, acting as if it really means what it explicitly says (and promises)' might be not only 'the most effective way of disturbing its smooth function-ing' (220), but also the way help it overcome its repetition compulsion. We will return to this in the final chapter.

In at least this regard (although there are very many more regards), Žižek's discourse is double. It theorises – but only so far – and then refuses to theorise further: in it, Lacan is (Hegelian and is) 'right',

Marx is (Hegelian and is) 'right', and Žižek has access to the true readings of these true positions. His theoretical ground is affirmed and thereafter asserted beyond question (a paradigm case of 'positing the presupposition', something he is fond of diagnosing in his examples). The complex theoretical apparatus and tone of intellectual certainty is affected in order to delight and 'persuade', indeed 'recruit', on the basis of a wager that his (Adornian) Marx is right, and that the only way to 'act' is to try to snap people out of false consciousness (in a *Matrix*- or satori-zen-like moment of insight and awakening) by purporting to show them the truth. Žižek views this political theory as radical, when in actual fact 'radical' means crude, reductive and simplistic, arguably even placing strict censorious limits on thought and analysis and closing down all possibilities for intellectual or conceptual development from the outset. Indeed, Žižek's discourse does succeed in being a kind of 'anti-cultural studies' (if not anti-capitalist) approach – but not for the reasons he himself would give, reasons which centre on cultural studies allegedly being ideological and intellectually and ethico-politically feeble. It is, rather, anti-cultural studies insofar as it is *closed* to the possibility of development, it is *certain* that it already knows the truth, refuses to *think* politics or indeed to *read* any object at all, preferring tub-thumping and mantra-reciting in a closed and private professional academic yet nevertheless mystificatory language. Žižek, uncannily like Rorty, is ultimately anti-intellectual. Furthermore, Žižek's work is not really 'intellectual' or 'analytical', but is rather well-meaning post-Marxist *assertion* premised on the hope of mobilising a traditional politics of recruitment and vassalage.

If Žižek's position is the Lacanian 'fool', the 'court jester' who nevertheless wants to be taken seriously; and if the Rorty/Butler position is that of the more or less conservative 'knave', then these positions are equally problematic, and in no sense do they appear to be alternatives. What makes them problematic is the difference between their avowed investments and their orientations – that is, the difference between what they claim to want, or would like to see happen, and what they are doing about it, when their orientation is evaluated in terms of that claim. Both Butler's position of well-meaning marginal-subject-centred left liberalism and Žižek's well-meaning, voluntarist subject-centred post-Marxism can be construed as equally unaware of or inattentive to the nature of their practices' articulation and disarticulation with other practices and relations. Ultimately, both (and all such positions) seem content to believe that, just because they want their work to be an intervention, therefore it must be. Arguably, there is a gap between their explicit investments and the effects of their own actions. In the next chapter, we will consider means of closing that gap. But first it is necessary to consider further the nature of this distance between *investment* and *orientation*.

Of course, all positions and orientations must have some investment which constitutes but also thereby skews or biases them from the outset. In this regard, perhaps both Butler and Žižek constitute good examples of the way that investments organise orientations and apperceptions (paradigms). As Butler – who declares an interest in seeking 'to galvanize a minority rejection of the status quo' – helpfully points out, the problems of investment, apperception, and orientation are perhaps intractable:

> like most subjects who set out with purposes in mind, and find ourselves achieving other aims than those we intend, it seems imperative to understand the limits on transparent self-understanding, especially when it comes to those identifications by which we are mobilized and which, frankly, we would rather not avow. Identification is unstable: it can be an unconscious effort to approximate an ideal which one consciously loathes, or to repudiate on an unconscious level an identification which one explicitly champions. It can thereby produce a bind of paralysis for those who cannot, for whatever reason, interrogate this region of their investments. It can become even more complicated, however, when the very political flag that one waves compels an identification and investment that lead one into a situation of being exploited or domesticated through regulation. For the question is not simply what an individual can figure out about his or her psyche and its investments (that would make clinical psychoanalysis into the endpoint of politics), but to investigate what kinds of identifications are made possible, are fostered and compelled, within a given political field, and how certain forms of instability are opened up within that political field by virtue of the process of identification itself. (Butler 2000: 149–50)

Of course, as invested as Butler appears to be in certain types of political identity, she maintains that 'it will not do to invoke a notion of the subject as the ground of agency, since the subject is itself produced through operations of power that delimit in advance what the aims and expanse of agency will be. It does not follow from this insight, however, that we are all always-already trapped, and that there is no point of resistance to regulation or to the form of subjection that regulation takes' (151). A key point of resistance can be found, as seen earlier, from the identification of (if not with) contingency. Therefore, in terms of this theorisation, it would seem to be important and perhaps even urgent 'to investigate what kinds of identifications are made possible, are fostered and compelled, within [this theoretical] field, and how certain forms of instability are opened up within that political field by virtue of the process of identification itself' – 'especially when it comes to those identifications by which [it is] mobilized and which, frankly, [it] would rather not avow'.

Investments and Institutions

Laclau discusses the inevitability and effects of the constitutive 'investment' (or 'cathexis') in his contributions to *Contingency, Hegemony, Universality* (2000; and also in Laclau 2005). Indeed, here, Laclau conceptualises any intellectual work as devolving ultimately on the matter of the appropriation of a previously established tradition. Any new 'development' – in theory or practice – will necessarily be something of a reiterative performance, the limits of which will be provisionally determined by the sedimented character of the discursive disciplinary formation 'within' which the appropriation takes place. This was discussed in Chapters 1 and 2, where it was argued that the new appropriates, inhabits with, uses and abuses, and performatively elaborates and reiterates the extant, within and as irreducibly institutional contexts. As Laclau sees it vis-à-vis the theorist or thinker, any 'appropriation of a theoretical approach will be more or less orthodox, depending on the degree of identification that one finds with the "appropriated" author' (or, indeed, institution). However, 'any intellectual intervention worth the name will be "heterodox"' (2000: 64–5).

Laclau himself puts his cards on the table – or rather, those 'cards' or investments the he would most like to 'avow' – when he states: 'I am a Gramscian, not a Baudrillardian' (75). Yet, given his own deconstructively informed argument that simple fidelity and simple repetition are impossible (because fidelity always becomes infidelity in some sense, and repetition is always actually reiteration, introducing alterity), then to be 'worth the name' also means that one cannot simply be 'in' or 'of' any paradigm, school, or orientation. One cannot simply be a faithful and true disciple (at least not *in theory*'). Rather, Laclau's point is that here one is always only in an inventive relationship, identifying and disidentifying by degrees, rather than simply, purely or 'authentically' repeating identity-with. Indeed, in deconstructive terms, such a conception of identity or identification as if it were changeless *repetition* is strictly incompatible with the Derridean logic of *reiteration*, whereby the 're' of the iteration both alters *and* differentiates, echoing the former 'same' *and* introducing alterity and difference (Derrida 1977; Spivak 1997): there is no simple repetition, but only complex reiteration. Indeed, according to Derrida (1996), there is no simple identity, but only the partial and provisional efforts and effects of ultimately failed relations of identification and disidentification. In deconstructive terms, perhaps this is never more clearly so than when engaged in literally and thoroughly *reading*. However, to reiterate, in deconstruction, 'reading' is no simple or 'mere' activity; rather, as Derrida makes clear in that important passage:

> in every operation we pursue together (a reading, an interpretation, the construction of a theoretical model, a rhetoric of an argumentation, the treatment of historical material, and even of mathematical formalization), . . . an institutional concept is at play, a type of contract signed, an image of the ideal seminar constructed, a *socius* implied, repeated or displaced, invented, transformed, menaced or destroyed. An institution – this is not merely a few walls or some outer structures surrounding, protecting, guaranteeing or restricting the freedom of our work; it is also and already the structure of our interpretation. If, then, it lays claim to any consequence, what is hastily called deconstruction *as such* is never a technical set of discursive procedures, still less a new hermeneutic method operating on archives or utterances in the shelter of a given and stable institution; it is also, and at the least, the taking of a position, in work itself, toward the politico-institutional structures that constitute and regulate our practice, our competences, and our performances. Precisely because deconstruction has never been concerned with the contents alone of meaning, it must not be separable from this politico-institutional problematic, and has to require a new questioning about responsibility, an inquiry that should no longer necessarily rely on codes inherited from politics or ethics. Which is why, though too political in the eyes of some, deconstruction can seem demobilizing in the eyes of those who recognize the political only with the help of prewar road signs. (Derrida 1992: 22–3)

As Laclau elaborates it, the appropriation of and/or subordination to an author/ity will be partially determined by and will partially determine an extant hegemonic structure, insofar as hegemony 'defines the very terrain in which a political relation is actually constituted' (Laclau 2000: 44). There are two directions to be pursued here. First, that of the problematic of one's relation to 'tradition' and 'identification with an author' signalled by Laclau, and as it is dealt with in his thought. Second, though, in the background of and underpinning this reading, there are the directions (that were only partially and obliquely mentioned by Butler) signalled by Derrida, which devolve on the fact that 'because deconstruction has never been concerned with the contents alone of meaning, it must not be separable from [the] politico-institutional problematic'. The politico-institutional problematic is something that comes into view when it is acknowledged that every reading, every decision, every orientation and every sense of responsibility relates to an 'institution'. Here 'institution' means both noun and verb, of course; as well as both something 'theoretical' or 'conceptual' ('institutional model') and something 'practical' or 'physical': 'An institution – this is not merely a few walls or some outer structures surrounding, protecting, guaranteeing or restricting the freedom of our work; it is also and already the structure of our interpretation'. Derridean deconstruction is all about the displacement of theory/practice schemas, wherever they try to establish themselves and work to orientate what might still nevertheless be (paradoxically perhaps) referred to as 'theory' and 'practice'. Indeed, Derrida is adamant that the 'strongest responsibility' for intellectual activity is that of seeking to make the political implications of this problematic 'as clear and thematic as possible'.

In the terms of Laclau's discussion, his argument has the effect of imputing to the proper name, or particularly to the investment in it, a peculiar status: attachment to proper names is both central and yet tagged-on (supplementary), in Laclau's thinking of worth and intervention. In other words, Laclau argues that proper names work as *'points de capiton'*, structuring discourses, or controlling the slippage of signification; that is, effectively enabling predication and signification; which he argues is a precondition of stabilising discursive predication and identity (Laclau and Mouffe 1985). So, what proper names 'mean' becomes relatively fixed, in and by other relations (relations that they themselves intervene in and help to 'fix'). For Laclau, therefore, attachment to a name as the metonymic expression of a politics has a double status. In terms of his own theorisation, such attachment is a contingent, perhaps even arbitrary, but nevertheless orientating investment – like a fixed point in a Rortyan 'final vocabulary': a point (de capiton) beyond which the identities invested in it will not want to go, or, in Žižekian terms, a point beyond which they cannot go – because, for Žižek, 'it is possible to resignify/displace the "symbolic substance" which predetermines my identity, but not totally to overhaul it, since a total exit would involve the psychotic loss of my symbolic identity' (Žižek 2000: 222). Thus, Laclau can theorise cathexis with names, symbols, etc., as being constitutive of contingent political identities. But this reveals his *own* claim of investment in a name ('I am a Gramscian') as a contingent anchor; a statement of ethical investment. This seems fine, but it also masquerades as a simple process, as if stepping out of the complex processes of the contingency of identification, naming and establishment within which it occurs. To enter into a Žižekian or Rortyan mode, Laclau's act of naming is an exemplary 'final' point, or point de capiton within Laclau's 'symbolic identity'.

Accordingly, it is important to examine the conceptual, orientative and ethico-political consequences of such 'cathexis'. For, Laclauian logic should seem to make *Laclau's* attachment to any name not only 'strictly speaking' impossible 'in itself', but also problematic in ethico-political ways. This is a problematic point of his post-Marxism, a post-Marxism which, in his theoretical development of it, 'logically' ceases to be 'Marxian' in any other way than through this contingent, supplementary attachment to or anchorage in the evocation of 'Gramscianism' (75). This seems to jar with the 'logical' dimension of post-Marxism. So it seems important to establish what work this contingent identification with a name *does* in this particular disciplinary production. It was of course in Laclau and Mouffe's (1985) reading of Gramsci that something crucial was 'discovered in' Gramsci. As is noted very early in *Hegemony and Socialist Strategy*:

> the expansion and determination of the social logic implicit in the concept of 'hegemony' – in a direction that goes far beyond Gramsci – will provide us with an *anchorage* from which contemporary social struggles are *thinkable* in their specificity, as well as permitting us to outline a new politics for the Left based upon the project of a radical democracy. (Laclau and Mouffe 1985: 3)

So, something in the work of Gramsci – or, rather, in 'the social logic implicit in the concept of "hegemony"' – anchors their project. Hence they understandably declare a debt to Gramsci's thought. However, it is not actually *Gramsci* that enables their post-Marxism, but rather the *deconstructive effects* of their own deconstructed notion of 'hegemony' (as it were, precisely when it becomes *unanchored from* Gramsci). So, even the exciting conceptual possibilities opened up by the concept of 'hegemony' do not actually necessitate any *attachment to* Gramsci. This does not 'logically' explain the attachment, investment or identification. However, the deconstructive logic of the work of the archive, the lineage, and the inheritance (Derrida 1995b) does help to explain Laclau's reason for staking this claim, over and above the rhetorical possibility/inevitability that 'Gramsci' here functions as a connotative guarantee that this political theory has impeccable Marxian and ('therefore') real political credentials, even though it may move 'in a direction that goes far beyond Gramsci'.

The explicit attachment to the Gramscian archive echoes Derrida's (1994) injunction that everyone should read and re-read Marx, interminably, for the 'teleieopoetic' reason (Derrida 1996) that, as Mowitt defines 'teleiopoesis': 'what we believe to have happened to us bears concretely on what we are prepared to do with ourselves both now and in the future, [and that] the formation of such a memory is inseparable from historical, and ultimately political, practice' (Mowitt 1992: 2). Laclau's persistent privileging of or reiteration of Gramscianism is, then, at once 'logical' *and* 'illogical': post-Marxism is deconstructed Gramscianism, so it comes from and wants to stay with Gramscianism, in an ethico-political sense; but it is no longer purely 'Gramscian' (as if such a purity were possible). Furthermore, therefore, in this name-checking of Gramsci, it is also possible to discern another under-acknowledgement of the more immediate 'debt' to deconstruction. The over-playing of the debt to the lineage of Gramsci shores up the rhetorico-political force of being primarily 'properly Marxist'. The deconstructive supplement which enabled post-Marxism is downplayed, and implicitly represented as being something that sits comfortably and unproblematically with 'Gramscianism', as in: post-Marxism is that which fully puts to work a deconstructive understanding of the Gramscian notion of hegemony and it is therefore both deconstructive *and* Marxist. In this sense, the proper name has a job to do. *Its job is to stabilise post-Marxism as an entity*; to rein-in the 'internally' interruptive and destabilising effects of a threatening auto-deconstruction; and to subordinate deconstruction to the proper task of deconstructing other things 'out there'. Post-Marxism uses and abuses deconstruction in order to institute itself.

However, according to the logic of hegemony that Laclau also professes, the attachment to the proper name also works as an instrument of 'domination' (2000: 47). This is all a question of 'a moment of *investment* which . . . redefines the terms of the relationship between what is and what *ought* to be' (81). His 'I am a Gramscian, not a Baudrillardian' (75) constitutes and governs (or, indeed, hegemonises) his perception and apperception (his paradigm):

A Gramscian is what Laclau knows he should be. This names the investment of which he is conscious that enables his sense of post-Marxism. With this, therefore, Laclau puts the brakes on how far deconstruction 'should' go: no matter what it might do, no matter what a deconstruction might teach, it remains the simple case, 'I am a Gramscian', and pointedly *not* a Baudrillardian. Herein can be discerned a certain – quite Žižekian – 'emptying' of Gramsci in order to identify with Gramsci; at the same time as it might be speculated that preference for Gramsci over Baudrillard may be metaphysically and not just historically/contingently overdetermined, given Gramsci's discursive status are being a 'properly engaged' kind of Marxist, rather than an 'irresponsible' thinker of the simulacrum – something that might of course be read as another variant of the workings of a metaphysical theory-versus-practice schema. In maintaining this *assertion*, Laclau seems very like Žižek.

This insistent reference perseveres despite the inevitability of Laclau's own transgression and heterodoxy in the face of 'Gramsci'. So, even though one may well question the logical status of this *point de capiton*, it would nevertheless *make no difference*. We might be able to demonstrate 'logically' that Laclau is not a Gramscian at all – and we might only refer to *anyone* else's different sense(s) of what it is to be a Gramscian to do so. Nevertheless, Laclau's investment *will* remain. The ever-open intertextuality of the Gramscian text enables contradictory appropriations of the name. It also 'impossibilises' the possibility of a unitary or universal agreement about what 'it' is, means and does (Peters 2001). But, here, for Laclau, that makes no difference. Accordingly, this investment is at odds with the logic it has in some sense enabled. The proper is impossible, yet strangely necessary. The debate about what proper Gramscianism might be, or proper Marxism, or whatever, will be a debate which contests and attempts to fix the surplus/absence of a fixed unitary meaning to any term or discourse (Chapter 2). Each competing or different instance stakes a claim in the name, and performs what it thinks that name properly necessitates or obliges. Put bluntly, Laclau's declared Gramscianism can only be what Judith Butler calls, in the same volume a *parodic performance*, according to (yet transgressing) his own terms (78).

The 'domination' of Laclau's declared investments by the signifier 'Gramsci' problematizes the deconstructive commitment to radical democracy *per se*. Indeed, John Protevi actually explicates a relation between deconstruction and democracy that, as it were, *logically bypasses* any need for a detour through Marxism at all (which is not the same as saying that reading the texts of Marx or Gramsci is not valuable), when he argues:

> What, then, does deconstruction do? It diagnoses and intervenes when the skewing *coup de force* at the institution of a body politic forces certain elements to bear the weight of the institution in force by forcing them into economically exploited, politically dominated and culturally marginalized positions. This exploitation, domination and marginalization is revealed in the concrete call for justice made by others forced into those positions . . . Deconstruction is justice, that is, 'deconstruction is already engaged by this infinite demand of justice'. Deconstruction also finds its 'force, its movement or its motivation' in the 'always unsatisfied appeal' to justice . . . We might want to say here that *democracy* is the future, the 'to come' of this transformation, intensifying itself to the point where instituted bodies that muffle or distort the calls of others are overflowed and reinscribed in other contexts. Deconstruction is democratic justice, responding to the calls from all others. (Protevi 2001: 68, 69, 70).

If 'Gramsci' – or indeed arguably *anything* other than the attachments to justice and to radicalising democracy – dominates Laclauian post-Marxism, then this in itself is problematic. For, regarding any 'domination' of and by *any* particular proper in the face of the question of radical democracy, John Mowitt argues that:

> It is a matter of inscribing within one's own position the possibility and necessity of a position which is obscured by what one opposes. Radical democracy ought to involve listening to those whose voices have been drowned out by the very voice of advocacy. Textual politics seek to frame the conditions under which this would be possible, and if the articulation of this politics requires that we hesitate suspiciously before the category of discourse, I believe the stakes warrant doing so. (Mowitt 1992: 221)

Post-Marxism should 'know' that it should conceive of itself as a repression of the impossibility that permeates it, and as such that it is contingent, non-necessary, and structurally incomplete. Moreover, in his approval of Butler's notion of parodic performance, Laclau must also be conceding that the elaboration of the theory of hegemony by/as post-Marxism is itself something of a parody. As a contingent articulation it mimes itself (what it thinks it should be) into itself, and only through un-avowed investments and identifications – investments and identifications that are less than conscious and that are identifications with and investment in institutions, their protocols, procedures and conventions, rather than simply with any named author.

In the sense of being both a theoretical paradigm and an institutionally located and practically orientative 'institution', post-Marxist discourse cannot but be subject to 'forces' or 'logics' that affect all institutions. And, of institutions, Derrida insists that:

> what we call an institution must sometimes remember what it *excludes* and selectively attempts to doom to being forgotten. The surface of its archive is then marked by what it keeps outside, expels, or does not tolerate. It takes the inverted shape of that which is rejected. It lets itself be delineated by the very thing that threatens it or that it feels to be a threat. In order to *identify itself*, to be what it is, to delimit itself and recognize itself in its own name, it must espouse the very outlines of its adversary, if I can put it thus. It must wear its adversary's features, even bear its name as a negative mark. And the excluded thing, whose traits are deeply engraved in the hollows of the archive, imprinted right on the institutional support or surface, can end up in turn becoming the subjectile that bears the memory of the institutional body. This is true for the founding violence of states and nations and the peoples it never fails to suppress or destroy. And this never takes place once and for all, but must necessarily continue or repeat itself according to diverse processes and rhythms. But this is also true, on an apparently more modest scale, of academic institutions, philosophy in particular. (Derrida 2002: 5)

The 'apparently . . . modest' deconstructive refusal of simple distinctions and demarcations between putative 'realms' (such as theory and practice, inside and outside, private and public, micro and macro, etc.) adds a dimension to all theory, such as performativity or hegemony, which is underdeveloped within post-Marxist discourse. Post-Marxism can clearly be said to require the supplementation of attention to themes such as identification, investment, institution, constitutive exclusion and violence, to a much more thoroughgoing extent than it has so far undertaken. To do so would promise to transform the character of post-Marxist discourse analysis to a perhaps unprecedented degree. Indeed, this is nothing less than the 'textual politics' challenge to post-Marxist discourse analysis. Should discourse analysis decline the challenge, the suspicion has to be that – to borrow Butler's words – they 'do not want to think too hard about what it is they are doing, what kind of discourse they are using; for if they think too hard about what it is they are doing, they fear that they will no longer do it' (Butler 2000: 265). In the terms of post-Marxist theory itself, this is most likely to be approached as being a matter of 'decision'.

Laclau contends that 'decisions are contingent displacements within contextual communitarian orders', which can only 'show their ver-isimilitude to people living inside those orders' (85). To take this present work as an example, Laclau's point here could be said to relate to the way that a decision, such as the one taken by this study, to read quite closely (and doubtless quite 'abusively', too) Laclau's own texts will only make sense (as if 'immediately', 'transparently', 'obviously' or 'directly') to people who are already part of the community of close reading invested in closely reading these texts. At this point, the problem of circularity and tautology of point and purpose arises again. However, what also arises is the point that within such community contexts, improper and even apparently abusive reading is in a sense obligatory and necessary, in order to preserve what Laclau calls the ethical dimension of the 'community'; by interrogating it, calling it into question, and apparently, or indeed effectively, trans-gressively abusing the community. As such, any affront constituted by this reading may only be the justifiable affront of suggesting that all of post-Marxism's talk of ethics and the ethical may well only amount to 'empty symbols' – empty symbols used by a community in the effort to (re)produce itself, through symbols of itself (85). Indeed, this must precisely be the case, for Laclau, given that he argues that:

> If the ethical moment is essentially linked to the presence of empty symbols in the community, the community requires the constant production of those symbols in order for an ethical life to be possible. If the community, on top of that, is to be a democratic one, everything turns around the possibility of keeping always open and ultimately undecided the moment of articulation between the particularity of the normative order and the universality of the ethical moment. (85)

Accordingly, perhaps the most worthwhile thing that could be done for the impossible society or community of post-Marxism is to *undecide* it, to challenge it, to accuse it, and to rattle its attempts at stability: 'The only democratic society is one which permanently shows the contingency of its own foundations – in our terms, perma-nently keeps open the gap between the ethical moment and the normative order' (86), argues Laclau. In the next chapter, a strategy of *interdisciplinary* intervention will be developed from this insight. But first, there are some final observations to be made about Laclauian intervention.

For, having now just reiterated all of these ethical declarations and prescriptions, another 'secondary' but irreducibly central dimension of Laclau's own discourse should now be turned to: namely, the *way* he writes. This was addressed above in terms of the subscription to 'logic', of course. And it is clear that it is intricately imbricated in questions of performance, authority, and institutional disciplinary conventions. But, for a deconstructively informed thinking and writing, there are irreducibly ethical and political factors relating to style, presentation, and the *ways* in which one discourses, factors that post-Marxism tends to overlook. Nevertheless, they have political implications.

Derrida famously argued that one must always attend to the 'ethics of discourse' (1977), and, moreover, that 'everything is summoned from an intonation' (1998: 48). It is in this sense that Laclau's mode of address, his discourse, goes on to betray another 'gap', between declared and avowed ethical injunctions and the normative order. This can be seen in Laclau's address/redress to Butler (183–6), where he uses some surprisingly hostile metaphors as well as adopting a problematically supercilious or sententious tone. So, even though Laclau may not be 'wrong' when, for example, he characteristically divides Butler's critique of his arguments into what he calls 'three kinds of statements', what is nevertheless problematic is the nature of the divisions when considered either in terms of a Derridean quest for an ethics of discourse of the lesser violence, or when considered in terms of Laclau's own theorisation of the limitations and impossibilities of any representation. That is, Laclau denounces statements of Butler's that he claims 'misrepresent what I am saying', statements 'which omit a vital point of my argument', and 'those which make critical claims that contradict one another' (188). The problem with this denunciation arises in the face of Laclau's own theorisation of 'representation' – specifically his consistent arguments about the *impossibility* of a true or – more relevant here, a *neutral* – representation, and (because representation is constitutively limited and partial or tendentious), the constitutivity of 'misrepresentation'. If one could 'correctly' represent another's representations, this would equal a mechanical, slavish repetition of the very sort that Laclau not only claims he disapproves but also deems to be constitutively impossible. Indeed, what should be recalled here is that, according to his own terms, to engage with Laclau in anything other than a 'heterodox' manner would not be an engagement 'worth the name'. The question is: what does Laclau *expect*, and what does he *want* from Butler's – or anyone's – engagement with his work? Despite agreeing with Butler that 'translation' is necessary to politics, and despite claiming to be against limiting discursive 'tropoi' (Laclau 1999: 102–3; 2000: 78), Laclau nevertheless *actually* refuses any other terms than his own.

In addition to such observations, Laclau's very metaphorics warrant attention, too, not least because, as Stuart Hall reminds us, 'metaphors are serious things' because 'they affect one's practice' (Hall 1996: 268). In this sense, both the tone and the implied ideals of his response to Butler should be observed: 'First, Butler introduces her usual war machines – the "cultural" and the "social" – without the slightest attempt at defining their meanings, so it is impossible to understand what she is talking about except through some conjecture' (188). Now, the fact that, for Laclau, Butler's concepts and arguments are 'weapons' and 'war machines' implies that thinks he is under attack. To defend himself, he counterattacks by insisting on the importance of literal or explicit precision. Quite what that would be, when the literal 'is the first of all metaphors' (Laclau and Mouffe 1985: 111) must remain something of a 'conjecture'.

In fact, what Laclau regularly does in this encounter with Butler is twofold (and in this regard his encounter with Butler is exemplary of his treatment of all others). First, he takes *any* different terminology to his own and declines to accept it, often refusing to countenance that there are any similarities, affinities or compatibilities with his own, and deeming the other to be incorrect. This is, in fact, something like a general rule of engagement for Laclau. It is his hegemonic and hegemonising strategy. The second rule of engagement is to subordinate the other to his own meaning, drawing the other's discourse into his own, redrawing the other in terms of his own. This too is hegemonising. (The same process can also be seen to be at work in his preface to Žižek's *The Sublime Object of Ideology* (1989), wherein he frames the disagreements between himself and Žižek as being things that must ultimately tend towards consensus, but moreover, a consensus in which the other comes round to accepting Laclau's rectitude (Laclau 1989: xi).) When Laclau speaks of 'the aspect of her approach to which I feel closer, and which makes me think that in the end our political positions are not really so far apart, whatever the differences in our theoretical grounding of them' (192) – namely, their implicit agreement that 'there is no universality which is not a hegemonic universality' (193) – one can see that even in affiliating, Laclau clearly draws Butler's terminology into line with his own meaning (and even then it seems that he must point out some more errors of reading on her part). This whole movement is an exemplary performance of what Laclau thinks hegemony and hegemonising is and does in general. Indeed, it is regularly reflected as a strategy in his own work. To discern his hegemonising of Butler, then, is also to discern more fully his understanding of what hegemony is, does, and the way it works. It is also to add fuel to the fire of the Mowittian critique of the discourse paradigm as reductive, exclusionary and even anti-democratic (see Chapters 1 and 2); a critique which was also evidenced in the reading of Laclauian 'logic', above. Accordingly, there is an awful lot taking place in a passage like this:

> one concept which, in my terminology, is particularly close to her notion of 'translation' [is] that of 'equivalence'. She even identifies the notion of 'difference' in my work with that of 'exclusion' or 'antagonism', which is clearly incorrect, for in my approach, 'difference' means a *positive* identity, while all antagonistic reordering of the political space is linked to the category of equivalence. I have tried to distinguish, in the logics constitutive of the social, two kinds of operation: the logic of difference, which institutes *particular* locations within the social spectrum; and the logic of equivalence, which 'universalizes' a certain particularity in the basis of its substitutability with an indefinite number of other particularities – the distinction broadly corresponds, in linguistics, to that of relations of combination and substitution, or between the syntagmatic and the paradigmatic poles. In a populist discourse, for instance, the social space tends to be dichotomized around two syntagmatic positions and the ensemble of identities weaken their differential characters by establishing between themselves an equivalential relation of substitution, while an institutional discourse multiplies the differential-syntagmatic positions and, as a result, reduces the equivalential movements that are possible within a certain social formation. (193–4)

In this passage, at least two things deserve emphasis. Both relate in different ways to two dimensions of this political discourse. The first is, perhaps obviously, that Laclau *excludes* Butler's different notion of difference and antagonism. Butler's notion of difference and antagonism, as seen earlier, is perhaps very 'subjectivist', in its emphasis on social antagonisms as arising simply because subjects variously bump up against each other in different 'antagonistic' ways (31). Laclau counters this subjectivism, first by reiterating the tenets of his own theory (political antagonism relates to the universalization of a particularity and not to different particularities as such) and then, implicitly, by evoking the importance of a mediating instance – *either* 'populist discourse' *or* 'institutional discourse'.

Focusing on the question of differing conceptions of difference and difference's relation (or not) to antagonism is, inevitably, a stock in-house polemic of post-Marxist discourse analysis. But adjudicating between them here is of less significance in this context than pointing out the ramifications of what Laclau says (as well as of the *way* that he says it) for the theorisation of 'effective' politics vis-à-vis institutional practices such as those of academia. For, Laclau's statements can be read as meaning that *institutional* academic protocols are not related to or suited to effective *political* antagonistic polemics and, hence, in Laclau's terms, 'institutional discourse' is not particularly politically efficacious, because the institutionalisation of a discipline constrains it to reducing equivalential movements. Thus, in a certain respect, this suggests that 'the best' political movements are those of a *greater violence*, of greater reductivity and simplification (such as those – allegedly – of 'populist' discourses; or maybe like, say, Žižek's or Rorty's reductive and simplified arguments), insofar as they entail the exclusion of listening to, or even hearing and respecting the other. The ('populist', reductive: 'practical') increase of equivalential universalization and oppositional reductivity seems directly proportional to political effectivity. As such, and quite contrary both to Derrida's conviction about deconstruction being the search for the lesser violence and Laclau's purported affiliation to an ethico-political orientation of radical democracy, the politics Laclau nevertheless here subscribes to, or implicitly advocates, are not those of the lesser violence, but are rather those of greater violence, insofar as this schema relates radical political force with disrespect for and reduction of the other. (As will be argued in the final chapter, it is nevertheless possible to theorise and implement a less violent intervention from the same premises.)

At the same time, Laclau's evaluation of the political status of 'institutional discourses' is that they are not political, because of their multiplication 'of the differential-syntagmatic positions', which reduce 'the equivalential movements that are possible within a certain social formation'. So, Laclau's definition of the political *is* populist discourse (Laclau 2005), and arguably this paradigm cannot think the political outside of a dichotomous space of equivalences. What can be seen in Laclau's argument, then, is a double movement: on the one hand, the hegemonisation of Butler's thought; on the other, the removal of 'institutional discourses', like this very one, from the 'terrain' of the political. The theory versus practice schema returns with a vengeance here to skew post-Marxism away from the deconstructive textual-institutional political paradigm. This is ironic because the central category of the theory of hegemony – *articulation* – can be deployed to repoliticize institutional space, not through violent reductivity, but rather through the intimate over-fidelity of deconstructive 'reading'.

The return of this schema exacts a heavy toll, because, ironically, it ultimately means that within the post-Marxist paradigm there would seem to be no other choice available but that of adopting either a Žižekian strategy of polemical reductivity and tub-thumping, or a Butlerian or Rortyan strategy, entailing the belief that 'a critical intellectual' should (banally) 'use the very terms that she subjects to criticism, accepting the pre-theoretical force of their deployment in contexts where they are urgently needed' (Butler 2000: 159), believing that journalistic public debate somehow *simply does* connect, impact, and make a calculable difference, in proper (external) political contexts out there, and that this thereby constitutes the be-all and end-all of responsible political intervention. Within the post-Marxist paradigm, such would seem to be the best conceivable approaches for politicised intellectuals – to try to increase the equivalential movements. In more than one way, then, the logic of hegemonic politics that is 'rationally' delineated or identified by post-Marxism is in tension with its explicitly avowed ethico-political 'preferences'. This, perhaps, names what Slavoj Žižek would call one key 'obscene underbelly' of the theory that, in the case of Laclau, wants to champion both 'Gramsci' and 'radical democratic politics': it does so in the face of 'knowing' that the most effective politics are the anti-democratic politics of the greater violence – the monstrous double of deconstruction; the politics not of listening to or being open to the other, but excluding all others. The issues that such a possible conclusion opens out onto demand attention. This is because intervention in post-Marxism overlooks the reserves of its own central category, *articulation*. Thus, to echo Laclau and Mouffe (1985: 3), it is possible – indeed necessary – to develop the notion of articulation in a direction that goes far beyond the way the term is conventionally understood.

Notes

1. It is quite unusual for thinkers to settle for *entirely* valuing one end of the binary at the expense *entirely* rejecting the other – *either* theory *or* practice; or, in the terms that Robert J. C. Young says have structured the debate on knowledge for at least two centuries, of valuing either 'useless' or 'useful' knowledge (1992: 99). Young finds that even in the arguments of extreme cases, such as Adam Smith's thinking on what kind of knowledge is to

be valued (*useful*, of course – a thinking that allegedly strongly influenced Margaret Thatcher (112–13)), the rejected or subordinated element nevertheless serves a supplementary function and must remain: in Adam Smith, Young points out, a measure of 'useless' 'cultural' education has the economic benefit of preventing the workers from falling into unmanageable superstition or dangerous barbarism, for instance, and so cannot be eradicated from even an avowedly use-orientated paradigm (121). Young's argument is that debates on the university, on the status and role of knowledge and intellectual activity, have transformed and swung quite dramatically for the last two hundred years or so, but always within the discursive limits set by a binary between the 'useless' (non-utilitarian) and the 'useful' (utilitarian).

2. Godzich reminds us that 'presently we tend to use the term ['theory'] to mean a system of concepts that aims to give a global explanation to an area of knowledge, and we oppose it to praxis by virtue of the fact that it is a form of speculative knowledge' (Godzich 1987: xiii), but that this is a recent opposition, compared to 'the ancient relation between *aesthesis* and *theoria*' (xvii). Nevertheless, 'the act of looking at, of surveying, designated by *theorein* does not designate a private act carried out by a cogitating philosopher but a very public one with important social consequences . . . Only the theoretically attested event could be treated as a fact. The institutional nature of this certification ought not to escape us, as well as its social inscription' (xiv). The constitutive problematic of any theoria, argues Godzich, is that it must use *language*, and construct the reliability of its own claims. This causes problems that should be clear from our present perspective (xvi–ii). Ultimately, however, 'The problematic status of praxis in contemporary thought derives in great part from this situation. Conceived of in relation to theory, praxis is subject to the latter, and when the latter runs into problems, praxis appears as arbitrary or wilful . . . It is incumbent upon us now to deal with praxis, though it becomes rapidly clear that our old ways of dealing with it, beholden as they were to the supremacy of theory and the autonomy of *aesthesis*, will not do. Praxis thus stands as a rather mysterious entity presently, the figure of the agency (*Handlung*) that we thought we had lost when we secularized but that now returns without the godhead that adorned it, as the figure of history' (xvii). See also Chapter 1, above.

3. As Butler represents it, 'Identification is unstable: it can be an unconscious effort to approximate an ideal which one consciously loathes, or to repudiate on an unconscious level an identification which one explicitly champions'. However, she suggests – as if this were some kind of a *solution* – that 'psychoanalysis' is therefore crucial to cultural-political analysis, because it can enable analysts to 'interrogate this region of their investments'. There is however a big problem with this; which is that psychoanalysis simply does *not* help to clarify, simplify, or decide things. For the first question would be: *which* psychoanalysis (the very question Butler initially raises (6)); then, that of which way to represent, construe, and construct any scene; how to select what is significant and how to interpret this; and so on. In short, therefore, the issue remains textual, contingent and political. Wheeling in psychoanalysis as if it amounts to some kind of saviour actually solves nothing, and in fact merely defers the unavoidable task of referring everything back, once again, to the question of knowledge itself – to the universal fact that the precondition of *any* formal knowledge (18) is abstraction: the inevitable production-construction of a fiction masquerading as the actual.

4. John Mowitt observes that 'one finds [in Žižek's Lacanianism] a clear repudiation of something like the method of historical materialism as a way to get at the affiliation between capitalism and psychoanalysis', and goes on to note that '[a]lthough Žižek does acknowledge the historical specificity of capitalism – his whole account of fetishism hinges on the distinction between feudalism and capitalism – the homological orientation of his discussion leads one to assume either that psychoanalysis is essentially a derivative hermeneutic or that it is foundational in a way that makes its commitment to historicity quite difficult to assess' (Mowitt 2002: 206).

5. The allusions here are to the Derridean themes that Žižek would seem to reject. For 'teleiopoiesis' see Derrida (1997). For 'conjuration' and 'spectres' see Derrida (1994).

Four – Post-Marxist Cultural Studies' Theory, Politics and Intervention

Philosophers have hitherto only interpreted the world in various ways; the point is to change it.

(Karl Marx 1845)

What remains still to be conquered is the repetition compulsion.

(Jacques Derrida 1998a: 22)

Relations and Effects

Stuart Hall deems 'the discursive metaphor' with which this book has been concerned, and which is central to post-Marxist discourse theory and cultural studies, to be so 'extraordinarily rich' as to entail 'massive political consequences'. Indeed, he ventures, 'if I had to put my finger on the one thing which constitutes the theoretical revolution of our time, I think that it lies in that metaphor' (Hall 1996d: 145). At a stroke, then, post-Marxism and cultural studies are articulated (at least theoretically, or metaphorically), given that this paradigmatic 'metaphor' is so central to them both. However, Hall's enthusiastic evocation of 'the theoretical revolution of our time' and the 'massive political consequences' of this metaphor begs several questions. It seems to involve a mismatch of concepts, or a dissymmetry. For, how can a *metaphor* have massive *political* consequences? What is *revolutionary* about a *theoretical* revolution? And, to add the question begged by my own articulation of post-Marxism and cultural studies, what is the precise nature of their articulation?

These questions ought to be approached sequentially. This is because what underpins Hall's reasoning is the by now familiar rationale (reiterated and examined in various ways throughout this book) that 'metaphors are serious things', because 'they affect one's practice' (Hall 1996: 268). All orientations and practices are under-pinned by some form of theory or organising metaphorics, however tacit or unacknowledged. When it comes to intellectualised constructs like 'discourse' as it functions in these academic contexts, Gayatri Spivak's term 'concept-metaphor' helps to remind us that the notion in question is neither simply conceptual, absolutely necessary or essen-tial, nor free from metaphor. But nor is it simply metaphorical. Rather it is 'neither and both', a concept-metaphor which exerts troping, structuring and guiding effects on the orientations organised by it. In this sense, then, the adoption in cultural and political studies of the concept-metaphor of 'discourse' signals a paradigm change in those fields – an 'internal' theoretical revolution. But, in what way could a theoretical revolution entail *political* consequences? The pragmatist or traditional political thinker may contend that a merely intellectual theoretical revolution organised by a new metaphorics is unlikely to be of consequence to practical politics and that Hall's interest in an academic 'theoretical revolution' could be taken as an overestimation of the political consequentiality of academic work. We saw this position exemplified by Rorty, in the previous chapter. In other words, what are the grounds for contending that the (academic) discursive metaphor holds 'massive political consequences'?

The keystone of the contention is that 'discourse', when understood in Hall's sense, sweeps away the straightforward distinction between, say, academic and political. In other words, discourse recasts realms previously held to be distinct, showing them instead to be articulated – both contiguous and stitched together. Thus, any 'academic versus political' or 'theoretical versus practical' type of perspective – any proposition of necessarily and strictly demarcated realms – is precisely the sort of thing that the metaphor of discourse should actually transform. This is because the notion of discourse effectively decon-structs such putative boundaries and shows that demarcations, realms and contexts are not simply distinct or separate, but abut, leach into each other, and are diversely and dynamically interconnected and interimplicated. In a sea of discourses among discourses, institutions themselves are not simply unitary, free or unrelated. Rather, all institutions and discourses are complexly ensnared, imbricated or reticulated within, and articulated to yet other institutions and dis-courses. Thus, the discourse metaphor and its ensuing paradigm asserts the fundamental complexity and textile-like interimplication of institutions, the acts within and between them, and other contexts, sites and scenes. In other words, facile schemas proposing supposedly discrete locations and agencies, like the 'inside' (of the university) versus the 'outside' (of the 'real' world), or theory versus practice are shown to be missing a dimension: the dimension of articulation, or the unavoidability and complexity of relation. Consequently, the chain of dominoes that is set up to fall down with the arrival of discourse begins, theoretically-speaking, with the inception, adoption or development of the concept-metaphor in the institution, an institution that is itself reorientated in response to the metaphor it now uses (it starts to see things otherwise, and to act differently: a 'theoretical revolution'), a reorientation which cannot but impact upon the other scenes and institutions with which it is articulated or variously connected – at least *in theory*.

This is the logic of discourse. The image is one of a complex system of links, knock on effects, reaction formations, transformative encounters, relays, contagions and mutations, structured in dominance, but fundamentally contingent (See Chapter 1). Yet does this mean that such a theoretical revolution will *necessarily* have massive political consequences? What are its knock-on effects? As we have seen, Hall has always been concerned that the *way* the post-Marxists use the notions of discourse and articulation seems to suggest that they think that 'there is no reason why anything is or isn't potentially articulatable with anything' (Hall 1996d: 146) – or, in other words, as if they think that just anything can have an effect on anything else. That is why Hall mistrusts post-Marxist discourse theory, because its 'critique of reductionism has apparently resulted in the notion of society as a totally open discursive field' (Hall 1996d: 146). In this, he expresses a worry that has been formulated by others about Laclau and Mouffe's approach (many of which are included in Sim 1998). All such concerns are versions of the one identified by Hindess and Hirst that was discussed in the prior chapter: namely, that in theoretical production it can all too easily be the case that 'concepts are deployed in ordered successions' in order to produce the *effect* of analysis and apparent solutions, although too often 'this order is the order created *by the practice of theoretical work itself*: it is guaranteed by no necessary "logic" or "dialectic" nor by any necessary mechanism of correspondence with the real itself' (Hindess and Hirst, quoted in Spivak 1999: 316). In other words, does discourse really propose that anything is 'potentially articulatable with anything', which Hall thinks is so preposterous? The answer is yes and no – it all depends on the sedimented institutional relations of a context. Furthermore, despite

Hall's criticisms of the openness allegedly implied by discourse, it is actually only in terms of a discourse paradigm that his assertion of the political consequentiality of a theoretical revolution can properly make sense. Hall's caveat is simply that we must pay attention to the matter of the institutional context. This is what he thinks Laclau and Mouffe's approach overlooks.

In a defence of his retheorisation of culture, politics and society as discourse, Laclau (1996) argues that the idea that discourse theory asserts that anything can be potentially articulatable with anything else is at once 'logically' correct but nevertheless actually incorrect. For, he argues, the theory of discourse and articulation does not propose that 'everything that is logically possible [will become] automatically, an actual political possibility'. On the contrary, he explains, whilst there is no theoretical reason why any conceivable connections and transformations could not become an actual possibility, 'there are inchoated possibilities which are going to be blocked, not because of any logical restriction, but as a result of the historical contexts in which the representative institutions operate' (1996: 50). Accordingly, the post-Marxist theory of discourse asserts that society is not and will never be 'a totally open discursive field' precisely because of the limiting effects of the operation of established institutions in particular historical contexts.

What should be isolated in all of this is the argument that the prime movers – or indeed, often, the prime blockers, limiters or resisters – of political contexts are 'institutions'. This point is crucial to my argument. For it means that in order to be other than merely metaphorical, in order to be analytical rather than descriptive, the theory of discourse and the practice of discourse analysis must necessarily focus upon the workings and interrelations of these crucial social and political forces, called 'institutions'. Of course, many may contend that this has already been done, for a long time, and that precisely such a focus – the analysis of the political and social force and consequences of institutions – is already central to sociological, social and political studies of all orders, and that accordingly the means of engaging with institutions in culture, society and politics are already well established. Perhaps post-Marxism need only become more sociological or empirical? However, Laclau has consistently interrogated and rejected all approaches that he calls classical, orthodox, positive, positivist, empirical or empiricist. Laclau's argument is that empiricist approaches are unconvincing because they are logically mistaken (skewed by a 'referential' thinking – see Chapter 1), or that is, *precisely because they are empiricist*. In other words, it is the case that post-Marxism essentially rejects on principle, or at least strenuously critiques and deconstructs, all but broadly deconstructive approaches. Remember that the deconstruction of referential and empirically descriptive conceptions of political agency was central to the move from 'orthodox' Marxism to post-Marxism in the first place (Chapter 1). It is synonymous and simultaneous with the development of the concept-metaphor of discourse. So, given the question of how to engage with the specificities of institution, and given the centrality of deconstruction to post-Marxism, then, 'logically', the only way for post-Marxism to approach institutions is via what is often called the 'detour' of deconstruction. It is a 'detour' because it is apparently not 'direct'. However, the argument here has been that it is necessary to approach anything with one eye on the question of the (institutional) paradigm, which means that the apparent 'detour' is not at all a digression.

'Discourse', the paradigm-revolutionising metaphor of post-Marxism and cultural studies, arrives in the wake of and owing to a deconstruction of traditional approaches to culture and politics. Therefore, deconstruction surely constitutes the most appropriate approach, the best way for post-Marxism and cultural studies to engage with institution and institutions. At this point it may be worth referring the reader back to the Preface. For, as has been argued from the very first line of this book, Derridean deconstruction (what Mowitt calls 'the textual approach') is to be construed as precisely an engagement with the political effects of institution. The title of Samuel Weber's book *Institution and Interpretation* (1987) encapsulates its enabling insight: deconstruction homes-in on the important relationship between institutions and interpretations, and lays bare its political implications. Derrida himself emphatically makes it plain: *'Deconstruction is an institutional practice for which the concept of the institution remains a problem'* (Derrida 2002: 53). In my Preface, Derrida's (1992) exploration of the topic of 'university responsibility' was shown to be bound up with the ethics and politics of acts of institution – instituting, establishing: a problematic of reading/rewriting. This, for Derrida, is an irreducibly and fundamentally *textual* matter. As he argues unequivocally, 'the interpretation of [anything] is only produced by simultaneously proposing an institutional model, either by consolidating an existing one that enables the interpretation, or by constituting a new model to accord with it'. Accordingly, all interpretation entails that the interpreter 'assume one or another institutional form'. 'This', Derrida adds, 'is the law of the text in general' (Derrida 1992: 21–2). Deconstructive readings focus on this, and seek out the political implication. This, argues John Mowitt, is something quite different from a 'discourse approach', which does not foreground the problematic of reading *as a problematic*, and moreover all too happily assumes an uninterrogated institutional form, and does not look for the political implication of this.

So, deconstruction proposes a reciprocal relation between 'text' (or way of reading a text) and 'institution'. It is not simply a hermeneutic or straightforwardly interpretive operation because, as Derrida reminds us, deconstruction is not solely concerned with the 'contents' of meaning, but rather with the contextual/institutional constitution of those 'contents'. As we have seen, John Mowitt calls the hermeneutic entity, continuum, or field 'produced' by a discipline or a paradigm the 'disciplinary object'. Thus, whilst disciplinary objects may not even be real (they may be utterly misconstrued or interminably debatable), they nevertheless have effects – first and foremost, of course, on the discipline that proposes and is organised by them. Moving from this insight, Mowitt goes on to argue that the effect of the post-Marxist discourse paradigm on cultural studies amounts to a simplification of the (both logically and historically prior) textual approach, and to something of an inoculation (or 'disciplining') of the politicisation that an avowedly textual/deconstructive (antidisciplinary or anti-disciplining) approach affords.

This is because the notion of discourse so clearly invites an externally-looking and macro-political perspective: it offers a fertile way of talking about the contingent processes of the world. However, Mowitt reminds us, this is a move that is at once enabled by deconstruction (it views the world as text-like) but that also amounts to a move away from a very important aspect of deconstruction; namely, a uniquely political 'institutional' focus (the focus on textual construction as institutional). For, in post-Marxist theory, the adoption of the disciplinary object of discourse precipitates a rush to the macro-political perspective. This move to the 'macro' is justified and enabled by an acceptance of the broadly deconstructive claim of the consequential and politically salient relation between text, interpretation, and ('its') institution; or indeed, between what passes for knowledge, accordingly what proper or legitimate practice, approach and orientation are deemed to be, and mode of organisation. But post-Marxism rushes to the macro on the basis of but also at the cost of what might schematically be called the 'micro-political' perspective of the textual approach of deconstruction. In other words: if

'*Deconstruction is an institutional practice for which the concept of the institution remains a problem*', then the discourse of post-Marxism does not resist and actually facilitates *the forgetting of the political problematic of the institution.*

This is the same as saying that post-Marxist discourse theory does not adequately theorise the politics of its own institution. The discourse approach certainly happily takes *other* institutions, agencies, movements, formations and contexts as its object of study. But it does so without deconstructing its own position. The discourse approach to politics and scholarship of post-Marxism directs its deconstructive insights externally, using deconstruction in the analysis of macro-political phenomena, 'out there'. To reiterate Mowitt, this can unwittingly lead to a reduction in theoretical purview wherein the objects 'seen' by the academic gaze are treated as if they straightforwardly present themselves to the academic's consciousness, without the constitutive intervention of the theoretical paradigm or perspective itself. But, he argues, this cannot be so. Mowitt follows the Derridean argument, as we saw in Chapters 1 and 2, to argue that such a view is naïve. I have tried to show that this naïve view – wherein the scholar is somehow the immediate viewer of the transparently objective world – is also impossible in the terms of the post-Marxist paradigm itself (although this seems rarely considered). Objects and discourses do *not* 'present themselves' *as such*. What Rancière calls the partition of the sensible is contingent; so much so that even ontology is, strictly speaking, ontopolitical. The inevitability of contingency, construction, mediation, and indeed what Žižek calls 'anamorphosis', in perception/interpretation is fundamental to post-Marxist discourse theory. Nevertheless, the orientation of discourse analysis amounts to an approach which at once relies upon and also simplifies the theory of the text, and along the way comes to overlook the institution as a theoretical and political problematic. As such, discourse skews the orientation away from a complex engagement with the question of university responsibility that, I have argued, is fundamental to – even definitive of – cultural studies, as a 'project' rather than a discipline.

This can be restated recalling the terms of John Mowitt's vital argument: post-Marxism, and its use of discourse, is *disciplinary*; whereas an impetus and orientation of both the textual approach of deconstruction and cultural studies can be characterised as *anti-disciplinary*. This is the difference between 'seeing' objects of study 'out there' and consequently studying them in traditional (panoptical) manner, as is the case in discourse analysis; versus problematising the constitution, production and circulation of 'knowledge' *per se*, by drawing attention to its contingent institutional and theoretical frames, and exploring the question of their ethico-political implication. This institutional textual perspective is largely absent from post-Marxism. Instead, the discourse approach proceeds in what might be termed the politically presumptuous and quite possibly ineffectual manner of holding forth on this or that subject 'out there', as if one's responsibilities had been carried out by the act of discussing this or that topic. Now, my argument is not that one should *not* analyse, explore and discuss macropolitical topics and themes. Rather, it is first of all that this activity in itself does not necessarily have the desired political consequences, and does not necessarily constitute an intervention. Furthermore (as discussed in the preceding chapters), simple subscription to such a procedure actually stakes a claim in a problematically journalistic notion of politics, academia, and intervention – what I called in Chapter 2 a soap-box conception of politics. Against this, this work has sought to emphasise the complexity of politics, the undecidability of causality; a complexity that the textual approach of deconstruction does much to elucidate in its focus on institution and interpretation, but with which post-Marxism seems uninterested.

The reason I have insisted on this difference is quite simply because an argument does not necessarily make any difference to anything. As McQuillan points out, it is very easy – too easy – to call for change, and all too many academic and intellectual works are organised merely *as* calls for change, 'as if the call itself changed anything' (McQuillan 2001: 120). But, a call for change does not necessarily change anything. This elementary observation really must be remembered above all else if change is indeed part of the aspiration of cultural studies or post-Marxism – if, in short, they aspire to be anything other than disciplines. What this means is that when it comes to academic work, on any subject, with the aim of intervention, what is at least as important as the particular object, topic or issue of attention is the matter of establishing the conditions of possibility for what Derrida calls 'being-heard' (1974: 63), or what Arditi and Valentine (1999) call 'polemicization': how to become intelligible and relevant, how to gain the appropriate sort of attention or effect the appropriate alterations in the contexts that would count. This, Derrida reminds us, is an issue that is 'structurally phenomenal and belongs to an order radically dissimilar to that of the real sound in the world' (1974: 63). Accordingly, the prime problematic that is currently lacking in cultural and political studies, and the prime problematic that needs to be institutionalised within them is that of working out *how* to make academic work in cultural and political studies *become able* to make a definite difference. My argument is that deconstruction's textual approach offers the resources by which to articulate academic and political work.

What is crucial to emphasise is that this privileging of the textual over the discursive does *not* involve a bifurcation of the micro from the macro (as if the textual approach were merely 'looking at books', while the discourse approach were 'looking at larger structures and movements'). Indeed, the very perception that on the one hand political studies is concerned with macro-political issues (such as 'political will formation') whilst on the other hand deconstruction is concerned with 'texts' is itself a skewing disorientation (Protevi 2001). This work has tried to emphasise the politicality of the determination of the text (Mowitt 1992; Derrida 1992). Of course, a text is only political if one manages 'to recognize the structural moment of the text . . . that commits it to a critique of the enabling conditions of disciplines as such' (Mowitt 1992: 24–5). So the textual paradigm *'impossibilizes'* any micro/macropolitical bifurcation. In addition – and this too is crucial – it demands of political and cultural studies, in particular, a clarification of the mechanisms of articulation and causality that they think are implied in their own calls for this or that alteration or this or that intervention, and their claims that this or that insight or even 'theoretical revolution' holds 'massive political consequences'. As Mowitt sees this:

> By refusing the antidisciplinary scope of the textual model, we implicitly condone critical readings that exhaust their oppositionality without seeking to transform the institutional conditions of their own authority. Of course, such a transformation cannot be achieved simply by adopting a paradigm that invites one to reflect on its enabling conditions. But by the same token it just as surely cannot be achieved by endorsing a paradigm that "mere readings" must give way to action when "real" social issues are at stake . . . The point is to develop the institutional means whereby this insight is not exhausted in isolated moments of interpretation, and this implies inscribing such an insight in the paradigm that organizes the production of interpretive statements. (Mowitt 1992: 217)

Intervention is irreducibly a matter of articulation, relation, and reticulation. Phrased like this, the character of articulation is more readily construed as *textile, interwoven* – *textual* – than it is under the concept-metaphor of 'discourse', which carries a connotation of disconnected *speech* and straightforward ongoing *conversations*. This work has therefore proposed that the theoretical category of articulation needs to be rethought along these lines. First, in terms of its intra- and inter-disciplinary and intra- and inter-institutional ramifications, rather than on the basis of some model of the inside and the outside of the university; and, second, in ways which avoid what deconstruction would call the 'phonocentric' simplifications of conceiving discourse in terms of *speech* and *presence*. This is not to reject the value of the 'political will formation' with which post-Marxism in particular is so concerned (Laclau 2005). It is rather to *supplement* and hence transform this interest. The reorientation of politically engaged work in cultural studies that is proposed here insists upon the contingent institutional dimensions of academic practice. This should not be allowed to recede from view. This is because, outside of the institutional problematic, politicised academic work too often simply pins its hopes and orientation on a belief in the political efficacy of itself as a kind of journalistic publicising that will magically have the desired effect. This in itself rests upon the shaky foundations of a belief in means-end rationality, a 'monkey-see, monkey-do' version of political causality, and a phonocentric viewpoint that is largely blind to the institutional.

Instead of assuming that academic work somehow *just is* consequential in the manner intended by those who call for change (the first lesson of 'Deconstruction 101' is the deconstruction of intentionality), the real challenge today is to rethink cultural political studies' relation to (*within*) the political and to reorient work in light of this. In light of the orientation developed in previous chapters, it seems clear that this requires a deliberate re-engagement with the familiar topic of disciplinarity, or rather, interdisciplinarity. Indeed, today intervention requires a new interdisciplinarity.

This is absolutely not to evoke some notion of the concord of the disciplines, of establishing clear and fluent dialogue between them all; which is a traditional, idealistic and impossibly utopian dream. This must be acknowledged at the same time as affirming that cultural studies must nevertheless strive to 'connect'. Crucially, though, it must seek to do so by producing work that is not *simply* for, *within* or *of* cultural studies. In other words, there are paradoxes and double binds attendant to this interdisciplinarity, that must be addressed and engaged. They arise because the challenge is to produce work that can be intelligible and effective in other relations and *other* contexts. This means that, to intervene, cultural studies must effectively cease to be recognisably, familiarly, 'itself'. This is because 'intelligibility', 'legibility', and the capacity to 'be-heard' must be approached in light of the Derridean deconstruction of the conditions of possibility for intelligibility or legibility. In light of Derrida, legibility and intelligibility are to be understood as 'structurally-phenomenal', or that is, institutional. According to the Derridean understanding of institution with which this book began: 'An institution . . . is also and already the structure of our interpretation' (Derrida 1992: 22–3). What this means is that, insofar as any discipline is recognisable and identifiable purely as it exists in and as particular contexts, protocols and technical languages, then to intervene *elsewhere* requires *the transgression of those (its own) protocols*, the adoption of different protocols and different technical languages, and the infestation of different contexts. As such, this is to advocate cultural studies ceasing to appear to be cultural studies, in the name of particular interventions.

Let me be clear: this is far from a call for cultural and political studies to 'go public', in newspapers, or to go on the polemical offensive. Rather, if the aim in these fields is to intervene in other contexts, to seek to precipitate crises in the fields or contexts where they are deemed to be most needed for ethical or political reasons, then the strategy should not be anything like polemical or journalistic denunciation. Rather, interventional efforts should seek to operate as faithfully as possible to the protocols that would make these interventions first intelligible and second compelling within the relevant contexts. This can only be done by using the appropriate discursive protocols, methodological and technical languages and procedures. This may seem obvious or straightforward. However, the theoretical reasons underpinning this argument perhaps require further explanation if it is not to be misconstrued as merely another banal call for public deliberative dialogue.

This is not a call for open and frank public deliberative dialogue. It is not this precisely because such a notion overlooks the theoretical and practical consideration of *language, institution,* and *hegemony,* that has been central to this work. In fact, in the context of these considerations, the notion of interdisciplinarity conjured up here is a far cry from the contemporary myth of interdisciplinarity as friendly conversation, jovial cooperation or nebulously 'productive encounters'. Early theorists of interdisciplinarity (such as Roland Barthes (1977) or, further back, Bachelard (see Weber 1987)), already foresaw that interdisciplinarity entailed resentment, resistance, hostility and enmity rather than friendly 'productive encounters'. The reasons for this are, as Mowitt (2003) explains, because it will always be 'our way' that seems to us to be the 'right and proper way' to do interdisciplinary work . . . well . . . *properly*: the others' methods will always be weird, worrying and inferior. As such, concludes Mowitt, the very idea of interdisciplinarity as (if) happy general collaboration occludes an impossibility: it is constitutively conflictual and antagonistic.

So a politicised interdisciplinarity – the tendentious and strategic *becoming-interdisciplinarity* with, as it were, ulterior 'ethico-political' motives – would necessarily have to be 'multilingual' or chameleon-like, insofar as disciplines, contexts and communities have their own specialist languages. So, interdisciplinary interventions must necessarily be executed in the language of the other, so as to be intelligible according to the key frames of particular local contexts. There is a subtle irreducible interplay of 'hospitality' and 'hostility' at work. All disciplines and institutions are 'hostile' to – i.e., exclude – the other (the other methodology, the other language, the other orientation, the other values, the other discipline). They are only likely to be able to be 'hospitable' – i.e., able to include – the same (that which uses the 'right' methodology, the right language, right terms of reference, archive, examples, etc.).

Ultimately, then, this means that interventional interdisciplinarity needs to be actualised not simply in the pages of cultural studies and political studies journals and books. Rather, if it is to intervene into other institutional contexts, this entails intervention into other disciplinary productions. It must appear not as cultural studies work, but quite literally work under *the other heading*. (This is generalisable beyond the university, as there is no production or context that is not in some respect disciplinary, in this sense. Indeed, attempting to intervene 'outside' the university only raises the stakes, as we will see.) Thus, this strategy of intervention cannot be simple or straightforward. For, first of all, as both deconstruction and the theory of hegemony anticipate, it will meet resistance. Indeed, resistance will not necessarily be 'external'. The extent to which ostensibly politicised academics will resist, ignore or reject this strategy could in fact be read as a sign of the extent to which these contexts have been disciplined (in the pejorative sense). Or, as Butler puts it, resistance might be read as a sign of the extent to which people may 'not want to think too hard about what it is they are doing, what kind of discourse they are using; for if they think too hard about what it is they are doing, they fear that they will no longer do it' (Butler 2000: 265). The contention here is that, for reasons set out by deconstruction and post-Marxism, there is likely to be quite a lot of resistance, and that this is especially so because we are currently in an era of the intensification of disciplinary compartmentalisation and regulation.

The contemporary academic context is characterised by endless disciplinary assessment, and increasing enclave isolation. One of the key forms that this takes is through various auditing techniques which implement the imperative to conform to the figure of 'the specialist' or 'expert'. The political implication of this is that the contemporary academic condition becomes one of enclave *isolation* and the *disarticulation* of academic work from intruding into any other context. There is, in other words, a disarticulation of academic fields. It is in this light that a new interdisciplinarity could constitute what Mowitt construes as a political strategy of *antidisciplinarity*. This is not a denial of disciplinarity. Rather it is to focus *on* disciplinarity as being a key locus or 'condition of possibility and impossibility' for intervention.

It is crucial to note that such an interdisciplinary effort on the part of cultural studies towards counter-compartmentalisation would precipitate a disciplinary legitimation crisis *in cultural studies itself*, first and foremost. This may seem counterproductive – a bit like shooting the horse one is riding. However, such a strategy of 'striking at oneself' (to borrow an apt phrase from Žižek) is called for precisely in order to try to 'break the hold that the vocational or professionally oriented disciplines have had on the commerce between the university and society', as Mowitt suggests. (Mowitt 1992: 218). This antidisciplinary orientation entails *playing* the micro- and macro-political techniques that are instrumental in 'enclaving', 'policing', and depoliticising (by professionalising) academic work in order to achieve specific interventions in 'the other scene'. The disarticulation of academic work from any other scene is perhaps most clearly visible in the need to publish recognisably proper work in fully compliant assessable and auditable academic journals. Of course, such production is not obviously intervention into some *other* scene. *This* interventional strategy, on the other hand, precludes conflating intradisciplinary production (publishing in 'our' journals) as interdisciplinary intervention. This is not to say that one should not publish in one's own disciplinary contexts. It is rather to point out that this is not political intervention into the *other* context. It is intervention into one's own disciplinary context – as it were *intravention* as distinct from *intervention*.

In short, this reorientation plays on what Derrida revealed to be the unstable frontiers between hospitality and hostility – hospitality cannot conceptually or semantically be divorced from hostility, he argues (Derrida 1998: 14); nor fidelity from infidelity – the most faithful reading deconstructs the text and so revealing its bias becomes a kind of infidelity, unfaithful transgression (1987). In short, this is a deconstructive strategy, a strategy of reading/rewriting. The resources for discerning, reading, revealing, and returning-to-sender intellectually and politically deleterious texts of *any* order, discipline, institution or modality are readily available in the deconstructive close engagement with texts and their institutionally produced meanings. This might schematically be called a 'micropolitical' strategy. But the border between the micro- and the macro-political, as well as between theory and practice, between 'reading' and 'rewriting', becomes uncertain here.

The Necessity of Articulation

This can be explained further by returning to the concept-metaphor of *articulation* – although this, the central category of post-Marxism and cultural studies, is not usually approached in such a way. As it stands, articulation is usually either understood to evoke some kind of fundamental hybridity and eclectic identification at play in the establishment of cultural and political identities; or, when it comes to the political, articulation is taken to refer to rhetorical or symbolic connections between groups. In his most recent writings, Laclau has moved entirely away from anything like an institutional problematic and now exclusively theorises politics as a straightforwardly phonocentric matter of 'rhetoric' (2004). To this extent, articulation and, accordingly, politics, remain under-theorised. But there is a lot more to articulation than meets the eye (or ear). This under-theorisation necessarily has consequences for academic, intellectual and political orientation, of all orders. So, the precise nature of the articulation of post-Marxism and cultural studies should be explored further.

In light of the advent of 'the discursive metaphor', the theory of discourse, in post-Marxism and cultural studies everything can be theorised as hinging on articulation. What something is and what it does is always a matter of articulation: 'effects' are matters of connections, relations, reticulations, interruptions. In fact, articulation is to be construed as the central concept of both cultural studies and post-Marxism. The same can be said for deconstruction, given that Derrida's discussion of dissemination can be construed as a differently inflected account of the necessary possibility of the failure of intentionally-directed articulation. To use one of Derrida's motifs, a letter might not arrive at its destination (1987). If it does arrive, this is testament to a high degree of inter-institutional organisation and stability. But, even in contexts of great stability, 'letters' (meanings, signifieds, messages, etc.) can and do go astray and have unintended receptions and consequences. In other words, political causality is far from necessarily simple or predictable; and thinking – as Derrida ceaselessly reiterated – ought to engage with the irreducibility of things going awry.

In cultural studies, the centrality of articulation remains apparent even when the word itself is not explicitly used. This remains the case even when it is deployed without necessarily accepting post-Marxism's particular theorisation of it. (Often, cultural studies has a distaste for the theoretical categories and 'jargon' of post-Marxism and post-structuralism, which are even pejoratively called 'post-structuralist deconstructionism' (Young 1999). Nevertheless, however casually or technically, one or another notion of articulation is central to cultural studies). To take one representative example: Tony Bennett conceptualises the responsibility and interventionality of cultural studies through the following evocation of articulation. 'The ambition of cultural studies', he asserts, 'is to develop ways of theorizing relations of culture and power that will prove capable of being utilized by relevant social agents to bring about changes within the operation of those relations' (Bennett 1997: 52). This is what we might call a pedagogically inflected understanding of the articulation of cultural studies: In it, cultural studies is imagined to be responsible only to the extent that it is the *teacher* of political activists 'out there'. The sense attached to articulation is multiple: First, articulation is a synonym of Bennett's 'relations of culture and power'. Second, cultural studies academics are articulated to politics to the extent that they are trying to work out how those ('relevant social agents') involved in politics can 'bring about changes within the operation of [relevant social] relations'. But ultimately, in this version cultural studies is political only to the extent that 'relevant social agents' turn to cultural studies for edification about politics. Thus, politics hinges on articulations, as does intervention: the proper intervention of cultural studies in this account is articulation construed as the direct connecting up of 'theoretical' (academic) and practical ('political') realms. Bennett's fairly representative version of what it is that would make cultural studies political is, however, phantasmatic. Articulation is central to it, but the mechanisms of intervention that it assumes are both euphemistic and untenable. No one can be assumed to come running to cultural studies for political advice, so this should not be the paradigmatic organising assumption or expectation of cultural studies. Nevertheless, there is clearly much of value in Bennett's formulation. Richard Johnson clarifies this when he points out that 'we have to fight against the disconnection that occurs when cultural studies is inhabited for merely academic purposes or when enthusiasm for (say) popular cultural forms is divorced from the analysis of power and of social responsibility' (Johnson 1996: 79). Johnson's point is extremely valid, as is Bennett's injunction to seek to intervene. However, a number of dubious presuppositions and euphemistic argumentative steps hamper their arguments and mean that the manner of cultural studies interventionality that they subscribe to does not actually add up.

A rethink about articulation should acknowledge that articulation is not just about speech and language and connections between groups. Or rather, it is (also), but only to the extent that 'speech and language' are understood through a deconstructive theory of hegemony. This can be clarified by recalling the debate between Laclau, Rorty and Derrida. Responding to Laclau and Rorty's disputes about politics, academia, responsibility, deconstruction and pragmatism, Derrida observes that 'the question of language is essential to everything that we are discussing here', and that 'if there are differences between us, this essentially derives from a question of language' (Derrida 1996: 77). As the previous chapters have sought to show, this 'question of language' is indeed a key problematic, but it is one that is certainly not merely linguistic. It is irreducibly institutional. This is because, as Derrida phrases it, 'force is the other of language without which language would not be what it is' (quoted in Protevi 2001: 59). In this context, the word 'force' might be replaced with the word 'discipline'. In other words, language is not to be construed as merely a matter of semantics and semiotics. Rather, as Derrida makes plain, it is precisely because 'deconstruction has never been concerned with the contents alone of meaning, [that] it must not be separable from this politico-institutional problematic' (Derrida 1992: 22–3).

The 'politico-institutional problematic' is in this sense *textual*, before being 'discursive'. It involves language, but is not simply linguistic or rhetorical. It is rather tied to and illustrative of the work of institutional paradigms as efforts to police, hegemonise, and restrict dissemination. As Samuel Weber puts this: 'the function of establishing identities, of imposing determinations and of enforcing lines of demarcation can be conceived only as an effect of what we call "institution" and of "institutionalization"' (Weber 1987: xiv). In substantially overlooking this, post-Marxist discourse theory has (ab)used deconstruction to *impose* determinations and enforce lines of demarcation where the textual approach of deconstruction would seek to *expose* such operations. In this, the textual approach of exposing and deconstructing determinations, lines of demarcation and their effects is political insofar as it exposes establishments to their own biases. If one approaches this from the question of the (human) subject, and if, as Mowitt's reading of disciplinarity suggests, the subject is not construed as prior to discipline, but rather as 'arising' in and through it, then attending to the work of disciplines is political insofar as disciplines are irreducibly engaged in 'the social production of subjectivity' (Mowitt 1992: 37). In effect, this is ultimately to suggest that the textual approach of deconstruction constitutes a *more politicised* approach than discourse analysis because it deliberately searches out instances, acts, styles, strategies, habits, histories and effects of discipline. As if opposed to this, the post-Marxist discourse approach arguably seeks to discipline. (This is perhaps nowhere more apparent than in the exchanges of *Contingency, Hegemony, Universality* (2000), wherein Butler, Laclau and Žižek each obdurately refused to accept that each others' language, terms and concepts were in any way acceptable; instead each urged the others to use *their* terms and concepts.)

In this respect, Derrida's insistence on the ethical and political importance of the 'question of language' recasts the textual and putatively micro-political *approach* in a better light than it recasts post-Marxist political studies' macro-political *focus*. For, what Derrida seeks to clarify are the reductive and/or policing effects of contexts in which 'a certain type of propositional form governs, and where a certain type of micrology is necessarily effaced' (1996: 78). This work has characterised post-Marxist scholarship as revelling in precisely such a problematic 'rigour' and 'strictness'; as well as being organised chiefly by a (problematic) macro-political perspective, in which 'a certain type of micrology is necessarily effaced'. As Derrida sees it: 'Owing to this macroscopia or macrologic . . . [what] tends to prevail are theses, positions, position takings, positionings' (1998a: 40). This takes place at the expense of intimate analysis. Against this, and instead of allowing one's work to be 'swept along by swelling, choruslike rhythms' of the 'macro', Derrida urges intellectuals to pay attention to 'the minutiae of the letter, that is, those microscopic or micrological displacements where I might incorrigibly persist in hoping things get decided' (1998a: 40). As he says in response to the arguments of Rorty and Laclau, 'what interests me . . . are other protocols' (1996: 78).

This is also why, from a position more explicitly orientated towards the textuality of cultural rather than the discourse of political studies, macro-political studies can start to seem to operate according to a rather inadequate and under-interrogated notion of political causality, and can come to seem reductive, simplistic, and banal (despite the best intentions of political theorists themselves). On the other hand, once one starts to examine cultural practices or discourses (and one's 'relation to'/'construction of' them) in their textual complexity and micrology (Derrida 1998a: 40), the notion of articulation becomes so complex and/or aporetic – and to make things so complex for analysis – that political studies style accounts of politics and hegemony seem cumbersome, crudely metaphorical and even gestural. This is why, although post-Marxist political theory feels itself to be adequate – indeed, 'perfect', according to Laclau (2004: 322) – Stuart Hall argues for the constitutive and ineradicable *impossibility* of such adequacy when it comes to the problem of working out 'culture's relations and its effects' (Hall 1992: 286).

Post-Marxism thinks that its account of cultural-political relations and effects *is* adequate. But both cultural studies and deconstruction deem an *adequate* account to be impossible, given the complexity and textuality of 'discourse'. This different stance generates at least two different modalities of work (textual versus discursive), which, although they may appear to be contiguous, are actually heterogeneous. That is to say, although discourse theory is enabled by and deeply indebted to textuality, it remains a formalised, procedural simplification of it. In addition, although it is clearly the case that post-Marxist macropolitical theory has influentially informed cultural studies, it nevertheless also jeopardises the antidisciplinary potential of cultural studies because it lacks a focus on the complexity of textuality, articulation, and a dynamic engagement with the micrology of institutional power. As was seen in Chapter 1, post-Marxist discourse theory may well amount to a formalisation and theoretical legitimation of diverse political projects (cultural studies included), but *qua formalisation* (and, indeed, *legitimation*), discourse theory has so far involved a certain depoliticisation.

In this sense, the textual, deconstructive, micropolitical focus will be able to enrich, reorient, and indeed *politicise* post-Marxism and cultural studies. Paradoxically, however, this 'enrichment' would also amount to what deconstructive language would call an 'impossibiliza-tion' of post-Marxism and 'the discourse approach'. Ironically, that is, deconstruction was the condition of possibility of post-Marxism, but it also amounts to its condition of impossibility. Post-Marxism can be deconstructed, and its biases, decisions and 'violences' come to light. *Vis-à-vis* cultural studies, post-Marxism is therefore necessary but insufficient. Cultural studies is not just discourse analysis. (Nor is discourse analysis *just*.) Deconstruction's micropolitical antidisciplin-ary textual politics suggest a transformative *addition* to macropolitical scholarship. Through more rigorous attention to *articulation* (the condition of possibility of post-Marxism and cultural studies), each can be brought into a more fruitful relation through, as it were, the harrowing ordeal of the undecidability of all articulation (the condition of impossibility of post-Marxism and cultural studies *qua* 'subjects supposed to know'). This undecidability is always more perceptible in a textual approach than in a discourse approach.

The Necessity of Institution

The characterisation of post-Marxist discourse as formalising, legit-imising, disciplining and institutional on the one hand, does not mean that, on the other hand, cultural studies and deconstruction are simply 'anti-' all of these things. It does, however, mean that these processes, and the institution, should remain a *problem* for cultural studies. This is because, far from being something to be 'rejected', on the contrary institutions are immeasurably culturally and politically constitutive. As such, institutionalisation must be actively addressed. In post-Marxist discourse theory, as we have seen, institutions are said to enable or block political possibilities, meaning that they are to be regarded key players in hegemonic politics. Institutionalisation is certainly not simply 'depoliticisation', then. In many respects it is a condition of possibility for any kind of political force or leverage at all.

To clarify, let's revisit this familiar problematic. Stuart Hall argues that institutionalisation is always to be treated as 'a moment of profound danger' – adding however that, in cultural studies, 'dangers are not places you run away from but places that you go towards' (Hall 1992: 285). Similarly, Lola Young casts the topic of the institutional location of cultural studies in this light: Cultural studies, she argues, 'was originally a radical, political project – associated with the late 1960s and 1970s but in existence in a variety of forms before then – a project which sought to resist institutionalization, even whilst courting it' (Young 1999: 4). This is a very similar view to the ones examined at the beginning of Chapter 1, of course. In it, the reasons why cultural studies both courted and resisted the institution are said to relate to what Hall calls the unavoidability of the political 'game of hegemony', and what Derrida variously thinks in terms of motifs such as '*poleros*', or interimplicated sentiments and acts of hostility (polemos) and desire (eros), gaining 'leverage', 'derailing' established networks, and so on, as discussed throughout this work. Young cites numerous canonical cultural studies texts and authors to have made similar arguments, and continues: ' "Antidisciplinary", "trans-disciplinary", "interdisciplinary" and "post-disciplinary" have all been used by those involved in the subject to describe its academic status' (4). In other words, Young's *very first* claim about the nature of cultural studies' political status relates exclusively to the argument that the university institution is *de facto* 'political'. Cultural studies is something that definitively 'sought to resist institutionalization, even whilst courting it'.

So, Young's first definition of cultural studies – a definition bolstered and propped up by the arguments of many other central cultural studies figures – is aligned with Derrida's characterisation of deconstruction as '*an institutional practice for which the concept of the institution remains a problem*'. Unfortunately for her argument, however, the next significant move that Young makes is characteristic of a wider tendency in cultural and political studies in general. It is deeply problematic, and entirely different from the move I am advocating instead. Namely, she very quickly *drops* this enabling insight about the institution, and, effectively, *abandons* the whole politico-institutional problematic:

> There is an idealism inherent in cultural studies as a political project which has been acknowledged and which still provokes criticism: perhaps the subject's early practitioners' initial ambitions were too great. And certainly the utopian tendency should not mask the problems embedded in the assertions of 'marginality' and 'disciplinary transgression' which recur in historical accounts of the cultural studies project: the conservatism of the academy militates against sustained, radical change. It is an illusion to believe that cultural studies could ever become something other than institutionalized once it set foot inside an institution: there is little scope for transgression or operating outside of disciplining structures and practices in most universities. (1999: 5)

Upon this melancholy note, of resignation to the disciplining structures of institutionality, Young's argument moves to relocate the continuing intervention of cultural studies as (if) something squarely 'outside' the university. (So, cultural studies intervenes by studying things like racist representations in the media.) She does so straightforwardly in terms of a by now familiar deployment of one meaning of 'articulation', wherein cultural studies' very emergence and its ultimate institutionalisation is considered to be related (articulated) to wider social, cultural and political 'shifts' (immigration, ethnic subcultures, feminism, etc.), and in which it is represented as having been at the intellectual vanguard, coming as a first university response to these wider political changes (See also McRobbie 2005). Then, Young proceeds to represent cultural studies as having intervened in this historical moment of cultural transformation primarily insofar as it blazed a trail, set the terms and the standards for subsequent institutional responses and reconfigurations in different disciplines, and beyond:

> In spite of being vilified along with media studies, amongst others, as being a 'Mickey Mouse' subject, . . . [over] the last ten or so years, ideas and analyses which are now firmly embedded in media discourses have increasingly come to resemble closely the kind of cultural textual analysis that has been nurtured through cultural studies. It is somewhat ironic then that there have been repeated attacks on the subject in the media . . . It is also the case that critical and theoretical paradigms derived from, and influenced by cultural studies, have seeped into the study of a wide range of disciplines: History, English Literature, Geography, Sociology and so on. I am not suggesting that cultural studies was solely or even primarily responsible for the changes in thinking suggested here: it has been, however, a key element in the movement of disciplinary boundaries, and is symptomatic of wider shifts in political and intellectual sensibilities. (5)

According to a Žižekian ideology-focused reading, cultural studies could, because of this, be regarded as the exemplary institutional recuperation and 'hegemonisation' of that which was 'emergent' or 'other' by the dominant hegemony in its dominant institutions. (Needless to say, this relates to the discussion of 'theoria' in Chapter 1.) A Žižekian ideology-critique such as this, whilst always being provocative in its focus on capitalist hegemony/ideology, is however another of the very things that the post-Marxist deconstructive theory of discourse, articulation, and the textual focus on 'institution' nevertheless undercuts and essentially 'impossibilizes'. This is because the discursively and textually understood concept-metaphor of institution frustrates Žižek's anti-capitalist focus on 'ideology', at least insofar as institutionalisation is not synonymous with commodification. Žižek's worry, of course, is that the distance between the two terms (institutionalisation and commodification) is diminishing – albeit asymptotically – all the time. The textual approach, however, focuses upon the political chance implied by the unavoidable *différance* between institutionalisation and commodification (or the inevitable failure of complete hegemonisation), whilst Žižekian ideology-critique flattens and ignores this *différance*, viewing institutionalisation *as* commodification, and thus allowing the problematic of the institution to recede from view, or to be recast as a subordinate, secondary matter, 'symptomatic' of the 'primary' problem of capitalism. But, my contention is that even if one wants to address 'directly' the so-called 'primary' problem of capitalism, as Žižek claims to, this cannot but be done outside of engaging with putatively secondary institutional matters. In this way, Žižek's anti-capitalism is itself a 'utopian' problematic (i.e., 'of no place', not anchored to the actual), that therefore needs to be inverted and displaced onto the matter of institutions in order to even hope to become effective in any consequential sense.

In a different way, but with equally unfortunate effects, from this point in her account, the politico-institutional dimension of the problematic of cultural studies totally recedes from Lola Young's consideration of cultural studies. For Young, with a view that may be taken to be representative of that held by many others within cultural studies, cultural studies is regarded as something which simply *is* institutionalised now, and that's that. Because of this resigned acceptance of cultural studies' institutional pacification and domestication, her ensuing discussion of *what* political action and the 'interventionality' of cultural studies *is* becomes skewed. By now it is easy to recognise its familiar form, as this has been plotted in the earlier readings of the debates between Butler, Derrida, Laclau, Rorty, and Žižek, in the previous chapter. For, the themes Young chooses to draw out, at the cost of letting the institutional problematic recede, is 'the question of the appropriate political formation within which cultural studies should organize' (8). With this, Young's argument at once falls into what Derrida would once have called the 'metaphysical trap' of a very straightforward notion of politics and intervention as devolving on conscious intention and political will formation with academia's political credentials determined by its conscious and deliberate relation to this (articulation). This is a metaphysical notion of articulation. It is also irreducibly euphemistic. Thus, the problem is not only establishing *what* an 'appropriate political formation' is, but also clarifying what the phrase 'within which cultural studies should organize' might possibly even mean let alone oblige. The 'metaphysical' dimension – in Derrida's sense of a prioritisation of the possibility and value of 'presence' – can also be seen clearly in Bennett's (and, indeed, Rorty's) argument that academic work (or 'theory') can only be 'useful' if it 'will prove capable of being utilized by relevant social agents to bring about changes within the operation of those relations' that it theorises (Bennett 1997: 52). In this sense, the role of 'theory' is either to formalise and justify 'practice' (in precisely the way that McRobbie argued post-Marxist 'theory' justified and intellectually legitimated cultural studies as 'practice': see McRobbie 1992: 720; Gilbert 2001: 191; See also Chapter 1). Or, theory might somehow offer an extra insight for political practice – it might, in other words *teach* those who practise. These are both arrogations that betray a metaphysical (logocentric) conception of the relation of academia to the political. Put bluntly, it assumes that political action is carried out (presumably on the much-fetishized, mythical 'street') by graduates of cultural studies. This thinking of the politics of institutional academia is somewhat wanting.

Many theorists, including but far from exclusively those associated with deconstruction or cultural studies, have argued that politics needs to be rethought. This is unlikely to be a simple, delimitable or terminable task. But as we have seen, in arguments of Young, Bennett, Rorty, Hall, Žižek and Laclau, the 'metaphysical trap' risked when conceptualising the political is tenacious. Young herself discusses the ferocious cultural studies 'debates about what constitutes political action' (1999: 9; see also Hall 2002), but nevertheless quickly reverts to a metaphysical narrative and its attendant conceptual schema, which runs: In the beginning, cultural studies was *de facto* political because, by virtue of studying newly emergent but hitherto 'excluded others' in a disciplinarily hidebound context, it was instrumental in an ethico-political reorganisation of disciplinary boundaries. That reorganising moment has now passed, however; the proof being that nowadays very many disciplines do their own version of 'cultural studies'. Consequently, cultural studies is arguably the model of the new institutional norm. It only remains politically effective in two ways: on the one hand, insofar as it can raise the political consciousness of its students; and on the other, insofar as it can raise the political consciousness of other disciplines.

Now, even though this final 'cross-disciplinary consciousness-raising' argument may sound like the institutional focus for which I am recruiting textuality, it does not quite add up to it. For, in fact, the institutional problematic has here largely fallen off the agenda; only to have been replaced by a fixation on (presumably) 'free' or 'autonomous' individuals and groups engaged in face-to-face liberal public debate – replaced, that is, by a wager that cultural studies' teaching can consciously educate others and that these others might somehow 'do something' with the knowledge cultural studies has given them. Now, this argument is made with no evident irony by Young, even though her text is full of references to 'disciplinary boundaries' and the 'conservative' character of disciplines and institutions. In addition to this, it betrays an impossibly utopian belief that everyone in every discipline *will be able* and *inclined* to familiarise themselves with and keep abreast of the ongoing work in every other discipline. To see the problems here, one might only enquire into how many microbiology, physics, genetics, law, theology, informatics, neuro-psychology, and management journals you or I have read recently. Not very many, one might reasonably expect. (Keeping abreast is not only unlikely; it is simply impossible.)

The problem appears to be one of an under-theorisation of the scope and reach of the meaning and political implications of disciplines and boundaries as *complex mechanisms*, rather than *things*, like, say, garden fences. Quite other than this conception, I have sought to represent boundaries as institutional paradigms that enable and delimit thinking and orientate action, and whose existence can be seen in and as language. The culmination of the former stance on academia and politics ignores the latter's attention to the institutional field and proposes that the only other way for cultural studies to be political is for academics to get themselves into real relationships with specific, local cultural/political practices of their own choosing. Thus, for Young, the answer to the question of responsible political intervention is basically simple: today, articulation (connection, relation, intervention) should be 'actual', face to face, hands on, (meta)physical. Engaged academics should 'really' connect up with whatever they seek to intervene in (1999: 13).

Now, this has the benefit of reconfiguring cultural studies as 'the other' of the traditional academic posture of disinterested and impartial observer, whilst also demonstrating the importance and necessity of this reconfiguration (Young adds: 'Some colleagues – particularly those based at more traditional establishments – find

the suggestion that cultural studies' academics should become involved with those who work in the media, in government offices, in
the legal profession, derisory, and [she quotes Jameson] "chilling"'
(1999: 13).) But it has the disadvantage of implying that cultural
studies is either to be non-academic 'action' or ethnographic 'field-
work'. Of course, the fact that very soon after publishing this argument Lola Young, so to speak, 'put her money where her mouth was',
by taking a position as Head of Culture at the then recently formed
Greater London Authority is surely testament to her commitment to
'doing cultural politics' (she remained as committed to practical
matters of black culture, history, art and politics in her cultural/
political administrative office as she was in academia). But, the
theoretical and political question that should be maintained here is:
does this traditional notion of politics offer a *model* of intervention for
cultural studies? Is this metaphysical conception of intervention really
the paradigm of political action that cultural studies should seek to
emulate?

It deserves to be noted that this sort of 'cultural studies success
story' shares a narrative form with that of Stuart Hall. On this matter,
Jeremy Gilbert has suggested that 'the key reason that Stuart Hall
acquired such totemic status as the pivotal figure within British
cultural studies, despite the fact that his only single-authored work
was a collection of mainly journalistic political commentaries, was
precisely his crucial function as mediator between cultural studies as
an academic interdiscipline and these wider political tendencies'
(Gilbert 2003: 146). Does the responsibility of cultural studies remain
to get down and dirty with some real political movement and then
articulate this for or to others, whether academically or journal-
istically?

Far be it from me to disparage the achievements of such figures as
Young and Hall. However, further be it from me to accept that these
(and the handful of other examples of cultural studies 'successes' that
might be gestured to) somehow furnish us with an exemplary or
exhaustive model of what cultural studies intervention ought to look
like. Indeed, any 'Try to Re-enact the Stuart Hall Success Story'
version of cultural studies seems suspect precisely because in it con-
spicuously select isolated cases of 'success' are held up as the model of
supposedly generally achievable ideals, against an overwhelming
backdrop of a more general and widespread failure. (As well as being
premised on scarcity, and perhaps also celebrity, this model also
skews or 'hegemonises' the very notion of what constitutes proper

orientation and successful intervention.) In other words, I am suggesting that rather than supposing that cultural studies ought to try to repeat or literally re-enact either its own trail-blazing institutional history or simply to try to emulate the same kinds of success as its iconic figures, what is required is a less nostalgic version and a more theoretically and ethico-politically justifiable pragmatic strategy of intervention. I have argued that this necessarily hinges on an inclusion within the purview of its theorisation an attention to the necessary contingency of institution that is unique to a deconstructive textual approach to cultural and political studies. I have also suggested that it implies the necessity of politicised interdisciplinarity.

The difference between this understanding of interdisciplinarity and many other appeals to interdisciplinarity rests on the reconceptualisation of interdisciplinarity predicated on a deconstructive attention to the institution conceived as a political problematic *per se* – and moreover, one in which 'transparent communication' is, strictly speaking, *impossible* – and certainly never neutral – because of the unavoidability of heterogeneous disciplining paradigms. Contra Habermasian sensibilities, no matter how 'clearly' one tries to speak, misunderstanding and unintelligibility are not only inevitable. They are the norm. To the extent that they are avoided, this is evidence of hegemony as effective discipline.

The (Dis)Articulation of Post-Marxism and Politics

Interestingly, Lola Young also touches on the problematic of language, when she asserts that 'we need to be wary of being seduced by the apparent authority wielded by the rhetorical flourishes of post-structuralist deconstructionism. Current cultural studies has developed alongside radical reformulations of language which have encouraged us to demystify the workings of discourse: how then could we simply leave the place of theory and abstraction unquestioned?' (1999: 10) This is important. But, despite the sweeping anti-deconstructionist tone of Young's criticism (and its implicitly 'voluntarist' suggestion that there may be times when human subjects are not in some sense already 'seduced', 'mystified' or subject to and subjects of one or another form of 'authority', or *hegemon*), it is quite possible to agree with her on this point *and* to maintain an argument that definitively supports a deconstructive and post-Marxist cultural studies. This is because there is no *one* deconstruction. 'Post-structuralist deconstructionism' need not be mystificatory rhetoric. It should certainly not be grand system-building, given the blatant contradiction that this would entail. Deconstruction need not be – indeed, deconstruction is not – post-Marxist, post-structuralist 'deconstructionist' discourse. Nevertheless, the crux of the situation is encapsulated by Young, in this argument: 'If the cultural studies teacher represents anything then she or he should exemplify an attempt to resist the role of transparent mediator of knowledge and information' (Young 1999: 10). Effective here is a tacit alignment with the theory of hegemony (in one or another form), which already furnishes us with the reasons *why* one should reject any belief in the 'transparent mediator of knowledge'. For, when it comes to conceiving of the university as existing in and as a part of hegemony, representatives of deconstruction, cultural studies and post-Marxism alike have all argued that there is a strong political implication attendant to any and all academic work. This is something that we have seen throughout (Derrida 1992: 21–3; Mowitt 1992; Laclau 2004: 290; Weber 1987). This work has argued, however, that it is chiefly within the textual deconstructive (anti)paradigm that this 'implicit' dimension to the theory of hegemony can become most effectively explicit.

Consequently, it is – 'strictly speaking', as Laclau likes to say – unacceptable that the orientation favoured and invested in by Laclauian post-Marxism downplays this dimension and adopts instead the idioms of and identification with the discipline of philosophy; as Derrida might say, not only concerning itself with the 'contents of meaning alone' but also becoming a 'philosophy [which] *clings to the privilege it exposes*' (2002: 1–2). Herein lies a significant difference between post-Marxism as a disciplinary discourse and cultural studies as, at the very least, a problematisation of disciplinary discourse. In other words, the post-Marxist investment in disciplinarity divides post-Marxism and cultural studies from each other, placing them at odds. The difference can be seen clearly in recent work of Laclau, in which he asserts that 'our main intellectual task [is now] to rethink philosophy in the light of [psychoanalysis]' (2004: 304). Stuart Hall was indeed prescient indeed to discern in *Hegemony and Socialist Strategy* (1985) a move away from political investment and towards a straightforward investment in the discipline of philosophy. David Howarth recently confronted Laclau on this point (in Laclau 2004), pointing out that Laclau's work is orientated towards philosophical ('ontological') research and does not care to consider the messy stuff of actually existing ('ontic') arrangements in culture and politics. To this charge Laclau answers:

The first and main criticism is that I have concentrated on the ontological dimension of social theory rather than on ontical research. Now, this is a charge to which I plead happily guilty, except that I do not see it as a criticism at all. I have located my theoretical intervention at the theoretical and philosophical level and it is at that level that it has to be judged . . . I think . . . that hegemony as form – that is, as an ontological category – is perfectly theorized in my work . . . Howarth himself, quite correctly, distinguishes between a political theorist interested in describing and classifying different types of political institution and a political ontologist putting into question the very concept of political institution. Now, what would be the use of the second task if it could not transmit its effects to the first? (Laclau 2004: 321, 322, 323)

So, despite its analytical and deconstructive pretensions, it seems that Laclau is now content merely to put into question the results of the taxonomical labours of political theorists. This really puts the pejorative 'con' and '-ism' into deconstructionism. For, after the early efforts to move *'towards a radical democratic politics'*, as the subtitle of *Hegemony* proclaimed, Laclau now prefers to have 'located [his] theoretical intervention at the theoretical and philosophical level'. Thus, Laclau happily ignores the institutional-political critique that is central to deconstruction, or rather he formalises it as a repetitive 'putting into question of the very concept of institution', *in a nevertheless stable institutional form*, according to stable protocols and formal and policed procedures. Furthermore, there is a closure: hegemony is believed to be 'perfectly theorized'. Yet, the Laclauian theorisation of hegemony could only be said to be 'perfect' if the perfect theorisation of hegemony entailed staying at the 'level' of gestural metaphors, metaphors which *seem* clear but which, as we have seen, actually make 'rigorous' thinking, knowledge, means-end rationality, or 'phronesis' straightforwardly impossible (see Devenney 2004).

Of course, at the same time as this, what is apparent in the passage above is the claim that 'usefulness' has everything to do with the transmission of 'effects'. This is the insight proper to discourse theory. Unfortunately, Laclau has evidently lost interest in the question of their transmission to anywhere other than somewhere else within the same disciplinary space as his own work – a space that his own work seeks to hegemonise. This is as much as to say that Laclau has abandoned the fundamental analytical question of any theory of hegemony and discourse; the question that post-Marxism assumed but never successfully answered: the question of the transmission of 'effects'.

Discourse theory is a theory of texts produced by and ensnared in relations of articulation. In asking post-Marxism to examine its own status in terms of its own theory is to ask it to specify more thoroughly its institutional context and interventionality, rather than merely to assume that there *are* progressive political relations that *it is in* with 'other practices'. It is also, and by the same token, to ask post-Marxism to finish theorising its own central categories. This is clearly justified on a 'theoretical and philosophical level' on the basis of the observation that post-Marxism conceives of everything through a metaphor of relation but without actually thinking particular effects of relation or examining either the complexity or the less than conscious or other than intended aspects of its own relations. Paradoxically, as we see, Laclau now claims not even to want to study or to theorise *actual* relations because he doesn't think that such an orientation will add anything specifically, pragmatically, or consequentially, to the political conjunctures governed by such relations. For Laclau, the 'important task' remains 'a *formal* analysis of the logics involved' in identity and discourse constitution (Laclau 2000: 53). He concedes, 'I think that it is entirely true that starting from where we start imposes intellectual requirements of a particular kind. But I do not think of those requirements as "costs"' (2004: 320). This is a striking kind of disciplinary myopia, which arises because post-Marxism illogically proposes that its own preferred 'logical' discourse is necessary, that what it thinks it understands about the world *is* 'ontological' and that what it thinks it sees *is* 'ontic'. This flies in the face of its basic premise of contingency (and textuality) and of what post-Marxism calls the 'surplus of meaning'; what Derrida more appropriately calls 'dissemination' (which relates 'meaning' to its institutional production). But textuality, absence, incompletion, lack, dissemination and contingency are not one-sided. Lack and contingency does not reside solely or simply in the object 'out there'. It also refers to the undecidability introduced by the inevitable contingency of one's own hermeneutic frames. Ultimately, in arrogating this 'perfection' to itself, post-Marxist discourse is essentially radically anti-democratic and anti-deconstructive in orientation. It is a straightforward identification with the contingent institution of philosophy misconstrued as essential and universal.

This is the same as saying that post-Marxism does not deconstruct what it would call its own 'ontic' or institutional situation, its investments, and its constitutive, orientative biases. It does not deconstruct or even really 'use' its own central category of articulation.

This is further complicated or compounded when Laclau at the same time goes on to contend that 'the social link is a libidinal link' (2004: 326). Thus, 'the theoretical and philosophical level' becomes exposed as a chimera or shibboleth; for 'this libidinal dimension is crucial in keeping society together, as well as in explaining the moments of its radical disruption' (Laclau 2004: 326). As Laclau himself would be among the first to claim, identification and identity are rather less about 'logic' and rather more about 'ideological fantasy' – or, if you like, the logic of ideological fantasy. The problem, therefore, is that Laclau remains closed to the possibility that something like the libidinal link of post-Marxism's disciplinary sociality might exact any 'cost'. In the terms of this present argument, however, it is possible to see that *the cost is the orientation itself*. It manifests in a complete identification with the discipline of philosophy, an anti-democratic relation to academic discourse, and a disarticulation from the impetus to, or effort to establish, responsible political intervention.

The cost entailed by this becomes clearer when Laclau's essay, 'Glimpsing the Future' (2004), is considered. This essay has the subtitle and aim of 'sketching a possible agenda' for future work in 'social and political thought'. This agenda, however, is deeply problematic. It is spelled out in the essay's final sentence, which reads: 'Rhetoric, psychoanalysis and politics (conceived as hegemony): in this triad I see the future of social and political thought' (2004: 326). Laclau's argument is this: *Rhetoric* is important because 'if discourse is the terrain of constitution of all objectivity, rhetorical movements are constitutive of discursivity' (306). (Needless to say, perhaps, this is a complete forgetting of the insights of deconstruction – as it were, a regression from Derrida to Saussure.) *Psychoanalysis* is deemed to be important for many reasons, but mainly because 'by discourse I do not understand something restricted to the linguistic conceived in its narrow sense, but a relational complex of which enjoyment [*jouissance*] is a constitutive element . . . Moreover some of the categories that I employ, such as "radical investment", would be unintelligible without the notion of *jouissance*' (303). (This 'broadened' conception of discourse, unfortunately, also seems regressively subject-centred.) *Politics* is transparently important to 'political thought', of course, but only when conceived as hegemony.

Now, whilst there may seem to be nothing *necessarily* wrong with this agenda or this argument (given that work undertaken in terms of such a triad could be articulated in any number of ways), my contention is that there is a fundamental problem with the very effort to institute these themes *as* a 'triad': a rigorous, stable interlocking structure. For this effort implies that the approaches to any and every object or topic of social and political thought would have to be organised by, directed or refracted through these categories – enabled, limited, oriented, and, overall, hegemonised by them. This would make the task of social and political thought into the increasingly disciplinarily hidebound work of repetitive, accumulative description and diagnosis according to a stiflingly unified approach. There are a number of problems here. The ones to be emphasised relate to the matter of disciplinarity that has kept returning throughout this work. On the one hand, the investment in disciplinary strictures apparent here reiterates Laclau's identification with and primary interest in the university (yet without being interested in thinking or engaging the politics of the university in any way – it is, on other words, *imaginary* identification). On the other hand, and more importantly, this triad masquerades as the necessary, correct and adequate grounds upon which to establish the 'correct approach' with which to organise and orchestrate social and political thinking.

For a New Intervention

A different agenda is needed here. According to the arguments this work has elaborated, such an agenda should be established from an awareness of the key insights of deconstruction, post-Marxism, and cultural studies; insights that hinge on the constitutive character and perennial problematics of institution, articulation and relation. For, these familiar and unavoidably central concepts appear, on second glance, actually to be under-theorised, under-developed and under-deployed in the very areas, theory and contexts to which they are central. This peculiar status of being central-yet-underdeveloped or central-yet-obscure recalls a deconstructive argument once deployed by Geoffrey Bennington against vociferously politicised cultural studies. Gary Hall recounts the argument; it runs: 'the last thing that is raised in all this talk about the importance of politics for cultural studies *is* the question of politics . . . Politics is the one thing it is vital to understand, as it is that by which everything else is judged. But politics is at the same time the one thing that *cannot* be understood; for the one thing that cannot be judged by the transcendentally raised criteria of politics is politics itself' (Hall 2002: 6). In a similar vein one might say post-Marxist theory has yet to get to grips with its own central category of articulation, its fundamental insight and condition of possibility. The central category is stable only to the extent that it relies on a certain 'blindness', a blindness to the fact that it is actually a rather vague and metaphorical notion; thus revealing this condition of possibility to be a 'condition of impossibility' – central yet excluded. In this light, my closing considerations will amount to an effort to rethink the *strategic* implications of articulation/relation for elaboration and application in and as a deconstructive post-Marxist cultural studies 'to come'.

To reiterate: the most usual question posed about work seeking to intervene consequentially, ethico-politically, is generally represented as being that of *what* to articulate with. To this, I have sought to emphasise that, no matter what the verdict, the crucial and generally overlooked dimension is working out the answer to the question of *how* to do so. This work has suggested that academics tend to be so preoccupied with the former question that the latter rarely even arises, and where it does it is presented as something that is obvious or simple – as if a *simple* matter of articulation. As if, in other words, articulation is simple and understood. But this contains a tautology, saying as it does that academic work is articulated to politics to the extent that it is articulated to politics. Of course, the plausibility of asserting this link may seem compelling. But it does not answer the question of *how* to articulate *otherwise*, how to *intervene elsewhere*. This is in fact the most pertinent and pressing *unanswered* or at least *under-answered* question for engaged academics and intellectuals today. Even though this question mark strikes me as glaring, to a great extent the discourses of both cultural studies and post-Marxism seem to forget it and instead are chiefly dominated by disputes about *what* valid or proper political themes actually are. Worse, their discourses too often amount to simple descriptive accounts of various 'political discourses' going on 'out there'. Although this work has schematically suggested that this is particularly the case with work in post-Marxist political studies (given its in-built bias towards 'macro-political' focus on 'discourses'), it is nevertheless also the case that cultural studies more widely is not immune from the impulse to indulge in ego-gratifying macro-political diagnostic pontification.

The disputes about what is or is not a valid political theme, what 'we' should be for and against, and so on, is inevitable, just as it is stimulating, vital and vitalising. Yet it misses and occludes the crucial point. As Lola Young characterises the debate: 'A repeated criticism of all things "post-modern" – a theoretical turn closely associated with cultural studies – is that "real politics" [are said to] have been *reduced* to *cultural* politics, and the politics of representation, and that cultural production and analysis has been depoliticized through the lack of engagement with economic processes' (Young 1999: 6). Young uses this criticism to stage a defence of the political importance of 'representation', especially insofar as it bears upon ethnic cultures. But it deserves to be noted, once more, that this account reveals that the wider criticisms of cultural studies have the same structure as the general form of criticisms made by many within cultural studies about the 'textual' approach: both misconstrue 'the cultural' and 'the textual' as necessarily meaning 'separate from and exclusive of the political'. Now, Young's account is fair, but what I have attempted to suggest, *also*, is that such arguments about things becoming 'depoliticized' through the 'lack of engagement' with this or that are themselves rarely backed up with a thoroughgoing explanation of precisely *how* anyone banging on about this or that ('the economy', 'the government', 'the media', or whatever disciplinary object it may be) is or is not politically effective, interventional or consequential. For, as McQuillan pointed out most baldly, a *call* for change should not be conflated with a change itself. To this one should add that a discourse *on* a theme (in the sense of an academic discussion about something) does not necessarily intervene into the discourse *of* that theme (in the sense of impacting on it in any way).

In cultural studies, then, the question remains phrased as being that of which sorts of wider political discourses (such as those construed in terms of class, race, gender, sexuality, technology, ecology, media, culture, the arts, education, legislation, etc.) are 'progressive' and so should be 'articulated with' (somehow) by cultural studies. This is often as far as the discussion goes. But, once the topic has been chosen, *how* does the academic work itself intervene? This is a more difficult matter than simply 'being for or against' this or that. Even when construed as a matter of being for or against one or another thing, Lola Young points out that cultural studies' and other such academic efforts to respond to matters of social, cultural, economic and political exclusion and marginalisation has led to it being condescendingly 'characterized as a refuge for black people, gay people, women and other self-named oppressed groups who whine about their victimhood, even whilst they celebrate it' (1999: 5–6). The question of whether this is a fair judgement or unfair accusation is secondary to the fact that cultural studies and its critics are embroiled – 'performatively', as it were – in 'debates about what constitutes political action' (9).

So, if 'doing' cultural studies is not necessarily 'interventional' in any particular direction, might it possibly be made to become so? If so, under what conditions, and given what provisos? If there are grounds for doubting that 'significant others' from other disciplines and other practices will automatically turn to cultural studies or post-Marxist theory for information or advice about how to be political – and it seems clear that there are strong grounds for insisting on the dubiousness of such an assumption – then it should be asked: what contribution might a deconstructive post-Marxist cultural studies offer instead as an alternative model of the political interventionality of academic work? What other theory of practice and practice of theory is available to academics *qua* academics?

Whatever else it may entail, it seems clear that a deconstructive theory of intervention must build upon the proposition of deconstruction that the best political interventional supplement would be what Derrida called the 'quest for the lesser-violence' as an ethico-political aim plus effort to engage with the other, not in one's own (disciplinary) language, vernacular, or idiom, but in that of the most relevant 'other' (hospitality/hostility, fidelity/infidelity). Although this is not literally the explicit argument of Derrida's *Monolingualism of the Other* (1998), this title clearly suggests that 'the other' is to be regarded as 'monolingual', speaking only its own language, and resistant to the other. In other words, one should not assume that the powerful (or, indeed, the weak) other of our attention will speak 'our' language, or have any 'use' for it. Similarly, one should not assume that in speaking 'our' language one *can* be intelligible to the other. This is where interdisciplinarity understood in light of deconstruction differs from most traditional conceptions of interdisciplinarity. For, from this point, it becomes clear that the obligations and strategy must consist not of speaking one's own easy fluency to one's own 'community', but rather in speaking the language of the 'other'. Whilst this may not appear to be a serious issue *vis-à-vis* 'debate' *per se*, the problem arises, as discussed above, when it comes to disciplinary 'legitimation' – and disciplinarity itself.

The strategy to develop here derives from deconstruction. It is that of seeking to be hyper-faithful to what one is engaging – indeed, to become a 'monster of fidelity', as Derrida termed it. This is because the monster of fidelity, for Derrida, ultimately amounts to 'the most perverse infidel' (1987: 24). The faithful and attentive reading of texts that constitutes deconstructive practice led Derrida to produce many transformed and transformative readings of key texts; readings which have prompted the many different disciplines within which those texts are central to reassess their own relation to them, and also to their own practice.

In this light, it should be clear that if intervention *is* the aim, it is not appropriate simply to choose the objects or orientations one prefers, or to discuss objects and topics according to one's own simple preferences. Rather, both the matter of the *object* of study and the matter of the *idiom* (and context) of the study become fundamental ethico-political considerations. Of course, this has arguably always been the case. As is clear to both Stuart Hall and Richard Johnson, for instance, there is a strong sense in which random or gratuitous acts of studying whatever one likes in whatever way one fancies unequivocally goes against the constitutive problematic of cultural studies – despite, or rather, *because of* its investment in the exploration of 'alterity'. For the *point* of cultural studies, so conceived, involves a sense that its work comes in response to ethically significant or politically consequential *exclusion*. Quite contrary to this, the arbitrary selection of any old or new object and any old or new approach can work to confirm the stereotype that cultural studies is an inconsequential 'Mickey Mouse' (in)discipline. So, even though cultural studies can also be said implicitly to claim the principled right to study *anything* (because its object or field is potentially limitless, and because it is interested in 'alterity'), nevertheless the mere studying of *anything*, when divorced from the question of responsible intervention, is indeed to make cultural studies 'irrelevant', in its own terms. This is what Johnson is criticising when he argues that 'we have to fight against the disconnection that occurs when cultural studies is inhabited for merely academic purposes or when enthusiasm for (say) popular cultural forms is divorced from the analysis of power and of social responsibility' (1996: 79).

But, if the professionalisation of academia is making it increasingly more disciplinary, more demarcated, more compartmentalised, more hived off and discursively or structurally 'disconnected' both from the much-fetishized 'great-out-thereness' of the world and even from the other disciplines 'in here'; and if, as many have suggested, there are no (longer) any clear political formations 'out there' for and within which cultural studies or academia more generally could be said to have a clear role (Brown 2001; Hardt and Negri 2000; See Chapter 2), then what political strategies are theoretically available, for intervention?

This very problematic – professionalisation and compartmentalisation leading to disarticulation – suggests a need for politicised response. In other words, if the question is 'in what political problematics might post-Marxist cultural studies possibly be able to intervene effectively, given the professionalization and compartmentalisation that has led to its disarticulation from other contexts and scenes?', then the answer is in the question. For, the political problem here is clearly *institutional* and *disciplinary*. Accordingly, the proposal here is that in a sea of disciplinarity it would be helpful to institute and maintain a distinction between work that is unproblematically *disciplinary* versus work which is *interruptive*. (See also Chapter 2) An *interruptive* orientation is to be opposed to a *smoothly fluent* orientation. The interruptive in this sense is not something *ad hoc*, opportunist, inward-looking or simply tactical. Rather, it can remain related to an ethico-political strategy derived from deconstructive, cultural studies *and* post-Marxist injunctions and orientations. In other words, this is to argue that, on the one hand, effective work must remain 'a politically committed questioning of culture/power relations which at the same time theoretically interrogates its own relation to politics and to power' (Hall 2002: 10). But, on the other hand, it is *also* to acknowledge that this very orientation in itself perhaps inevitably cannot but become both enclave and standard, predictable, business as usual, and ultimately inconsequential even in its own limited context. To paraphrase Martin McQuillan (2003), there comes a point when yet more work on Foucault and football ceases to be cultural studies, or when discussing power relations in the kitchen (Rancière 1999) or gender politics in *Sex and the City* ceases to *do* anything. This is why the proposal here is that *both* the 'choice' of the object and the 'choice' of analytical idiom become paramount theoretical and practical considerations and practices for any interventionally-minded work.

Of course, the matter of the ethical and political dimensions and ramifications of the choice of the privileged object of study has arguably always been a key consideration within cultural studies, given its early critique of canons, biases and dominant values. Objects in cultural studies have traditionally best been selected in terms of exploring their relation to progressive politics. 'Progressive politics' itself is, of course, and will always remain, a disputed notion. Nevertheless, this criterion deserves to be maintained. It has historically been built into the cultural studies paradigm and value system because, as Hall unequivocally explained, the object of study called popular culture is preferred and is deemed important in cultural studies because it 'is one of the places where socialism might be constituted. That is why "popular culture" matters. Otherwise, to tell you the truth, I don't give a damn about it' (Hall 1994: 466). This sentiment is instructive. But the acute problem is that of articulating such sentiments positively or effectively *to* any political process, in popular culture or elsewhere. It is here that the proposal for a transformation in the particular kinds of objects *and* in the 'language' and location of engagement comes to the fore. For, the question of the ethical and political dimensions and ramifications of the academic language of cultural studies has yet to be commensurably developed in cultural studies or discourse theory, even though the resources to do so are already present in their theoretical repositories. Despite this, the question of academic language is most regularly approached as being one of 'theoretical versus practical', or 'academic versus political', 'post-structuralist versus normal', or suchlike. But such unhelpful binaries are actually stifling or stultifying when it comes to addressing the ethical and political question of language, which is institutional and political.

Thus, to clarify, the argument is that an effective, interruptive, politicised deconstructive cultural studies cannot simply be the study of arbitrarily selected objects, nor *necessarily* the prolonged study of its traditionally preferred topics – those construed as objects of Art, Literature, Philosophy, media, TV, film, subcultures, the canon, disciplinary boundaries, conventions, identities, and so on and so forth. This is because, in fact, the cultural studies of these very objects and topics could be said to have become traditional, smoothly fluent, and not in any sense ethico-politically interruptive. So, rather than living in the repetition of studying such traditional objects, attention ought now to be given to such 'discourses' as the cultural-political effects of professionalization, compartmentalisation, managerialism, and bureaucracy themselves. These are doubtless articulated to the wider discourses of efficiency, effectivity, performance, performativity, productivity and production. As already indicated, others could be added. These can be provisionally singled out because they relate to a process that might be called depoliticising *'enclavisation'*. But this list is far from exhaustive and it is far from the first time that something like this has been said. Peters (2001) deals with little else in his study of the importance of the work of Derrida, Deleuze, Lyotard and Foucault for approaching the politics of 'managerialist-techno-capitalism'; and the same can be said of the work of Readings (1996), Rutherford (2005) and the contributions to Kilroy et al. (2004), among others; all of whom join a growing list of politicised academic works seeking to engage with the political dimensions of the increasing corporatisation of education, for instance. In this regard, this listing of themes is merely a further call to arms. But in another it is a concrete suggestion for an antidisciplinary reorientation.

It is important to point out that this reorientation would not even substantially move the focus away from the 'properly cultural' object of cultural studies. So, this is not a renunciation of culture as a domain that 'seizes hold of your soul' (Hall). Nor is any of this a forgetting of the 'project' or 'spirit' of cultural studies *or* post-Marxism. In fact, this proposed reorientation presupposes and seeks to prolong and deepen them both. For any analysis (say, of instances of political issues in technoscience, managerialism, or bureaucratisation) that seeks to be interruptive or otherwise effective will be orientated in terms of questions and issues of marginalisation, exclusion, domination, hegemonisation, violence, and value; including those questions of age, class, gender, race, sexuality and other such sedimented dimensions that are central to cultural studies' and post-Marxism's identity and values. Indeed, such a thematic reorientation as this will both transform and remain faithful to the political object of deconstruction, cultural studies, and post-Marxism.

The problems really arise *vis-à-vis* what I have been calling, for shorthand, 'the question of language', which is the same as saying, the institution, discipline. This is because, in remaining faithful to the effort to intervene by attaching to the other, this requires a new kind of disciplinary 'transgression': the transgression of *one's own* familiar style of disciplinary discourse; in effect, transgressing one's own identity, in/as attaching to what one seeks to alter. (Žižek has called this 'striking at the self' (2000: 122–3), and advocated it as a strategy to change the terrain of apparent possibilities on offer in a conflict.)

Derrida was consistently (some might say uncharacteristically and paradoxically) *unequivocal* on the subject of the double bind attendant to any apparently univocal injunction. He regularly pointed out that every injunction activates two incompatible demands. Such a double bind can also be seen to be activated here. For, attaching oneself to what one seeks to alter is an easy thing to *say*, but is an immensely difficult thing for academic work to *do*. This is because, in the world of increasingly discrete and policed institutional demarcations, realms and disciplines, each with heterogeneous discourses, languages, protocols, practices, procedures, values, histories, canons, and orientations, then 'attaching' to what one wants to alter opens up huge problems of language, translation, legibility, intelligibility, authority, and – something that those working professionally within academia are likely to be very familiar with – one's own 'auditability', 'accountability', 'viability' and *'assessability'*. The latter considerations are closely tied not only to employability, promotion and redundancy, but also to funding and departmental maintenance or closure in the contemporary corporate university. Institutional existence often depends on academics being able to demonstrate (to an externally imposed 'theoria'; see Chapters 1 and 2) that what they are doing *is* good and proper work in their particular field. However, the interventional strategy proposed here is not compatible with easy disciplinary recognition or contemporary norms about what good disciplinary work is supposed to be.

Despite the familiar claims to the contrary, 'dialogue' across discrete specialised fields is far from straightforwardly possible. So to attempt this new interventional interdisciplinarity in today's transformed context of intensified bureaucracy and 'enclaving' is already to enter a minefield. Nevertheless, it would seem to be the best chance for intervention into other contexts available. It is certainly an approach which, in overidentifying with and taking literally the ideals of intervention and interdisciplinarity actually tests any commitment to inter- (never mind anti- or post-) disciplinary work, obliging as it does a transformation in *our* conventions, norms, protocols, paradigms and procedures before (indeed, without) simply polemically pointing out the deficiencies in those of the other. In short, this intervention relies on 'striking at the self' insofar as it actively prevents and closes down the tendency towards smoothly fluent disciplinary comfort, complacency or maintaining delusions about engagement whilst existing in enclave isolation. Indeed, operating solely within the fleshed out disciplinary quarters of political or cultural studies could be said to constitute a sort of political inoculation, and to foster the smooth repetition of the very disengagement rightly decried by many in cultural studies.

Interdisciplinary intervention activates all of the double binds and contradictions entailed by interdisciplinarity articulation in a disarticulated enclave context. It must also inevitably be somewhat messy, tangled, less than grand or glorious. In fact, because it requires an intimate engagement *with* – and not simply *about* – the other, it is unlikely that the kind of interventional reorientation that is being proposed here will be greeted as the sort of political engagement of which many within cultural studies still dream. That is because that dream of intervention is based on some ideal of a physical and present audience of eager learners crowded around one's feet, eager to learn from academic subjects supposed to know. Quite opposed to this, this strategy of articulation involves navigating the ethics of discourse and hospitality/hostility repeatedly considered by Derrida (1977; 1981; 1996; 1998). The 'other', here, must neither be fetishized (in the way that the marginal, the abject, the subaltern, etc., have too often been fetishized within cultural studies) nor regarded as a monstrosity (in the way that the dominant, the hegemonic, the status quo, etc., has also sometimes reciprocally been characterised). Rather, the other context, the other scene, or practice must be approached not only as an interlocutor, but even as a 'host'. The strategies for a non-violent intervention in a context that cannot be dominated must be negotiated performatively every time. They will not be the same twice. Accordingly, this interventional strategy is strictly antidisciplinary, as it were, in essence and in application.

This would be the new 'disciplinary transgression': the acceptance of the other's terms of debate. This might be called a deconstructive strategy of hyper-fidelity, over-fidelity, or indeed 'literalisation': taking literally, reading faithfully the other's texts, productions. Insofar as it relies on overidentification, it bears striking similarities to Žižek's strategy of overidentification with that which one seeks to transform. As we have seen, according to Žižek, overidentifying with an institution or its set of claims tends already to start to deconstruct it, revealing the 'inherent transgression' of the power that propounds those claims (whilst itself limiting, policing and transgressing them). As Žižek sees this:

> my notion of 'inherent transgression', far from playing another variation on [the] theme (resistance reproduces that to which it resists), makes the power edifice even *more* vulnerable: in so far as power relies on its 'inherent transgression', then – sometimes, at least – *overidentifying* with the explicit power discourse – *ignoring* this inherent obscene underside and simply taking the power discourse at its (public) word, acting as if it really means what it explicitly says (and promises) – can be the most effective way of disturbing its smooth functioning. (Žižek 2000: 220)

With this, Žižek suggests a strategy that seems similar to deconstructing any particular discourse, text, or set of claims; but one which does not have the drawback of being called or telegraphed as 'a deconstruction', nor of being carried out in the 'proper language' of a 'proper' disciplinary version of deconstruction. Rather, in this version, 'the other' is enjoined to engage in a discourse in which a specifically constructed intellectually and ethically engaged position is deployed in an attempt to question and to lever at the cracks or fault lines in the other institution or edifice (Derrida 1992). This may smack of the dream of a Socratic dialogue between the disciplines. But it need not appeal to a facile image of dignified old gentlemen discussing philosophy beneath the olive trees – that 'arboreal' image of academe that Deleuze and Guattari rejected. This ideal should be acknowledged for what it is: constitutively impossible; overlooking the constitutive character of discrete, heterogeneous, and often mutually untranslatable language games within demarcated disciplinary contexts. Wherever such an ideal may be actualisable, it will be local, temporary, and will not take place according to hypothetical 'universal' norms of transparent communication, but rather according to constitutive reference to a shared problematic, archive, set of procedures, terms of reference and vocabularies.

This should be construed as the quest for new instituting events, reinstituting events, within an irreducibly institutional socio-political field. The *disciplinary* question may well be: What would remain of post-Marxism and cultural studies in such a strategy? This is to be recognised as a *disciplinary* question – one prompted by an identification with disciplinarity itself rather than any purported interventional aim or project. Of course, complete disciplinary disidentification is neither really possible nor desirable. Disciplines are institutions that have a central political status. But, to use an explanatory matrix given by Žižek: 'let us imagine an individual trying to perform some simple manual task – say, grabbing an object that repeatedly eludes him: the moment he changes his attitude, starts to find pleasure in just repeating the failed task (squeezing the object, which again and again eludes him), he shifts from desire to drive' (Žižek 2005: 10). In our discussion, the conservative disciplinary impulse is the move to drive, the move away from the desire to intervene elsewhere.

Nevertheless, in answer to this disciplinary question, it will be best to focus on what Laclau has called *the* political referent – the *demand* – and the constitutive character of the ethical. In this sense, a primary ethico-political 'referent' can be regarded as this or that claim for justice. This could be another characterisation of interventional efforts: As such, the work of cultural studies and post-Marxism consists in the effort to reinscribe, deepen, develop and preserve radical democracy. This takes the form of the exploration of antagonism, of the constitutive tendentiousness of instituted interpretation, and the ethical and political relations between interpretation and practice. This deconstructive orientation is to be deployed in the interdisciplinary effort towards effective, motivated, tendentious engagement, the effort of what Derrida called derailment and redirection, the transformation of protocols through revealing the contingency and bias of their current form. In other words, what remains of cultural studies and post-Marxism are efforts of *reinstitution* and of making differences that could be said to count. As Wittgenstein asserted, 'Our task is to be just. That is, we must only point out and resolve . . . injustices . . . and not posit new parties – and creeds' (quoted in Owen 2001: 139). Some of Laclau's recent representation of the political is in agreement with this Wittgensteinian assertion. This hinges on the claim that, *vis-à-vis* any existing social situation, something better can *always* be imagined. This has lead Laclau to claim that the distance and difference between the 'is' and the 'ought' is 'the root of the ethical': 'the experience of the fullness of being as that which is essentially lacking. It is, if you want, the experience of the presence of an absence' (2004: 286). In other words, 'justice', for Laclau, 'is only the name of an absent fullness, the positive reverse of a given situation which is negatively lived as "unjust". I do not know what a just order would be, but I know that justice is lacking' (293).)

The problematic of the political work of institutional fields is at the forefront of this strategy of intervention. Without a deconstructive, discursive and textual awareness of the politically consequential orientating work of disciplinary paradigms, this institutional dimension threatens to remain obscured. The textual approach ('deconstruction') allows a peculiar insight into, and perhaps the best degree of purchase upon, its workings, to the extent that it looks for the *exclusions* and aspires to institute 'democratic justice, responding to the calls from all others' (Protevi 2001: 70).

The Necessity of Deconstruction

All of this means an unequivocal recommitment to deconstruction. (This is not the same thing as a repetition of deconstruction.). Stuart Hall sums it up when he asserts that he remains 'a post-Marxist and a post-structuralist, because those . . . two discourses . . . are central to my formation and I don't believe in the endless, trendy recycling of one fashionable theorist after another, as if you can wear new theories like T-shirts' (Hall 1996d: 148–9). This is because, for Hall, the question always to be asked is what any intellectual effort is *for*. When intellectual work is being done, *what* is being done and *why*? Without addressing this, cultural studies risks attaining the status of being little more than a theoretical butterfly or dilettante:

> That is to say, unless and until one respects the necessary displacement of culture, and yet is always irritated by its failure to reconcile itself with other questions that matter, with other questions that cannot and can never be fully covered by critical textuality in its elaborations, cultural studies as a project, an intervention, remains incomplete. If you lose hold of the tension, you can do extremely fine intellectual work, but you will have lost intellectual practice as a politics. I offer this to you, not because that's what cultural studies ought to be, or because that's what the Centre managed to do well, but simply because I think that, overall, is what defines cultural studies as a project. Both in the British and the American context, cultural studies has drawn the attention itself, not just because of its sometimes dazzling internal theoretical development, but because it holds theoretical and political questions in an ever irresolvable but permanent tension. It constantly allows the one to irritate, bother, and disturb the other, without insisting on some final theoretical closure. (Hall 1992: 284)

In this light, insofar as deconstruction is the performative-interpretive exposure of any institution or establishment to the enabling limitation that is its own contingency and constitutive, contradictory bias, then deconstruction is a drawing of attention to the violence of institution, in the hope of inciting acts of re-institution with a view to the 'lesser violence'. For Mowitt, 'the point is to develop the institutional means whereby this insight is not exhausted in isolated moments of interpretation, and this implies inscribing such an insight in the paradigm that organizes the production of interpretive statements' (1992: 217). As Derrida wrote, in an early work: deconstruction 'instigates the subversion of every kingdom, which makes it obviously threatening and infallibly dreaded by everything within us that desires a kingdom' (Derrida 1982: 22). Nevertheless – and this is part of the point of deconstruction – it is also always the case that *anything* constituted/instituted/established, *resists* (Derrida 1987: 88). Institutions become sedimented and policed. Projects become disciplines. Desires become drives (repetitions). For deconstruction, the point is to change it. Derrida held that 'the best liberation from violence is a certain putting into question, which makes the search for an *archia* tremble' (Derrida 1978: 141). This is very different to Laclau's *repetitive* 'putting into question' of political theory – which is, so to speak, a *putting-into-question without putting-into-question*, existing as it does as a regular repetition of the same in the comfort and safety of its his own stable disciplinary context.

Deconstruction also demonstrates that every obligation activates contradictory and reciprocally subversive injunctions. Thus, even though it seems certain that what Derrida called 'clear conscience certainty' must be exposed to the ordeal of undeciding, the problem is that so too must the *certainty of uncertainty* – the certainty that *this* way or that way, our way or their way, is *the* right and most responsible way to do it. Laclauian or Žižekian post-Marxism are cases in point. They do not deconstruct their own certainties, their own discipline. Ultimately, then, this remains all about *institution*: the very thing that is central to post-Marxism that post-Marxist discourse has yet to face up to. The way to engage this is through deconstruction. The object of deconstruction is *institution* and *the* institution, *establishment* and *the* establishment. In facing up to the necessity of intervention, a first task will be to acknowledge and examine the extent to which, and the ways in which, our activities might be versions of what Judith Butler criticised in certain forms of action: namely, uncritical, unthinking repetition. As Butler suggests, perhaps inertia and repetition signify that those who live in repetition 'do not want to think too hard about what it is they are doing, what kind of discourse they are using; for if they think too hard about what it is they are doing, they fear that they will no longer do it' (Butler 2000: 265).

Bibliography

Adorno, Theodor, and Horkheimer, Max (1972), *Dialectic of Enlightenment*, London: Herder & Herder.

Åkerstrøm Andersen, Niels (2003), *Discursive Analytical Strategies: Understanding Foucault, Kosselleck, Laclau, Luhmann*, London: The Policy Press.

Althusser, Louis (1970), *Reading Capital*, London: Verso/New Left Books.

Althusser, Louis (1971), *Lenin and Philosophy*, New York: Monthly Review Press.

Arditi, Benjamin (2003), 'Talkin' 'bout a revolution: the end of mourning', *parallax*, 27, April–June.

Arditi, Benjamin, and Valentine, Jeremy (1999), *Polemicization: The Contingency of the Commonplace*, Edinburgh: Edinburgh University Press.

Bal, Mieke (2003), 'From cultural studies to cultural analysis: "a controlled reflection on the formation of method"', in Paul Bowman (ed.), *Interrogating Cultural Studies: Theory, Politics and Practice*, London: Pluto.

Barthes, Roland (1977), *Image – Music – Text*, London, Fontana.

Beardsworth, Richard (1996), *Derrida and the Political*, London and New York: Routledge.

Bennett, Tony (1997), 'Toward a pragmatics for cultural studies', in J. McGuigan, (ed.), *Cultural Methodologies*, London: Sage.

Bennington, Geoffrey (1994), *Legislations: The Politics of Deconstruction*, London: Verso.

Bewes, Timothy (2001) 'Vulgar Marxism: the spectre haunting spectres of Marx', *parallax* 20, July–September, pp. 83–95.

Brown, Wendy (2001), *Politics out of History*, Princeton, NJ: Princeton University Press.

Butler, Judith (1990), *Gender Trouble: Feminism and the Subversion of Identity*, London: Routledge.

Butler, Judith (2000), in Judith Butler, Ernesto Laclau, and Slavoj Žižek, *Contingency, Hegemony, Universality: Contemporary Dialogues on the Left*, London: Verso.

Critchley, Simon (2003), 'Why I love cultural studies', in Paul Bowman (ed.) *Interrogating Cultural Studies: Theory, Practice and Politics*, London: Pluto.

Daly, Glyn (2002), 'Globalisation and the constitution of political economy', in Jeremy Valentine and Alan Finlayson (eds), *Politics and Post-Structuralism: An Introduction*, Edinburgh: Edinburgh University Press.

Daryl Slack, Jennifer (1996), 'The theory and method of articulation in cultural studies', in David Morley and Kuan-Hsing Chen, (eds), *Stuart Hall: Critical Dialogues in Cultural Studies*, London: Routledge.

Derrida, Jacques (1974), *Of Grammatology*, Baltimore and London: Johns Hopkins University Press.

Derrida, Jacques (1977), *Limited Inc*, Evanston, IL: Northwestern University Press.

Derrida, Jacques (1978), *Writing and Difference*, Chicago and London: University of Chicago Press.

Derrida, Jacques (1981), *Dissemination*, trans. B. Johnson, Chicago and London: University of Chicago Press.

Derrida, Jacques (1982), *Margins of Philosophy*, Chicago and London: University of Chicago Press.

Derrida, Jacques (1987), *The Post Card: From Socrates to Freud and Beyond*, Chicago and London: University of Chicago Press.

Derrida, Jacques (1992), 'Mochlos; or, the conflict of the faculties', in Richard Rand (ed.), *Logomachia: The Conflict of the Faculties*, Lincoln, NE and London: University of Nebraska Press, pp. 1–34.

Derrida, Jacques (1992a), 'Canons and Metonymies: An Interview with Jacques Derrida', in Richard Rand (ed.), *Logomachia: The Conflict of the Faculties*, Lincoln, NE and London: University of Nebraska Press, pp. 195–215.

Derrida, Jacques (1994), *Specters of Marx: The State of the Debt, the Work of Mourning, and the New International*, London: Routledge.

Derrida, Jacques (1995), *Points . . .: Interviews, 1974–1994*, Stanford, CA: Stanford University Press.

Derrida, Jacques (1995a), *The Gift of Death*, Chicago and London: University of Chicago Press.

Derrida, Jacques (1995b), *Archive Fever: A Freudian Impression*, Chicago and London: University of Chicago Press.

Derrida, Jacques (1996), 'Remarks on deconstruction and pragmatism', in Chantal Mouffe (ed.), *Deconstruction and Pragmatism*, London: Routledge, pp. 77–88.

Derrida, Jacques (1997), *Politics of Friendship*, London: Verso.

Derrida, Jacques (1998), *Monolingualism of the Other; or, The Prosthesis of Origin*, Stanford, CA: Stanford University Press.

Derrida, Jacques (1998a), *Resistances of Psychoanalysis*, Stanford, CA: Stanford University Press.

Derrida, Jacques (2001), 'The future of the profession or the university without condition (thanks to the "Humanities," what *could take place* tomorrow)', in Tom Cohen (ed.), *Jacques Derrida and the Humanities: A Critical Reader*, Cambridge: Cambridge University Press.

Derrida, Jacques (2002), *Who's Afraid of Philosophy?: Right to Philosophy 1*, Stanford, CA: Stanford University Press.

Devenney, Mark (2002), 'Critical theory and democracy', in Jeremy Valentine and Alan Finlayson, (eds), *Politics and Post-Structuralism: An Introduction*, Edinburgh: Edinburgh University Press.

Devenney, Mark (2004), 'Ethics and politics in Discourse Theory', in Simon Critchley and Oliver Marchart (eds), *Laclau: A Critical Reader*, London: Routledge.

Docherty, Thomas (1993), *Postmodernism: A Reader*, London: Harvester Wheatsheaf.

During, Simon (1993), *The Cultural Studies Reader*, Routledge, London.

Forgacs, D. (1985), 'Dethroning the working class?' *Marxism Today*, 29, May.

Frow, John (1995), *Cultural Studies and Cultural Value*, Oxford: Oxford University Press.

Geras, Norman (1985), 'Post-Marxism?', *New Left Review*, 163, pp. 40–82.

Gilbert, Jeremy (2001), 'A certain ethics of openness: radical democratic cultural studies', *Strategies: Journal of Theory, Culture & Politics*, 14:2, November.

Gilbert, Jeremy (2003), 'Friends and enemies: which side is cultural studies on?', in Paul Bowman (ed.), *Interrogating Cultural Studies: Theory, Practice and Politics*, London: Pluto.

Girard, René, (1977), *Violence and the Sacred*, Baltimore and London: Johns Hopkins University Press.

Giroux, Henry A. (2000), *Impure Acts: The Practical Politics of Cultural Studies*, London: Routledge.

Godzich, Wlad (1986), 'Foreword: the tiger on the paper mat', in Paul de Man, (ed.), *The Resistance to Theory*, Minneapolis: University of Minnesota Press, pp. ix–xvii.

Godzich, Wlad (1987), 'Afterword: religion, the state, and post(al) modernism', in Samuel Weber, *Institution and Interpretation*, Minneapolis: University of Minnesota Press, pp. 153–64.

Gramsci, Antonio (1971), *Selections from the Prison Notebooks*, London: Lawrence and Wishart.

Hall, Gary (2002), *Culture in Bits: The Monstrous Future of Theory*, London: Continuum.

Hall, Stuart (1980), 'Encoding/decoding', in Stuart Hall, Dorothy Hobson, Andrew Lowe, and Paul Willis, (eds), *Culture, Media, Language*, London: Routledge.

Hall, Stuart (1990), 'The emergence of cultural studies and the crisis of the humanities', *October*, 53, 1990.

Hall, Stuart (1992), 'Cultural Studies and its theoretical legacies', in Lawrence Grossberg, Cary Nelson, Paula Treichler (eds), *Cultural Studies*, New York and London: Routledge.

Hall, Stuart (1994), 'Notes on deconstructing "the Popular" ', in John Storey (ed.), *Cultural Theory and Popular Culture: A Reader*, Harvester Wheatsheaf, London.

Hall, Stuart (1996), *Stuart Hall: Critical Dialogues in Cultural Studies*, (eds), David Morley and Kuan-Hsing Chen, London, Routledge.

Hall, Stuart (1996b), 'New ethnicities', in J. Donald and A. Rattansi (eds), *'Race', Culture and Difference*. London: Sage/Open University Press.

Hall, Stuart (1996c), 'The problem of ideology: Marxism without guarantees', in David Morley and Kuan-Hsing Chen (eds), *Stuart Hall: Critical Dialogues in Cultural Studies*, London: Routledge.

Hall, Stuart (1996d), 'On postmodernism and articulation: an interview with Stuart Hall', in David Morley and Kuan-Hsing Chen (eds), *Stuart Hall: Critical Dialogues in Cultural Studies*, London: Routledge.

Hardt, Michael, and Negri, Antonio (2000), *Empire*, Cambridge, MA and London: Harvard University Press.

Hobson, Marion (1998), *Jacques Derrida: Opening Lines*, London: Routledge.

Hunter, Lynette (1999), *Critiques of Knowing: Situated Textualities in Science, Computing, and the Arts*, London: Routledge.

Jameson, Fredric (1988) 'The ideology of the text', *The Ideologies of Theory*, 1, Minneapolis: University of Minnesota Press.

Jameson, Fredric (2002), 'From "The Cultural Logic of Late Capitalism" ', in Lawrence Cahoone, (ed.), *From Modernism to Postmodernism: An Anthology*, Second Edition, London: Blackwell.

Johnson, Richard (1996), 'What is cultural studies anyway?', in J. Storey (ed.), *What is Cultural Studies? A Reader*, London: Arnold.

Kant, Immanuel (1979), *The Conflict of the Faculties/Der Streit der Fakultäten*, New York: Abaris Books.

Kilroy, Peter, Nicholas Chare and Rowan Bailey, eds (2004), Auditing Culture, *parallax*, 10:2, April–June.

Kingsnorth, Paul (2003), *One No, Many Yeses: a Journey to the Heart of the Global Resistance Movement*, London: Free Press.

Kuhn, Thomas (1962), *The Structure of Scientific Revolutions (Third Edition)*, Chicago and London, University of Chicago Press.

Laclau, Ernesto (1977), *Politics and Ideology in Marxist Theory*, London: New Left Books.

Laclau, Ernesto (1980), 'Populist rupture and discourse', *Screen Education* 34.

Laclau, Ernesto (1989), 'Preface', in Slavoj Žižek, *The Sublime Object of Ideology*, London: Verso.

Laclau, Ernesto (1990), *New Reflections on the Revolution of Our Time*, London: Verso.

Laclau, Ernesto (1993), 'Politics and the limits of modernity', in Thomas Docherty (ed.), *Postmodernism: A Reader*, London, Harvester Wheatsheaf, pp. 329–43.

Laclau, Ernesto (1996), *Emancipation(s)*, London: Verso.

Laclau, Ernesto (1996a), 'Deconstruction, pragmatism, hegemony', in Chantal Mouffe (ed.), *Deconstruction and Pragmatism*, London: Routledge, pp. 47–68.

Laclau, Ernesto (1999), 'Politics, polemics and academics: an interview by Paul Bowman', *parallax*, 11, April–June, pp. 93–107.

Laclau, Ernesto (2000), in Judith Butler, Ernesto Laclau, and Slavoj Žižek, *Contingency, Hegemony, Universality: Contemporary Dialogues on the Left*, London: Verso.

Laclau, Ernesto (2001), 'Can Immanence Explain Social Struggles?', *Diacritics*, 31.4, Winter, 3–10.

Laclau, Ernesto (2004), 'Glimpsing the future', in Simon Critchley and Oliver Marchart (eds), *Laclau: A Critical Reader*, London: Routledge.

Laclau, Ernesto (2005), *On Populist Reason*, London: Verso.

Laclau, Ernesto, and Mouffe, Chantal (1985), *Hegemony and Socialist Strategy: Towards a Radical Democratic Politics*, London: Verso.

Laplanche, Jean, and Pontalis, Jean-Baptiste (1988), *The Language of Psychoanalysis*, London: Karnac.

Lechte, John (1994), *Fifty Key Contemporary Theorists*, London: Routledge.

Lyotard, Jean-François (1984), *The Postmodern Condition: A Report on Knowledge*, Minneapolis: University of Minnesota Press.

Lyotard, Jean-François (1988), *The Differend: Phrases in Dispute*, Minneapolis: University of Minnesota Press.

Maley, Willy (2001), 'The collapse of the New International', *parallax*, 20, July–September, pp. 73–82.

Marx, Karl (1845), *Theses on Feuerbach*, The Marx and Engels Internet Archive, http://www.marxists.org/archive/marx/works/1845/theses/index.htm

Marx, Karl, and Engels, Friedrich (1967), *The Communist Manifesto*, Harmondsworth: Penguin.

McRobbie, Angela (1992), 'Post-Marxism and cultural studies', in Lawrence Grossberg, Cary Nelson, Paula Treichler (eds), *Cultural Studies*. New York and London: Routledge.

McRobbie, Angela (2005), *The Uses of Cultural Studies: A Textbook*, London: Sage.

McQuillan, Martin (2001), 'Spectres of Poujade: Naomi Klein and the New International', *parallax*, 20, July–Sept, pp. 114–30.

McQuillan, Martin (2003), 'The projection of cultural studies', in Paul Bowman (ed.), *Interrogating Cultural Studies: Theory, Practice and Politics*, London: Pluto.

Morley, David, and Chen, Kuan-Hsing, eds (1996), 'Introduction', *Stuart Hall: Critical Dialogues in Cultural Studies*, London: Routledge.

Mouffe, Chantal (1996), 'Deconstruction, Pragmatism and the Politics of Democracy', *Deconstruction and Pragmatism*, London: Routledge, pp. 1–12.

Mowitt, John (1992), *Text: The Genealogy of an Antidisciplinary Object*, Durham, NC and London: Duke.

Mowitt, John (2002), *Percussion: Drumming, Beating, Striking*. Durham, NC and London: Duke.

Mowitt, John (2003), 'Cultural studies, in theory', in Paul Bowman (ed.), *Interrogating Cultural Studies: Theory, Practice and Politics*, London: Pluto.

Owen, David (2001), 'Democracy, perfectionism and "undetermined messianic hope": Cavell, Derrida and the ethos of democracy to come', in Ludwig Nagl and Chantal Mouffe (eds), *The Legacy of Wittgenstein: Pragmatism or Deconstruction*, Oxford: Peter Lang.

Parker, Ian (2004), *Slavoj Žižek: A Critical Introduction*, London: Pluto.

Peters, Michael A. (2001), *Poststructuralism, Marxism and Neoliberalism: Between Theory and Politics*, London: Rowman and Littlefield.

Protevi, John (2001), *Political Physics: Deleuze, Derrida and the Body Politic*, London: Athlone.

Rancière, Jacques (1999), *Dis-agreement: Politics and Philosophy*, Minneapolis: University of Minnesota Press.

Readings, Bill (1996), *The University in Ruins*, Cambridge, MA and London: Harvard University Press.

Rojek, Chris (2003), *Stuart Hall*, Cambridge: Polity.

Rorty, Richard (1996), 'Remarks on deconstruction and pragmatism'; 'Response to Ernesto Laclau', in Chantal Mouffe (ed.), *Deconstruction and Pragmatism*, London: Routledge, pp. 13–18, 69–76.

Royle, Nicholas (2000) 'What is Deconstruction?', *Deconstructions: A User's Guide*, Basingstoke: Palgrave.

Rutherford, Jonathan (2005), 'Cultural studies in the corporate university', *Cultural Studies*, 19:3, May, pp. 297–317.

Sim, Stuart (1998), *Post-Marxism: A Reader*, Edinburgh: Edinburgh University Press.

Smith, Anna-Marie (1994), 'Rastafari as resistance and the ambiguities of essentialism in the 'New Social Movements"', in Ernesto Laclau (ed.), *The Making of Political Identities*, London: Verso.

Sokal, Alan, and Bricmont, Jean (1998), *Intellectual Impostures: Postmodern Philosophers' Abuse of Science*, London: Profile Books.

Sparks, Colin (1996), 'Stuart Hall, cultural studies and Marxism', in David Morley and Kuan-Hsing Chen, (eds), *Stuart Hall: Critical Dialogues in Cultural Studies*, London: Routledge.

Spivak, Gayatri Chakravorty (1974), 'Translator's Preface', in Jacques Derrida, *Of Grammatology*, Baltimore and London: Johns Hopkins University Press.

Spivak, Gayatri Chakravorty (1997), *The Spivak Reader*, London: Routledge.

Spivak, Gayatri Chakravorty (1999), *A Critique of Postcolonial Reason: Toward a History of the Vanishing Present*, Cambridge, MA and London: Harvard University Press.

Spivak, Gayatri Chakravorty, and Gunew, Sneja (1993), 'Questions of multiculturalism', in Simon During (ed.), *The Cultural Studies Reader*, London: Routledge, pp. 193–202.

Storey, John (1994), *Cultural Theory and Popular Culture: A Reader*, London, Harvester Wheatsheaf.

Storey, John (1996), *What is Cultural Studies?: A Reader*, London, Arnold.

Valentine, Jeremy (2003), 'The subject position of cultural studies: is there a Problem?', in Paul Bowman (ed.), *Interrogating Cultural Studies: Theory, Practice and Politics*, London: Pluto.

Vitanza, V. J., (1997), *Negation, Subjectivity, and The History of Rhetoric*, New York: State University of New York.

Walsh, Michael (2002), 'Slavoj Žižek (1949 –)', in Julian Wolfreys (ed.), *The Edinburgh Encyclopaedia of Modern Criticism and Theory*, Edinburgh: Edinburgh University Press.

Weber, Samuel (1987), *Institution and Interpretation*, Minneapolis: University of Minnesota Press.

Wolfreys, Julian (2002), (ed.), *The Edinburgh Encyclopaedia of Modern Criticism and Theory*, Edinburgh University Press.

Wortham, Simon (1999), *Rethinking the University: Leverage and Deconstruction*, Manchester: Manchester University Press.

Young, Lola (1999), 'Why cultural studies?', *parallax*, 11, April–June, pp. 3–16.

Young, Robert J. C. (1992), 'The idea of a chrestomathic university', in Richard Rand (ed.), *Logomachia: The Conflict of the Faculties*, Lincoln, NE and London: University of Nebraska Press, pp. 97–126.

Young, Robert J. C. (2001), *Postcolonialism: An Historical Introduction*, Oxford: Blackwell.

Žižek, Slavoj (1989), *The Sublime Object of Ideology*, London: Verso.

Žižek, Slavoj (1990), 'Beyond Discourse-Analysis', in Ernesto Laclau, *New Reflections on the Revolution of Our Time*, London: Verso, pp. 249–60.

Žižek, Slavoj (1998), 'A Leftist Plea for "Eurocentrism"', *Critical Inquiry* 24:2, 988–1,009.

Žižek, Slavoj (2000), 'Class struggle or postmodernism? Yes, please!'; '*Da Capo senza Fine*'; 'Holding the place', in Judith Butler, Ernesto Laclau, and Slavoj Žižek, *Contingency, Hegemony, Universality: Contemporary Dialogues on the Left*, London: Verso, pp. 90–135, 213–62, 308–29.

Žižek, Slavoj (2001), *Did Someone Say Totalitarianism? Five Interventions into the (Mis)Use of a Notion*, London: Verso.

Žižek, Slavoj (2001a) *On Belief*. London: Routledge.

Žižek, Slavoj (2002), (ed.), *Revolution at the Gates: Selected Writings of Lenin from February to October 1917*, London: Verso.

Žižek, Slavoj (2005), *Interrogating the Real*, eds Rex Butler and Scott Stephens, London: Continuum.

Zylinska, Joanna (2001), 'An ethical manifesto for cultural studies . . . perhaps', *Strategies: Journal of Theory, Culture & Politics*, 14:2, November.

Index